The Church History of Providence Industrial Mission

Copyright 2006 Patrick Makondesa

All rights reserved. No part of this publication may be reproduced, stored in a retrieval system or transmitted in any form or by any means, electronic, mechanical, photocopying, recording or otherwise without prior permission from the publishers

ISBN: 99908-76-81-9
ISBN-13: 978-99908-76-81-9

Published by
Kachere Series
P.O. Box 1037, Zomba, Malawi

Kachere Theses no 5

Editorial Assistance: Elizabeth Ritchie
Layout and Cover Design: Caroline Chihana

The Kachere Series is represented outside Africa by:
African Books Collective Oxford (abc@africanbookscollective.com)
Michigan State University Press East Lansing (msupress@msu.edu)

Printed by Lightning Source

The Church History of Providence Industrial Mission 1900-1940

Patrick Makondesa

Kachere Theses no. 5

Kachere Series
Zomba
2006

Contents

Chapter One
The Early Period of PIM Ministry — 14

Chapter Two
Chilembwe's Approach to Conversion — 36

Chapter Three
Expansion of PIM beyond Mbombwe — 53

Chapter Four
Expansion through an Institutional Approach to Mission — 73

Chapter Five
Membership in PIM church — 100

Chapter Six
PIM's Ministry of Justice — 124

Chapter Seven
The Dark Period of PIM Ministry 1915-1926 — 143

Chapter Eight
PIM's Dawn of Hope — 160

Conclusion — 173

Bibliography — 175

Appendices — 180

Tables
Qualifications of each PIM teacher   85

Maps
Earliest centre of PIM at Migowi   54
PIM churches at Chiringa   62
Chilembwe's potential movements   142

Illustrations
Native hunting licence issued to Rev John Chilembwe   9
Chilembwe as a young man in America 1897/1898   17
Chilembwe baptizing   24
Pio Mtwere, once Chilembwe's gun bearer   27
Chilembwe's church in construction   32
The opening of PIM church in Chiradzulu in 1913   34
Rev John Chilembwe and Rev John Chorley   36
The earliest convert of PIM   38
Mrs Chilembwe and two PIM women   41
Mrs Flora Zeto Malekebu (Polished Diamond)   43
Dr Malekebu and the winners of the "Baby of the month" competition   44
The Thundu tree at which the first Hospital was established in 1927   45
The Church at Matapila   68
The Church in Harare, Zimbabwe   70
Foreign Mission Board Headquarters, New York as of 1940   75
Malekebu giving a speech at Meharry Medical College   95
Rev Wylie Chiwamba   105
John Grey Kufa: CCAP member   135
PIM followers being led to prison in 1915   145
The public execution at Zomba of convicted Chilembwe insurgents   152
The New Jerusalem Baptist Temple at Mbombwe built 1928-1933   169

Acknowledgements

I completed my Bachelor of Education majoring in Theology in 1997 at the University of Malawi, Chancellor College. I did not think of doing an MA immediately. The same year that I graduated I left for South Africa. While there I felt that the country was good and was planning to get a residential permit and start working. At the time my mind was beginning to settle down in South Africa, I received letters from Malawi. Of all the letters I received there was but one that reversed the whole situation. This letter came from Dr Klaus Fiedler. He suggested to me that it would be a better idea if I could continue with my studies rather than stay in RSA. After a week I received another letter from him with similar content but posted from Durban by Dr Isabel Phiri. I also received a similar message through email via Prof Landman of UNISA and I was told a copy was sent to my brother in Malawi. I took this very seriously and began to prepare for my return. After my return I was registered as an MA student with the University of Malawi in March 1998. I immediately started my work. To all this I am indebted to acknowledge with gratitude Dr Fiedler's encouragement, support and shaping of the direction of my academic endeavor. Special thanks also to Prof Christina Landman from UNISA for passing on the message to me while at Windsor West, Randburg, RSA. With equally sincere gratitude, I wish to acknowledge my thanks to Dr Isabel Phiri, who posted the message to me from Durban.

I thank the staff in the Department of Theology and Religious Studies at Chancellor College, University of Malawi, for providing advice and encouragement during the presentation of modules and the proposal that sharpened my ideas to develop this thesis. Special thanks go to the Rt Rev Dr F. Chingota for providing me with a book that widened my view in relation to the subject I was dealing with.

I wish to thank Rev Esker J. Harris, missionary of the FMB of NBC of USA, Inc. at PIM for constructive criticism and the provision of some information obtained from the FMB at the time of the establishment of the PIM pavilion. I also thank the staff at the Malawi National Archives in Zomba for some materials that have been used in this study.

Finally I acknowledge with gratitude my closest friend Melissa Kaunde for cheering me up every time I got tired going through the pile of materials that I gathered during the research. The following people should receive my thanks for their support in various ways: my brothers Wilfred, Joseph, Peter and sisters Grace, Rose and Martha; Samuel Perenje for hosting me for some of my research work, Bosco Mwasikakata, George Nasolo, Aaron Wallani, my mum and dad Rev and Mrs Makondesa and all PIM Christians who assisted me in obtaining information, to them all I say God bless.

ABBREVIATIONS

AIM	American Baptist Industrial Mission
BA	Bachelor of Arts
BD	Bachelor of Divinity
CP	Commissioner of Police
CCAP	Church of Central Africa Presbyterian
DRCM	Dutch Reformed Church Mission
FMB	Foreign Mission Board
Inc	Incorporated
MBC	Malawi Broadcasting Corporation
MNA	Malawi National Archives
MU	Missionary Union
NBA	National Baptist Assembly
NBC	National Baptist Convention
NIU	National Industrial Union
PIM	Providence Industrial Mission
SDB	Seventh Day Baptist
UMCA	Universities Mission to Central Africa
UNISA	University of South Africa
USA	United States of America
ZIM	Zambezi Industrial Mission

Introduction

THE PROVIDENCE INDUSTRIAL MISSION WAS FOUNDED IN FEBRUARY 1900 BY Rev John Chilembwe. Chilembwe's life and ideas were influenced by Joseph Booth through contact with him in 1892-1893, when Booth was establishing Zambezi Industrial Mission,[1] and in 1897 when Booth took him to America. Chilembwe was sponsored on his return to Malawi by the Foreign Mission Board (FMB) of the National Baptist Convention (NBC), USA, Inc.[2] In a letter to the Resident in Chiradzulu, Chilembwe wrote this about himself in response to a question regarding what authority he was under when operating and opening up schools:

> Regarding your request concerning the establishment of the PIM Schools, PIM was opened on February 1900. But touching the authority I will explain. After staying in America a few years I was ordained a minister and adopted as a missionary of the Foreign Mission Board of the National Baptist Convention.[3]

This statement shows that Chilembwe recognized himself as a missionary of the Foreign Mission Board.

Chilembwe centered his work on nothing else but mission work and society.[4] He received missionary support from the Foreign Mission Board of the National Baptist Convention, USA, Inc. The FMB sponsored two further missionaries for service at PIM during Chilembwe's period. These were Rev London N. Cheek (1901-1906)[5] and Miss Emma B. DeLany (1902-1906).[6] The mission experienced such development that in 1910 Chilembwe reported to the FMB that there was one missionary (himself), five churches, 800 members, seven native helpers and 625 pupils.[7] By 1912 Chilembwe efhad completed

---

[1] Harry Langworthy, *Africa for the African: The Life of Joseph Booth*, Blantyre: CLAIM-Kachere, 1996, pp. 32-33.
[2] Centenary Celebration brochure, Brief Overview of Providence Industrial Mission (PIM) 2000.
[3] John Chilembwe - Resident Chiradzulu, 12.1.1914.
[4] K.R. Ross (ed.), *Christianity in Malawi: A Source Book*, Gweru: Mambo-Kachere, 1996, p. 147.
[5] Cheek married Chilembwe's niece and took her to the USA at the end of his missionary work.
[6] Emma B. DeLany went back to the USA, and was later followed by her former student and houseboy Daniel Malekebu. She sponsored his education and later Malekebu became Chilembwe's' successor and the builder of PIM in 1926 after a period of eleven years of silence.
[7] Inscription on the memorial tower at the PIM built by Malekebu in the 1930s and officially dedicated by Rev M.B.K. Chiphuliko in 1995.

INTRODUCTION

construction of a large brick church, and he was known to have a well-dressed Christian community.

The mission flourished through hard work. Even though the Foreign Mission Board sponsored Chilembwe, he did not always receive his financial support. As a full time missionary, he struggled to raise resources by himself. Since the American missionaries left PIM in 1906, Chilembwe fought alone tooth and nail to bring his mission to a higher standard. He acquired a hunting license on 10th July, 1911, which was issued at Chiradzulu *boma* at a fee of one pound.[8] This license gave him the authority to hunt, kill and capture animals. He used to hunt elephants and this brought him money to support his mission work.

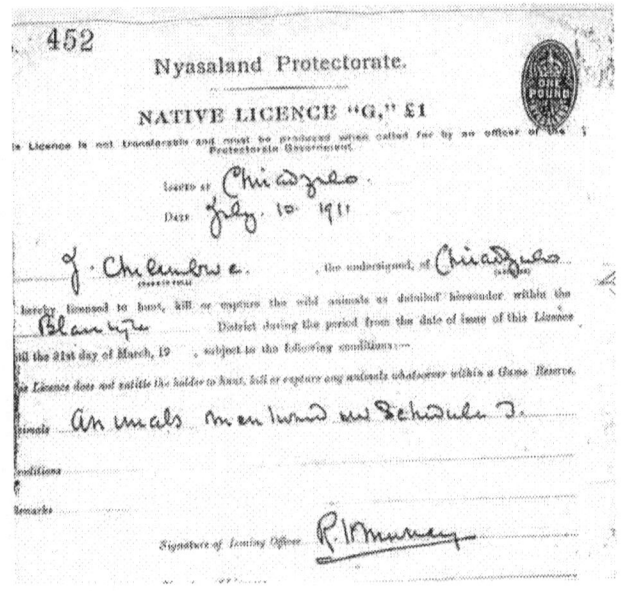

Native hunting license issued to John Chilembwe on 10th July, 1911.

Chilembwe used any means that would bring money to the mission. This led him to get into debt with H.E. Peters [Mlelemba].[9] In his letter dated 26. March 1914 Chilembwe states: "I am only laboured not for my own, but in the name of God for my countrymen. I am sure, it was by revelation of Christ I find you

---

[8] Native license 10.7.1911.
[9] H.E. Peters was a successful African businessman, a friend of Chilembwe who, apart from owning a shop in Blantyre, also ran his own school. Him and M.M. Chisuse were joint secretaries for the African Chamber of Commerce which was organized by African business entrepreneurs.

in the time of my struggling to be my constant helper."[10] Chilembwe was determined to pay back his debts as soon as he could as indicated in the same letter to H.E. Peters. "Believe I will square before I leave this country for Europe and America which will not be long."[11] Though in financial difficulties, Chilembwe remained faithful to his mission work by even requesting H.E. Peters to help him in prayer: "Pray for me that I may not fail for the money in my heart I value nothing for I have weighed the world and its riches and find nothing comparing the love I got for my people and our God."[12]

As a full time missionary, Chilembwe devoted himself to prayer for other people to achieve in their various positions in the society. In a letter to H.E. Peters about the Native Industrial Union, which was formed to help African Christian women and men to excel in their businesses, he wrote:

> I hope you will understand me, if possible show this letter to the chairman of said NIU for I am praying for him, that he may not sleep, while opportunity is before us ... now seems to me to be very time to send our efforts towards making the boys and young men of today, the Christian leaders of new negroes. Believe me."[13]

Chilembwe as a missionary also emerged as a harbinger of political independence for Malawi.[14] He was the heir of the "Africa for the African" vision of Joseph Booth but he transformed it in such a way as to reach the conclusion that armed revolt against colonial rule was necessary.[15] Chilembwe himself was shot and killed; many of his followers were executed and his big church was blown up by the British government in 1915. After that the church was not allowed to hold its meetings as it was banned by the colonial government. This led to underground worship of its devoted members till 1924. In 1926 Dr Daniel Sharpe Malekebu reopened the mission.[16] While Chilembwe was at PIM, Malekebu found his way to the USA following his teacher Miss Emma B. DeLany. Despite the resistance that came from his relatives, Malekebu was determined to go to America. He wrote "One thing I know, I made up my mind that, to that place called America I must go."[17] Malekebu kept his word. He found himself in New York, America, on August 19, 1905. Malekebu recalls

---

[10] John Chilembwe - H.E. Peters Mlelemba 26.3.1914.
[11] Ibid.
[12] John Chilembwe - H.E. Peters Mlelemba 24.4.1912.
[13] John Chilembwe - H.E. Peters Mlelemba 5.7.1909.
[14] It is for this reason that the government recognized Chilembwe as a national hero, and January 15, Chilembwe Day was gazetted as a public holiday.
[15] G. Shepperson and T. Price, *Independent African: John Chilembwe and the Origins, Setting and Significance of the Nyasaland Native Rising of 1915*, Edinburgh University Press, 1958, pp. 181-193.((6th printing Blantyre: CLAIM-Kachere 2000).
[16] R.J. Macdonald, "An Appreciation on Rev Dr Daniel Malekebu and the Reopening of the Providence Industrial Mission: 1926-1939", unpublished, 1975.
[17] Daniel Malekebu, "A Plea for Africa", unpublished, 1918, p. 9.

> "Due to the fact that I had no money, I was sent to Ellis Island N.Y. After staying there four days, one of the officers asked me, did I not have a friend in America who could stand or vouch for me. I told him I thought I did. The officers suggested to send a telegram. I did not know what they meant but I was glad to send anything. The telegram was sent to Florida Fernandina."[18]

After several accomplishments in America, time came for him to return to Africa as a missionary and medical doctor. Rosa Beckwith wrote the following poem in honour of Dr Malekebu.

> **Daniel S. Malekebu**
>
> **From Africa's Sunny Plain**
>
> At the border of the ocean stands a little heathen boy, with a heart fit for devotion, heart so soon to leap with joy.
>
> He had come from sandy desert, through the jungles, o'er the hills, and his feet are sore with walking, still he has a manly will.
>
> Now he's reached the grand old harbor, where the ships come floating in, soon he'll step aboard the vessel, then his voyage will begin.
>
> He will sail into a new world, pledge his heart and give his soul, in a school he will toil and study, till he's worth his weight in gold.
>
> Loyal to his duty ever, toiling onward day by day, with a will that naught can sever, stern and brave as soul can be.
>
> Many years have marked the training in this country for the lad, now he goes back to his homeland, making hearts of others glad.
>
> Toiling there among his people, teaching, preaching every day, pointing upward like a steeple, in a happy Christian way.[19]

While preparing to return to Africa while in Chicago, Malekebu wrote the following letter to his friends in 1918:

> Dear Friends,
>
> It is with unusual interest that I take the pleasure of writing you at this hour. Many years have passed since I left my fatherland to come to America for education. Many of you have prayed and helped me. My heart is filled with gratitude to you; more than I can express with pen and ink. The road has been hard and rough to be where I am today. You have very often heard the story, of how I walked two hundred (200) miles through the jungles of Africa, to come to this country for an education, and how I slept in trees, made bon fires to keep the lions and wild animals of Africa from devouring me. On the steamers, how I labored for my passage to America. Like Paul, while he preached the gospel of salvation,

---

[18] Ibid., p. 9.
[19] Ibid., p. 7.

labored for his sustenance. While trying to get an education, I have worked my way through colleges. Yea, in coal mines. Still I realize that OF MY OWN SELF I could not accomplish what I have accomplished, only through the Providence of God, and your prayers and assistance. I am glad that it has been so, for nothing is worth while, only that which we must pay a high price for; this makes me appreciate it all the more.

I appeal to you to think with me on this vital question of Africa and its redemption. After these many years of preparation in this country, now that the war is over, and soon I will be going home to carry the good news to my people. What do you want me to tell your people and mine? For they are anxiously waiting and expecting me to bring to them and show them something bigger than you or I have any idea after these years of preparation. Africa will afford, hereafter, the greatest field for usefulness with other people. Moneys are being raised, missionaries are being trained to go over when conditions are better. What then, shall there be lukewarmness and staleness of mind on your part, with these opportunities around us?

It is just as easy to have a great Institution in Africa, as to say we have one. I call your prayerful attention to our program, and the needs of Central Africa. The success of what God wants me to do in Africa will depend on the people of America, as you are his instruments. It is you, why I am here. It is through you I am where I am. What part will you take? How much will you give?

I am yours for the redemption of Africa,

Daniel S. Malekebu, M.D.[20]

Malekebu successfully returned to Nyasaland and officially reopened the mission on June 3, 1926.[21] As a medical Doctor graduated from Meharry Medical School in the United States of America, Dr Malekebu established the first hospital at PIM under a *thundu* tree in 1927. In 1928 the construction of the New Jerusalem Temple started and was completed in 1933.[22]

John Chilembwe and Dr Daniel Malekebu are no doubt the central figures of this book, and much they have in common. But they differ in terms of published coverage. Very little has been written about Malekebu,[23] much has

---

[20] Daniel Malekebu, "A Plea for Africa", unpublished, 1918, pp. 17-18.
[21] PIM Centenary Celebration brochure, Brief Overview of the Providence Industrial Mission (PIM) 2000.
[22] Ibid.
[23] Ibid., Roderick J. Macdonald, "The Rev Dr Daniel Sharpe Malekebu and the Reopening of Providence Industrial Mission 1926-39: an Appreciation", in R.J. Macdonald (ed.), *From Nyasaland to Malawi*, Nairobi: East African Publishing House, 1975, pp. 215-233; John K. Parratt, "The Malekebu Case", in A.F. Walls and W.R. Schenk (eds.), *Exploring New Religious Movements: Essays in Honour of Harold W. Turner*, Elkhart: Mission Focus, 1990, pp. 119-129.

been written about John Chilembwe.[24] This book is not to repeat what others wrote—though their books have been used with profit—but to present the PIM story from a different angle: not as political history but as church history, and to present it as a continuous history from the days of foundation (1900) through John Chilembwe's ministry, through the "hidden years" (1915-1926) and well into the ministry of Dr Malekebu up to 1940.

I write this history as an insider, a committed member of PIM. This may make me less critical at times, but it has also opened up to me venues of inquiry that an outsider might not have found. As PIM has kept few written records, I was excited to find the full 1914 membership list in the records of the PIM Pavillion. At Rev W.D. Manyika's home in Kanjedza I found Malekebu's old copy of "My Vision", and elsewhere I was given copies of Malekebu's correspondence with the Educational Authorities.

Much of the information was gathered through extended interviews, first in 1994 for my BA thesis "The Life and Ministry of Rev and Mrs Muocha"[25] and later for my MA thesis "The Ecclesiastical History of Providence Industrial Mission 1900-1940"f,[26] which provides the base for this book.

I want to thank all who assisted in my research, especially those from PIM, and I hope, that I have written their and our story.

---

[24] Still unsurpassed about the Chilembwe story is: George Shepperson and Tom Price, *Independent African. John Chilembwe and the Origins, Setting and Significance of the Nyasaland Native Rising of 1915*, Edinburgh: Edinburgh University Press, 1958. The 1987 paperback edition was reprinted by the Kachere Series in 2000 as the 6th edition. D.D. Phiri, *The Rev John Chilembwe*, London: Longman, 1976 shows Chilembwe as an educationalist, spiritual leader and Pan Africanist. G. Mwase's *Strike a Blow and Die* (ed. Robert I. Rotberg, Cambridge: Harvard University Press, 1967) contains much first hand information of the Rising given to Mwase by one of Chilembwe's followers when they were fellow inmates at Zomba Prison. The most recent book is D.D. Phiri, *Let Us Die For Africa: An African Perspective on the Life and Death of John Chilembwe of Nyasaland/Malawi*, Blantyre: Central Africana, 1999.

[25] BA, University of Malawi, 1996. This formed the base for Patrick Makondesa, *Moyo ndi Utumiki wa Mbusa ndi Mayi Muocha a Providence Industrial Mission*, Blantyre: CLAIM-Kachere, 2001.

[26] MA, University of Malawi, 2002.

Chapter One

THE EARLY PERIOD OF PIM MINISTRY

JOHN CHILEMBWE WAS BORN NEAR A HILL CALLED SANGANO,1 EAST OF CHIRAdzulu *boma* in the year 1871. His father, a Yao, was known as Kaundama.² John Chilembwe's other name was Nkologo.³ His mother was a Nyanja called Nyangu.⁴ Chilembwe's family migrated to village headman Chilomoni in Blantyre in search of land to settle on and cultivate. In this village there was a school at which Chilembwe was enrolled,⁵ and in 1891 he passed his standard three.⁶ As missionaries ran the schools, reading of the Bible and some form of worship were the order of the day before classes started. This practice had an impact in one way or the other on the pupils. While Chilembwe's conversion to Christianity may have had a basis in such a background, there is no evidence that he was baptized at this early stage.

---

¹T There is a growing story about the birth of Chilembwe. It is said that Chilembwe was not born in the normal way, his legs rather than his head were first to come out of the womb. I am not sure of how far the story is true but some people still hold it as something special to Chilembwe's birth.
² Kelvin N. Banda, in his book *A Brief History of Education in Malawi*, states that Chilembwe was born at Chilanga village about a mile from the district headquarters of Chiradzulu. The village of group village headman Chilanga can today easily be viewed from the Chiradzulu hospital as it is only 15 minutes walk. Chilembwe was born to a Nyangu of the Mpinganjira group of the Amaravi. Mpinganjira and Changamire had left Maravi and proceeded southwards settling in the area that is now part of Mangochi district. The Maravi group to which the family of Chilembwe belonged broke away from the Mpinganjira-Changamire group along with many other Nyanja speaking groups. The Chilanga group to which the Chilembwe family belonged settled at Sangano hill in Chiradzulu. It was at this Chilanga village that the woman of Nyangu married a Yao tribesman named Kaundama.
³ D.D. Phiri suggests that this was possibly the name he used before adopting the name John.
⁴ For more information on Nyangu read D.D. Phiri, *Let Us Die for Africa*, Blantyre: Central Africana, 1999, pp. 1-2.
⁵ D.D. Phiri, *Let Us Die for Africa: An African Perspective on the Life and Death of John Chilembwe of Nyasaland/Malawi*, Blantyre: Central Africana, 1999, p. 1.
⁶ A standard three education today means three years of schooling. In those days it meant about seven years; four years spent entirely in vernacular and then the remaining three concentrating on the learning of English besides other additional subjects. It was those years that included the learning of English that were referred to as *standards*; the preceding years were called *classes*.

Chilembwe's Call to Ministry

John Chilembwe's call to ministry can be traced back to the period of his contact with Joseph Booth, as early as 1893. Chilembwe, who had learnt some English through Blantyre Mission, went to Booth looking for a job. Booth praised God for sending a young man to him. However, Chilembwe seems to have felt a call within him even predating his contact with Booth, who acted as a passage to the fulfillment of his call and vision. In his letter to Booth seeking employment, Chilembwe wrote the following words in pencil. "Dear Mr Booth, You please carry me for God. I like to be your cook boy."[7] What comes first in his application is "God"; and "work" is to be of a secondary consideration to him. To Chilembwe, the call comes first, "work" becoming a means to its fulfillment. He seemed to have a burning desire that made him seek contact with Booth not for material gain but rather for spiritual gain. It was in this way that Chilembwe and Booth came into each other's lives in February 1893.

Booth's daughter, Mrs Emily Booth Langworthy, writes of Chilembwe: "Father was despairing of ever being able to find a dependable boy, when out of heaven's blue the right boy came to find us. His name was John. He was a very black boy with white teeth and a gleaming smile."[8] In describing Chilembwe as "the right boy," possibly, Mrs Langworthy observed special characteristics in him that would not be found in other boys of his age. This allows one to think that Chilembwe's character was worthy of a calling to gospel ministry, and he proved to be thoroughly reliable, honest and of a pleasant disposition.

When Chilembwe was taken into Booth's household, he began to excel in other areas, too With time, his English vocabulary improved and he was soon employed as Booth's interpreter not only in Blantyre, but also during his evangelical travels all over the Shire Highlands and the Lower Shire.[9] Chilembwe's request to Booth at the time of seeking a job to "carry me for God" was beginning to be fulfilled.

At Chilomoni Junior Primary School, Chilembwe had undergone instruction in Bible Knowledge as far as the catechumen class, but never sought as a member of the Scottish Kirk. On 17th July 1893, he was baptized by Booth and became Booth's first convert to Christianity. That marked Chilembwe's call to Christianity. His calling to ministry was being fulfilled little by little. Unsurprisingly, this gave him the chance to acquire skills and knowledge to effectively communicate to people of different cultures and beliefs thus preparing his future ministry as a pastor.

---

[7] D.D. Phiri, *Let Us Die for Africa*: p. 4.
[8] *Ibid.*, p. 5.
[9] *Ibid.*, p. 5.

His call to be a preacher began to emerge as he accompanied Booth during his preaching tours. As his interpreter, Chilembwe gained some experience of preaching the word of God. He did not always depend on or accompany Booth in his preaching sessions. He could take the initiative himself in going out into the field and preach. D.D. Phiri notes that from being Joseph Booth's interpreter, Chilembwe graduated to the role of a "zealous auxiliary preacher." Chilembwe in his own words once confided to Booth:

> I often preach in my native village, but the chief and many people will not hear now. One day after preaching my elder 'brother,' James Chimpele, came to me and said, 'You preached just now that God's message is to go to all people and tell a good message to them. How do you know?' I answered 'Because I can read it for myself both in the English tongue and in my own language, I have God's book.' He said, 'But perhaps white men have altered God's book to suit themselves and so they preach peace to us. Perhaps God's book does not say this to white men. Perhaps it says to them, go to all people take their land, kill the people, I give you power.' If God's word said to them what they preach to us, not to steal, not to kill, would they not do it? I cannot receive the words which the white men have brought.[10]

Chilembwe's own statement shows that he met resistance of some kind from his hearers. His cousin, Chimpele, was in the front line of the scoffers.[11] But Chilembwe was not the sort of person who would easily give up. It cannot be doubted that Chilembwe had in mind Isaiah's ministry, which had to face resistance. Still he had hope that one day things would work for his good.

Chilembwe learnt many things from Booth. For example, in 1894 Booth took him to Quelimane to clear his goods through customs; and Chilembwe was one of the seven African trustees for Booth's proposed completely African Mission in 1896.[12] It was from such trips and activities that Chilembwe received the training that would be important for his future ministry in the fulfillment of his call. The climax of the fulfillment and preparation of his call to ministry came when Booth took him to the United States of America in 1897. In early 1898 he began studies at Virginia Theological Seminary, Lynchburg

---

[10] G. Shepperson and T. Price. *Independent African: John Chilembwe and the Origins, Setting and Significance of the Nyasaland Native Rising of 1915*, Edinburgh University Press, 1958, p. 68.

[11] Morris Chimpele Chilembwe, one of Chilembwe's scoffers, soon became one of Chilembwe's right hand men, to the extent that he fully participated in the uprising and faced his death at Migowi where PIM church was then planted by Chilembwe's followers. His grave still is there just fifty metres from the present PIM church building near Mwananyani hill in village headman Garinet Kaduya. He was with Chilembwe on their way to Mozambique, fleeing colonial government soldiers." Rumours have it that he was mistakenly killed as Chilembwe, it later being discovered he was the nephew and not Chilembwe himself. This is probably the reason why the people at Migowi still hold the idea that Chilembwe was not killed but entered Mozambique. For more on this, see Patrick Makondesa "John Chilembwe in Migowi", unpublished.

[12] M.B.K. Chipuliko, "A Brief History of Rev John Chilembwe", unpublished, 1995, p. 1.

(founded in 1888). Dr L.G. Jordan, Secretary of the Foreign Mission Board, took Chilembwe to Rev William W. Brown who paid for his education.[13]

Chilembwe in America

While in America, Chilembwe and Booth parted company. One day in Philadelphia, at a large gathering of Afro-American ministers, Chilembwe said: "Mr Booth, we must now part company. God has brought me to good friends. I am now a man and can walk alone."[14]

Chilembwe did not attribute his presence in America to Booth but to God. He knew God had a special purpose for him; he knew he was called to ministry and all that happened was a step in the fulfillment of that call. He recognized God's presence at every juncture of his life.

Chilembwe as a young man in America (1897/1898). This picture originally appeared in the African American Black Baptist Convention magazine (David Stuart Mogg Collection)

While at school in America, Chilembwe did not want to see himself as inferior. Some American Negroes tended to assume an air of superiority towards the African Negro. However, true to his temperament, Chilembwe refused to remain quiet or indifferent before such arrogant pretence, coming even from fellow blacks. His reply to their pretension was to feign the air of an African of

---

[13] Today at PIM headquarters at Mbombwe in Chiradzulu, there is a building named "L.G. Jordan Memorial Library." It was given this name to honour the man that helped Chilembwe in time of need and managed to get facilitated the sponsorship of his education. Presently the building is used for the PIM pavilion, established as a landmark to the centennial celebrations of PIM 1900-2000. William W. Brown is remembered in one of the missions sponsored by the FMB in South Africa, Soweto, known as W.W. Brown Memorial Mission. W.W. Brown was the pastor of High Street Baptist Church at Roanoke, Virginia.

[14] G. Shepperson and T. Price, *Independent African, John Chilembwe and the Origins, Setting and significance of the Nyasaland Native Rising of 1915*, Edinburgh University Press, 1958, p. 93.

noble birth. When signing or giving his name, he would prefix it with the Yao title "che," which means "mister" and so when asked by the curious what "che" meant he would say it meant "prince", and that in Africa he was the son of a king.[15]

Chilembwe knew his calling, and believed that his presence in America was God's divine plan for the people of Africa to receive the light. It was in Louisville, Kentucky, USA where his dream of becoming an ordained pastor was fulfilled. When he was about to leave for home at the end of 1899, he became so ill with asthma that his American friends lost hope that he would ever recover sufficiently to return to Africa. Dr Jordan, the secretary of the Foreign Mission Board of the National Baptist Convention of USA Inc, even asked him if he had any last wishes to send to his people at home. In a spirit of confidence and optimism, Chilembwe replied that he could not die, for God had brought him to America to take the light to his people in Africa.[16] The following are Dr L. Jordan's words:

> Two years having gone by, and this bright eyed, open hearted young African had made rapid strides in his studies, but had become a victim of asthma. By order of his physician, he must return to Africa. We can never forget, at a farewell meeting at Newport News, Virginia, about 2 o'clock in the morning. With the rain coming down in torrents, the thunder fairly shaking the house wherein we dwelled, and the lightning playing about the electric wires on the front of the building, we supposed this young African dying. We had propped up his head with a chair to see him die. As we stood, after looking into his face with pity, we remember having said to him, 'Bro Chilembwe, if anything should happen, to you, what must I write to your people?' He was then to us breathing his last. Rolling his eyes towards us, unable to speak scarcely, he said 'Brudder Jordan, I no going to die. God bring me to this land to get light to take back to my people. He is not going to kill me here.' Deep in our hearts we admired his faith but would not have given a ten cents for his life. But the next morning he was yet living.[17]

To the American Negro Baptists, Chilembwe was not only an attractive figure in his own right but also a 'John the Baptist' making in the wilderness of Central Africa a path for American Negro missionaries. Such a missionary venture, they felt, would afford further evidence to the whites of the United States and the world in general that the Negro could succeed as well as they in any sphere of choice. It would be part of the great protest that was sweeping through Negro

---

[15] D.D. Phiri, *Let Us Die for Africa: An African Perspective on the Life and Death of John Chilembwe of Nyasaland/Malawi*, Blantyre: Central Africana, 1999, p. 11.

[16] G. Shepperson and T. Price, *Independent African: John Chilembwe and the Origins, Setting and Significance of the Nyasaland Native Rising of 1915*, Edinburgh University Press, 1958, p. 122.

[17] Pamphlet, The Sabbath Evangelizing and Industrial Association, No 4. 1899, in: Shepperson and Price, *Independent African*, p. 122.

America against its loss of civil rights since the failure of the Northern Reconstruction of the Southern States after the civil war; and a proud assertion of the Independent Negro spirit.[18] Indeed, by the end of 1904, when the National Baptist Convention had given to its members an account of its stewardship during the first phase of its relationship with Chilembwe's missionary enterprise, this point was made very clear:

> We serve notice on the world today that there will be no more begging for our own. There will be no more selling out below cost, there will be no more courting of favours, there will be no more divorcing ourselves from this soil, but there will be a standing until either Shiloh or our rights as American citizens come. Nothing but the gospel of Jesus Christ ruling every heart, in black and white alike, will bring these rights. Jesus will not come to this earth until at his appearance the world will sing this chorus. And the world will not sing this chorus until black men and white men who preach the doctrine of the brotherhood of Man and the fatherhood of God believe so supremely in that gospel that one shall not deny the other inalienable and sacred rights.[19]

It was in this spirit that Chilembwe returned to Africa. Phiri states that people, who are convinced that God has given them a special duty to fulfill amongst their people, or for their country, do not easily imagine that death will come to them in such fashion. Nor do they allow thoughts about death to cloud their minds.[20] Chilembwe successfully completed his studies in America and an entry in the class roll at his American College says that he was awarded the Bachelor of Arts and Bachelor of Divinity degrees (BA, BD). Specific detail is not recorded.[21]

Chilembwe as a Missionary

Chilembwe returned to Nyasaland fully qualified for mission work. He spoke of himself as an ordained minister and a missionary.[22] By early 1899, plans were underway for Charles S. Morris[23] to travel to South Africa to visit B.A. Jackson, who for some years had been associated with the National Baptist Convention's Foreign Mission Board. Lewis Jordan, secretary of the Foreign Mission Board, made an arrangement through the president of the ABIM, Cornelia Woefkin, to obtain financial backing from the American Baptist Missionary Union. One year's salary of $50 per month, for a year, was to be paid to Mrs Morris while

---

[18] G. Shepperson and T. Price, *Independent African*, p. 122.
[19] *Ibid.*, p. 123.
[20] D.D. Phiri, *Let Us Die for Africa*, p. 11.
[21] *Ibid.*, p. 116.
[22] John Chilembwe - Resident Chiradzulu, 12.1.1914.
[23] Charles S. Morris was from West Newton, Massachusetts, a member of the board of African Baptist Industrial Mission ABIM. After Booth's departure he became field secretary and missionary of the African Baptist Industrial Mission.

her husband was in Africa, and $500 was provided for the trip.[24] Apparently the former amount was to come from the ABIM and the latter sum from the Missionary Union (MU). Woefkin felt that instead of appealing to churches for money, and thus lessening normal contributions to the Missionary Union, a few individuals should pay the salary.[25] It is not clear what was contributed by the Foreign Mission Board of the National Baptist Convention aside from the services of Morris.

The main goal of the trip was for Morris to visit NBC interests in South Africa, with the purpose of investigating prospects for a site for an Industrial Mission. In addition, he planned to visit the American Baptist missionaries in the Congo and would stop in Liberia. Morris also planned to visit Malawi to help John Chilembwe become established as a missionary under the auspices of the ABIM. Morris and Chilembwe seem to have left the United States for Britain on 20th June 1899. In London they met with Robert Caldwell, the secretary of the Zambezi Industrial Mission (ZIM). Morris also met Dr Grattan Guinness, the Director, with his wife Fanny, of the East London Missionary Training Institute (ELTI).[26] Morris and Chilembwe together approached officials to gain a title for the land of what was to become Providence Industrial Mission. Morris also obtained for Chilembwe free passage up the Zambezi River.[27] As Morris reached Cape Town by early August, Harry Langworthy suggests that he possibly left London before Chilembwe. This argument can hold water in that Chilembwe himself seemed to act independently while in London, so at that time he could have been alone and not with Morris. In a letter to the Resident in Chiradzulu at the time when PIM was fully established, he wrote:

> Regarding your request concerning the establishment of the Providence Industrial Mission schools, PIM was opened on February 1, 1900. But touching the authority I will explain. After staying in America a few years and was ordained a minister and adopted as a missionary under the auspices of the Foreign Mission Board of the National Baptist Convention, on my return I thought it was best as I knew too well that I was one of the subject of British flag; to consult the leading members of the kingdom and after allowed to visit the house of commons where I obtained my right of getting a letter of Introduction to commissioner Sharpe who was afterwards became the governor of Nyasaland. After good conversation on the subject finally I was allowed to open my mission at Chiradzulu sub-district and afterwards I had opened out stations.[28]

---

[24] Harry Langworthy, *Africa for the African: The Life of Joseph Booth*, p. 102.
[25] Ibid., p. 102.
[26] Fanny and Grattan Guinness were the leaders of the interdenomminational Faith Mission Movement in Britain.
[27] Probably he obtained this from the ZIM which still ran the missions transport.
[28] John Chilembwe - Resident, Chiradzulu, 12.1.1914.

After Morris left Chilembwe in London, they never met, so that Chilembwe had to establish the PIM by himself. Morris was unable to go to Nyasaland or Congo, as previously planned, because the original plan to pass rapidly through South Africa en route to British Central Africa, apparently by going overland, was postponed by the many distractions in the Cape Colony. In Cape Town and Port Elizabeth he met coloured groups to raise interest and potential support. In Queens Town he met Rev Goduka of the African Native Church which had seventeen churches, 13 ministers, 814 members, 444 probationers and ten schools. He attracted their affiliation to the American Church as the African Baptist Church. On September 10th, Morris baptized two women leaders of the church in the presence of two thousand people. Morris spent a fair amount of time conferring with the leaders of the movement and visiting its centres. He was very optimistic about the prospects for Baptist and Industrial work in South Africa and more importantly to further this work than to go on to Nyasaland, or even Congo. However, the enthusiastic reception, the many calls to meet with interested groups, and the time spent proved more expensive than he had foreseen. His appeal for more financial support to complete the planned tour of investigation evidently was not met. Hence he was unable to go to Nyasaland and Congo. Instead he proceeded to Liberia where he spent some time recuperating from what probably was malaria.[29] In January 1900 he returned ill to the United States with his work incomplete.[30]

In London Chilembwe visited the House of Commons. He left London with a letter of introduction from officials of the British Government, possibly at the Foreign Office[31] to Sir Alfred Sharpe who, in 1900, was Commissioner of British Central Africa and was later to become the first colonial administrator to bear the title of Governor of Nyasaland. In February 1900, after a good conversation with Sir Alfred Sharpe, Chilembwe launched the Providence Industrial Mission (PIM) on the eastern side of the river Mbombwe, in Chiradzulu District. He named his church the First African Baptist Mission or Ajawa Providence Industrial Mission. Soon he dropped 'Ajawa' from the mission's title, because it was not a predominantly Yao venture. 'Providence' was an institution in New York that had helped fund Chilembwe's stay there. The name 'Industrial' Chilembwe borrowed from Booth. It emphasized the policy of his mission to combine the teaching of the gospel with that of industrial skills.[32] It is said that when he returned in 1900, the Central African

---

[29] Harry Langworthy, *Africa for the African. The Life of Joseph Booth*, p. 103.
[30] Some time early in 1901, Morris' travelling ended and he settled in New York to be minister of the Abyssinia Baptist Church.
[31] D.D. Phiri, *Let Us Die for Africa*, p. 15.
[32] Ibid. p. 15. Regarding the name Providence Industrial Mission, Shepperson and Price write that Chilembwe had undoubtedly taken his general concept of an Industrial mission from Booth's experiments between 1892 and 1897, and this had been sanctioned by the National Baptist Convention Foreign Mission Board which, even if it had no contact with Booth, would most

Times called him a "Pitiable travesty of true Christianity."[33] Chilembwe was the first African from his part of the world who had been to America and returned. He had come back from overseas not as slave, soldier or servant but as a religious minister, with the backing of one of the greatest forces of organized Negroes in the world. If the teaching and training of the Virginia Theological Seminary left much to be desired, it had conferred on Chilembwe the mark of increased social status. He returned home clothed in full clerical respectability more than a decade before the neighboring Blantyre Mission would ordain its first African ministers.[34] At the period when, as the Blantyre Mission paper put it, 'the direction of native wages [was] upward, especially skilled labour, [and] in native life the horizon of ideas [was] widening every year,'[35] he was for many Africans an example of a successful man: one who had taken advantage of the opportunities that white society offered him to claim a position of equality with the white man himself. He was an object of respect and envy: both attitudes that would add to Chilembwe's difficulties in starting mission work.[36]

Dr Daniel Malekebu recalls the time Chilembwe was busy searching for land where his mission was to be situated.

---

certainly have been aware of the discussion on Industrial missions in the American religious press. But where the adjective 'Providence' came from is difficult to say. Was it simply the reflection of pious hope? It is more likely that the term has American Negro connotations, and it may well have been suggested by the Providence Missionary Baptist District Association (PMBDA), the first grouping of United States Negro Baptists in Ohio, 1836; or by the fact that there were Negro Baptists at Providence, Rhode Island, as early as 1774, and that in a different Providence (New Providence in the Bahamas) American Negroes had been active as far back as the last decade of the eighteenth century. If this is so, the originators of its use for the title of Chilembwe's mission may have hoped that his centre would take its place in the Afro-American tradition of Negro Baptists, a tradition of highly independent activity that was set on increasing Negro status which Chilembwe, in a land where there were few Negro traditions other than tribal ones, may have welcomed as a support to him in his work of advancing the position of his people in the culture of the new technical west. It can also be a possibility that Chilembwe chose the name of an American church, by today's practice sometimes to name churches in Malawi after American Negro churches like the church in Migowi. This church was named Mt Cleveland Ohio Baptist Church after the visit of some American pastors from the FMB. Also the PIM church at Chiawelo, Soweto in South Africa was named First Institutional Baptist Church of Soweto after the First Institutional Baptist Church of Phoenix, Arizona in the United States of America when they became a mission sponsor of the congregation of Chiawelo, Soweto, in the early 1980s. Similarly the church at Sadzi in Zomba changed its name from Holy Cross Baptist Church to BM and E Baptist Church, Texas after being sponsored by the BM and E Baptist Church of Texas in building a church edifice at Three Miles in Zomba.

[33] Harry H. Johnston, *British Central Africa*, London 1898, pp. 203-204, John Buchanan, *A Lodge in the Wilderness*, London, 1906, p. 140. MNA.

[34] These first African Blantyre Mission ministers were Rev Harry Kambwiri Matecheta and Rev Stephen Kundecha. Both were ordained in 1911.

[35] Shepperson and Price, *Independent African*, p. 129.

[36] Ibid., p. 129.

> A few years after our arrival at Chiradzulu, Uncle and I happened to go to Blantyre and went in a church where they were having Sunday morning services. The missionary had an instrument that he played (an accordion) while the congregation sang. I was very much impressed with the services. When I went home, I gathered up a crowd of boys and made a grass hut for a church. I made the boys act as my congregation and I was the preacher. It was great fun for us all. I was greatly impressed at the appearance of the mission boys and girls and wished I could have been one of them.
>
> After some few years we heard that an African who had gone to America had returned and was going to make a mission at Chiradzulu. I remember when he passed through our village from Blantyre on his way to find a good place for his mission. Finally we learned that he had found one within about three miles of our village. This was in 1900."[37]

Chilembwe's more serious problem at the time was his taking up land in one of the parts of the Protectorate most convenient for European planters. While it is true that he was not the first African to buy land in British Central Africa, and that his demand in 1900 was a modest 93 acres, it nevertheless took some time before the title deed to the land which he had selected and purchased for £25:18s (about $130) was properly completed. Emissaries of the National Baptist Convention complained that this had been the result of deliberate delay by the commissioner, Alfred Sharpe, who first forced Chilembwe to have power of attorney from the Foreign Mission Board of the Negro Baptists, and then conveniently 'lost' it until another one was made available.[38] It is impossible to get at the truth of this allegation, but the administration may well have taken its time over the matter of Chilembwe's land transaction. Chilembwe, after all, was known to be one of Booth's first converts and the commissioner had just finished dealing with Booth after his 1899 petition. There was little love lost between the two of them: to Sharpe, Booth was a "shifty, undesirable, dangerous man"; to Booth, the Commissioner was a petty tyrant, ready to put an African into chains for the slightest offence.[39] Sharpe could hardly be expected, therefore, to go to undue pains to see that Chilembwe's land transaction went through quickly.

---

[37] Daniel Malekebu, "The History of my Life and my Work", unpublished, 1939, pp. 2-3.
[38] Journal of the Twentieth Annual Session of the National Baptist Convention, 12-17 September 1900 (Nashville, Tenn), p. 45-46, *Journal of the Twenty Fourth Annual Session of the NBC*, 1904, p. 37, *Mission Herald* Vol 44, September-October 1940, p. 17.
[39] Shepperson and Price, *Independent African*, p. 131.

*Chilembwe baptizing from Chilembwe's own photograph album
(courtesy of Professor George Shepperson)*

Probably he was annoyed with Chilembwe personally, not only because he came back to the Protectorate at a difficult time and was the type of African unlikely to take without question the directives of the administration, but also because, as it appears, he had offered him some form of office work which offer Chilembwe had refused.[40] Chilembwe's refusal to take up a job offered by Sharpe shows how faithful he was to his call, and he worked to see his vision being fulfilled. By the end of the year, Chilembwe had built sufficient buildings at Chiradzulu for a school of about a hundred, and a little mud church where he had baptized fifteen, and had begun to employ labour for more ambitious buildings. The first person Chilembwe baptized was his own sister Awanjilang'wa, also known as Mary.[41]

PIM's Early Missionaries

Early in 1901, the National Baptist Convention of USA Inc had decided that conditions in South Africa during the Boer war were too unstable to proceed with mission work at that time. Instead of deciding to support Morris to start a new mission in South Africa, they sent Rev Landon N. Cheek[42] to join

---

[40] Ibid., p. 131.
[41] Mrs Chilumpha of Mbombwe PIM, presentation on "The Women of the Past and Women Today", during the PIM Centennial Celebration, PIM, Mbombwe, 2000.
[42] Cheek was born at Canton, Madison County, Mississippi on 8 December 1871. He was thus of much the same age as Chilembwe. After a successful schooling, he had passed into the small Negro college at Jackson, Mississippi, for some higher education, and then to Western College, Macon, Mississippi, for Theology. In 1899 he applied to the NBC for a missionary post, was accepted and after appealing for funds from American Negro Churches he set out from New York in January

THE EARLY PERIOD OF PIM MINISTRY

Chilembwe in the already established work in Nyasaland.[43] He left on January 23, 1901 as a fully trained American National Baptist minister. Chilembwe no doubt was hoping that the American Negro newcomer to the PIM would take some of the burdens of work from his shoulders. However, Cheek's relationship with the whites was a problems was sometimes uneasy. He later wrote:

> My English friends were eyeing me as a veritable hornet who within thirty years would incite the natives against English rule. To the last day of our long and weary years they tried to trump my every move, even to build up our station, hoping that any day I would be discouraged and return to USA.[44]

The next Black American to help in the already established mission was Miss Emma B. DeLany.[45] She arrived in 1902, a year after Cheek. Malekebu describes Emma DeLany as a person with a genuine calling:

> This noble woman had the real call. She was willing to leave mother and father who were able to give her anything she wanted and needed, willing to leave her only sister and friends in general, to work for the redemption of Africa. The salary she received from home missions board was enough to make some say 'I would rather see someone going, let me help.' In 1901 she sailed for Africa, her mother followed her as far as Cincinnati, Ohio, advising her not to go but to let someone else go. And the last words of her father were these 'now daughter, if you must go you are going against my will. Remember I will never see you again on this earth.' He kissed her with tears falling from his eyes, then pushed her away and said 'goodbye'. Miss DeLany sailed for British Central Africa. Of the good she has done in Central Africa, the writer of this little pamphlet is a living example. After staying several years, she came home, and in 1912 she made her second missionary journey to West Coast Africa, Monrovia, Liberia. God will bless her work. The work she is doing and has done with very little human help, God has prospered it. Miss DeLany believes in putting religion and Christianity in everything she does, and

---

1901 for British Central Africa. Cheek became closely attached to the Chilembwe family. He married Chilembwe's niece, Rachel, and became the father of three children, one of whom, Ada, died in Africa.

[43] Harry Langworthy, *Africa for the African: The Life of Joseph Booth*, p. 104.
[44] Shepperson and Price, *Independent African*, p. 137.
[45] Emma DeLany was the same age as Cheek, and much the same age as Chilembwe. She was born at Fernandina in Florida, a daughter of Daniel and Anna DeLany. Her father worked for the United States Government as a pilot and owned a fine home in Fernandina. After an education at its Convent School, Emma DeLany had entered Spelman Seminary (now the undergraduate college for women at Atlanta, Georgia) in 1889, where she spent six years for further education, nursing training—for which she was awarded a gold-medal and preliminary instruction for the mission field. Soon after this she was employed by the Home Mission Society of Boston, Massachusetts, and worked for several years in Georgia, and then was elected as Matron of Florida Memorial College, Live Oak, Florida.

> those whom she teaches get the very essence of her godly life. At Spelman Seminary, her teachers were Northern white women who believed in cleanliness. She is the type of women we need in Africa, truthful, kind, honest, brave, she lives a clean, Christian, positive life."[46]

In the period before Chilembwe had both Cheek and Miss DeLany with him, his little mission was in such financial difficulties that Chilembwe was frequently out shooting in the bush. The sale of elephant tusks was profitable, but gun and game licenses were expensive too. The arrival of the two Black Americans signalled to him that the National Baptist Convention was ready to give him more tangible support. Soon regular cheques began to come from the United States. Chilembwe and Cheek devoted themselves to the tasks of teaching and preaching, and extended their congregations and influence not only in the immediate Chiradzulu area but through the neighbouring district of Mulanje into the Catholic Portuguese territories; and in may be, as far afield as the Rhodesias.[47]

In the early period of Chilembwe's ministry, there was famine and disease in Mozambique, which had increased the number of emigrants from there into British Central Africa in search of food and work.[48] This increase in the potential labour force of the area presented a challenge to Chilembwe. He soon built up a following amongst these migrant workers by actual penetration into their own homelands. He had gone into the Portuguese territories during 1901, on a hunting trip. While there, he found that many Africans were being thrown into prisons with execrable conditions, where women had often to give birth in the presence of men. By approaching the keeper of one of these prisons, and by pointing out to him that such things were not good in the sight of God, Chilembwe succeeded in securing the release of some of these captives.[49]

Chilembwe seems to have made several trips into Mozambique. During these trips he took the chance to share his faith and to preach the gospel of Christ. Though there was no real established work of PIM during this time in Mozambique, there is still evidence that Chilembwe preached there several times. As he writes, after one of his hunting trips in November 1910.

> Yes I had returned from my hunting trip nothing successful to please men, but I have done a great work in preaching the words of God to our

---

[46] Daniel Malekebu, "A Plea for Africa: African Life and Customs in Central Africa," unpublished, 1918. Malekebu claims to have written and published this pamphlet while preparing to sail for Africa. This was during the very busy time while attending Moody Bible Institute in Chicago.
[47] Shepperson and Price, Independent African, p. 139-140, but other evidence has not been found.
[48] These immigrants came to work in the European estates and some in missions. Such include Mr Pio Mtwere, who once worked as Chilembwe's gun bearer and later left and joined Nguludi mission following free education there.
[49] Shepperson and Price, Independent African, p. 139.

poor people until the Portuguese thought to lay hand on me, but they failed. I know this is the work I was born for.[50]

Pio Mtwere, once Chilembwe's gun bearer

It is through such evidence that one can see that Chilembwe used every opportunity to preach the word of God. He was an enthusiastic African preacher with a vision of bringing salvation to his fellow Africans. Possibly this was part of what he meant while in America when he said "God brought me here to take light to my people." As he writes to Peters in one of his letters: "I only heard the call of God for the salvation of the poor African Brother and lay foundation for future welfare in the right hand of God."[51]

At the time when Chilembwe was Booth's interpreter, he used to accompany him in his evangelical travels. During a visit one day to Chikwawa he met a half-caste girl, Ida, whose mother, a Makololo named Ndulaga, had been married to a Portuguese man. Later, when Chilembwe founded his own mission, Ida became one of his first girl students. Eventually he married her and she joined him as a capable member of his teaching staff.[52] While Chilembwe and Cheek worked in the area of evangelism, Ida Chilembwe worked hand in hand with Emma DeLany. They started a women's group which involved a weekly sewing class. The sewing machines were a great luxury and progress for the women.

---

[50] John Chilembwe - H.E. Peters Mlelemba 13.11.1910.
[51] John Chilembwe - H.E. Peters Mlelemba 13.11.1910.
[52] Some have claimed that Chilembwe married before going to America, and had one child. On returning he found that this wife was already married and so he took another. Other make out more probably that he did not marry until after he came back, while another story has it that he married in America and that his wife was a Negro American. See D.D. Phiri, *Let Us Die for Africa: An African Perspective on the Life and Death of John Chilembwe of Nyasaland/Malawi*, Blantyre: Central Africana, 1999, p. 5.

Regular forms of social life were springing up at PIM, and the celebration of Christmas was on its way to become a recognized feature of the mission's life with *nyama* (meat)[53] and games, to which the Africans in Chilembwe's following could look forward. Though small, there was nonetheless a corporate feeling, and pride was emerging at the mission. By 1904 this corporate spirit and pride had become recognizable. Miss DeLany expressed it very well in a letter to the women of the National Baptist Convention in America who had financed the first major brick building to be erected at the mission. She wrote:

> If I may compare the place today with the place two years ago, I would say that we have already reached a degree of civilization. In front of the house where one year ago only stumps, thorns and crooked trees were growing you will find today scarlet geraniums, a few blooming roses and other flowers, while the red leaf hedge forms the walks and divides the yards into squares. On either side of the walks in the back yard the thick soft grass that was planted in December has covered the place and the red hedge around it gives the appearance of a green velvet arch square with a red border. This with a few flowers gives the backyard a pretty appearance. Beyond the kitchen where the tall grass flourished and was burned each year simply to come back again, I had about an acre and a half of cotton planted. Certainly it is not growing nor bearing yet. But it makes the place look neat. To the right of the house a few hundred yards were dilapidated huts and another field of grass, trees, etc. Today you will find a brick church, certainly not a very handsome building, for architects here are self-taught, and native labour very crude, but nevertheless God's Temple reared to his glory.[54]

With the work of Emma DeLany and Ida Chilembwe, it seems the PIM centre improved socially, especially in the area of general cleanliness and domestic work.

The mission now established, Rev Cheek and Emma DeLaney left Nyasaland in 1905. The first to leave were Cheek and his family, taking with them Frederick Njilima and Matthew Njilima, aged eleven and twelve.[55] Later

---

[53] Meat was another luxury in an area that was often touched by scarcity of food.
[54] Shepperson and Price, *Independent African*, pp. 140-141.
[55] Frederick and Matthew Njilima were brothers, the sons of Duncan Njilima, one of Chilembwe's followers who was convicted of high treason and of being an accessory to the murder of the watchman at Mandala, in Blantyre on 24.1.1915. At the time of the Rising, Matthew and Frederick were being educated at Natchez College, Natchez, Missouri and Lincoln Ridge College, Lincoln, Kentucky respectively. Both these colleges were founded by Negro Baptists. The young Njilimas went to the USA in search of higher education, having been impressed by Chilembwe's attainments. Matthews died there. Frederick came back at the end of the First World War, having obtained a degree in Arts, and joined the Nyasaland Government. But soon he resigned because of racial discrimination in the Civil Service and emigrated to Tanganyika. There he became a reknown teacher over many years. One of the schools at which he taught was Tabora Secondary School, the country's best secondary school at the time. On his retirement he settled in Dar es Salaam. See D.D. Phiri, *Let Us Die for Africa*, p. 18.

the same year Emma DeLany left for the USA. Shepperson has it that they left in June 1906. This differs very much from Malekebu's own writings about his experience and dates of his trip to the USA following his teacher DeLany. Dr Malekebu himself wrote:

> In 1905 Miss DeLaney was to come home to America; she had promised to take me with her to America, but when my people heard this they came saying. 'We do not want you to go to America because we will never see you again. The American people will eat you.' I was quite small. I could not resist. I waited until Miss DeLany went away. By this time my desire and impression was greatly deepened to go to America to study to be a preacher and a doctor to help my people. I made up my mind that to America I must go. I remember leaving my people without saying goodbye, stealing away as it were, that I might overtake my teacher. But all in vain, I decided to go to the East Coast, walking over 300 miles, sleeping in trees and villages when I could. Many times in the woods a big fire had to be kept to scare wild animals. But I prayed that God be near me. You say did I see any lions? Yes, and snakes of all kinds. After reaching Beira, Portuguese East Africa, I saw a large body floating on the water. I asked what it was; they said it was a steamer going to England. I thought that was my chance. I made my way to the captain, and asked him if I could work my way to America. 'My steamer is not going to America', said he 'but to England.' 'I will work my way to England then,' said I. So I was given work on the boat. The name of the steamer was *SS Matebele* named after one of the tribes in South Africa. Seasick? Yes, I was. Upon reaching London, I wondered what would be the next thing to do. While in London I stayed at the Sherman Hotel near Waterloo station. It was very interesting to see those white waiters who were so very nice. They called me a black prince from Africa. Early in the morning before rising about 5 am, they brought coffee to my bed, every morning my shoes were shined. It was just great, I thought. In the same manner I was told that another steamer was about ready to go to America. I was given employment for my passage to America as I had done to reach London, England. My steamer this time was *SS St Paul*. I arrived in New York August 1905.[56]

As Dr Malekebu was the former student and houseboy of Emma DeLany, recounting of the dates of Miss Emma DeLany leaving Nyasaland can hardly be doubted. He himself wrote that he arrived in New York on August 19, 1905. Considering that Malekebu left Nyasaland following his teacher gives no room to doubt that by August 1905 Emma was already in America. When these missionaries left Nyasaland, Chilembwe once again was alone building up his mission.

---

[56] Daniel Malekebu, "The History of my Life and My Work", unpublished, 1940.

Chilembwe's Doctrinal Challenges

Other challenges that Chilembwe faced had to do with doctrinal issues. Chilembwe as a missionary and theologian had to face the challenges of Bible interpretation. The first time that he tried to argue theologically was a long while before he went to USA, while working with Zambezi Industrial Mission (ZIM). At ZIM, Booth may have been preparing him for the role of independent interpreter to the mission. It was about this time that Chilembwe was going out with parties of recently arrived missionaries from Great Britain to help them with their language difficulties and to witness the effects of their new enthusiasm in the African bush. One of these was a raid on an African 'beer drink' at Mbinda's village on Michiru Hill around Mitsidi: the zealous newcomers held up the proceedings in order to evangelize while Chilembwe interpreted.[57] Chilembwe had also at one time accompanied a young and zealous missionary, Alexander Hamilton, who arrived at Mitsidi shortly after the middle of July 1893. This time Chilembwe accompanied the missionary together with his fellow Yao, Gordon Mataka. In November 1894, the secretary of the Zambezi Industrial Mission was in Malawi investigating Booth's mission stations. He was Robert Caldwell, a Fellow of the Royal Geographical Society, and a man of some attainments.[58] The journal of the Scottish mission at Blantyre noted his arrival in January 1895 and observed that he had already made several changes in the mission and it's working. It is likely that Chilembwe helped Caldwell on some of his trips of investigation in 1895. Chilembwe certainly met Caldwell when he was in Africa. The secretary of Zambezi Industrial Mission must have thought enough of him to write to Chilembwe when he got back to London. It was through these interactions with missionaries at Mitsidi that Chilembwe later struck up a friendship with Caldwell. Some time after his return to England, Caldwell had sent Chilembwe a small broadsheet on which he had printed some verses that he had written about Africa. It was headed 'The Land of Ham' and started with a curse placed on Ham, the dark brother, that he should serve others eternally.

> Cursed let HAM be, and Ham's son CANAAN to ages unending;
> Servants of servants they shall be; Servants to SHEM and JAPHETH!

In presenting his argument Chilembwe wrote the following:

> Yes, that is true to be so, if it was long times ago, but by this time, is not so to be, says one of Ham's sons. Now Ham's son they shall be servants

---

[57] Shepperson and Price, *Independent African*, p. 55.
[58] Two years later he was to publish a practical grammar of Chinyanja, which ran into two versions (Shepperson and Price, *Independent African*, p. 66).

not to them now, dear white brothers and sisters. Yes our father was indebted long time ago, therefore now we are not servants anymore to them who are SHEM and Japheth's sons for many knoweth that our lord had paid all about us, through his exceeding bad death. We are in peace; we are saved by HIM, all is done; we are no more servants to SHEM's son and Japheth's son! No more. But one thing is this to be all the same, and be servants to Jesus...[59]

His argument was actually published in the Zambezi Industrial Mission journal in England for July and August 1896. The very fact that the letter was published might show the value being attached to it. Chilembwe ended his letter by even pleading for prayer for Africa to receive the light of the gospel, and that Africans should be true servants of Jesus forever.

At the time when Chilembwe was beginning mission work, Booth had made his peace with the government. He had thus entered again the Nyasa mission field, with the assistance of the Seventh Day Baptists of Plainfield, New Jersey, whose Sabbath Evangelizing and Industrial Association had backed him. This time he had selected in Thyolo, about 30 km south of Blantyre, a plantation of about 2001 partly cultivated acres; and between May and September 1900, the American Seventh Day Baptists had purchased it for about $15,000. It was to be the centre for another of Booth's Industrial Mission experiments. He called it the Plainfield Mission, after the New Jersey Sabbatarian church where he and his wife had been converted to the doctrine that the Sabbath as the proper day for rest and worship. It was after Booth's conviction that he decided to share his Sabbath doctrine with Chilembwe, asking Chilembwe to change the day of worship from Sunday to Saturday, the seventh day of the week. In his reply, Chilembwe wrote to him,

> Regarding your kind invitation I thank you most heartily, but regret to say that I am unable to fulfil for reason that I am almost overwhelmed by most important duty to perform. I am busy making bricks, as our old chapel is too small to hold our Christian congregation. Therefore the church devoted her to build a large church. As to be understood you are aiming that we should work together by changing Saturday into Sabbath day. Father what profit can a man got on Sunday or on Sabbath, are both days essential to the salvation of the souls of truth you have said. Certainly the truth of God will not part us for all the work I am doing and my life is partial to your crown But as the changing of the day is the question of the future I wish if I could see you tomorrow and try to accommodate you in your important request. Dear Papa Booth think not that I am unkind to you, you have my sympathy in all your suffering. I know you are God's fearing man, and as long as God's loving we are

---

[59] Shepperson and Price, *Independent African*, p. 67.

together. Desiring that God's blessing may rest upon you and successful dignify your effort. I am father.

Your dear son in Christ,
John Chilembwe.⁶⁰

Church Building Project

In the letter of 1911, where Chilembwe was arguing about the question of the Sabbath, he also mentioned his church being involved in a building project. This was a major building project that Chilembwe carried out alone without the assistance of FMB missionaries.

Chilembwe's church in construction (Courtesy Mr W. Sanderson)

Although he managed to raise up resources from his local congregation, largely in the form of labour,⁶¹ Chilembwe needed cash in order to purchase nails, iron sheets and planks, and so he took a loan from Haya Edward Peters Mlelemba. Though not a church member, he seemed to be a close friend to Chilembwe. Chilembwe borrowed £50, each pound of which earned interest of one pound, so that Chilembwe was supposed to give back a total of one hundred pounds. The period of the loan was not stated anywhere.⁶²

---

⁶⁰ John Chilembwe - Booth, 6.11.1911 in response to Booth letter of 1.10.1911, in Shepperson and Price, *Independent African*, pp. 547-548.
⁶¹ Most of the believers offered voluntary services. They kneaded mud, baked bricks and cut poles.
⁶² The exact date when the loan was taken is not certain but it was within the period of Chilembwe's construction of the church. This was probably 1909, since in 1914 Peters wrote

Chilembwe seemed to have given back some amount and Peters wrote to him claiming the balance. In his response Chilembwe wrote, "I am sending your letter to Dr Jordan for the balance of £84.10. I hope you will be quite sure to wait, I know next December was our agreement, and it will not go beyond that but the time of your grace is needed you had been so good in the beginning toward this first African Church."[63] The dates by which they agreed to settle the debts were not met and Mlelemba wrote to Chilembwe, comparing him to somebody named che Mussa who was able to settle his debts in time. Chilembwe called him to settle the issue calmly, but Peters Mlelemba refused. Chilembwe replied:

> I regret to hear that you have no time to come over here. And in addition you need not to compare me with che Mussa as you know too well that che Mussa is working for white people and he is getting his salary monthly. And I am poor handed man I only heard the call of God for the salvation of the poor African Brother and lay foundation for future welfare in the right hand of God. And according to my daily prayer, I thought I was led by the Holy Spirit to lean on you and ask help and I had boldly say lend me £50 and I shall pay the interest which, you kindly did it, but at the rate you set of £1 per a pound caused a failure that it was hard for me to make £50 to make the amount you gave to me, I reported I fail brother and you said you did not care anything but only you want me to keep your money and you know that I had returned £50, interest £27. And the remainder I shall pay you only give me time. My word I value and if you not value yours I am not responsible. I have the balance of £23 of you. Please find enclosed £1 leaving £22. Pray for me that I may not fail for the money in my heart I value nothing for I have weighed the world and its riches and find nothing comparing the love I got for my people and our God.[64]

Chilembwe was still struggling to settle the debt little by little till H.E. Peters noted that the debt had almost taken five years before it was settled. In his response Chilembwe wrote:

> On receipt of your letter dated 25.03.14 which you enclosed the receipt for £9. I understand the contents; it is true that five years has passed. It was due to the fact of my failure of what I expected with the amount I borrowed from, as you are aware of the fact too well. I pray that you will not hold my neck for the balance of the interest as you had already £42 interest beside £50 yours as I am only laboured not for my own but in the name of God for my country men I am sure it was by revelation of Christ I find you in the time of my struggling to be my constant helper... Believe

---

Chilembwe reminding him that the loan was then five years without being honoured fully. See Peters - Chilembwe 25.3.1914 in PIM Pavillion.
[63] John Chilembwe - H.E. Peters Mlelemba 13.11.1910. PIM Pavion.
[64] John Chilembwe - H.E. Peters Mlelemba 24.4.1912.

I will square before I leave this country for Europe and America which will not be long.[65]

Despite all those problems and struggles, Chilembwe's church was completed in 1913. He had it photographed by M.M. Chisuse,[66] and sent the pictures to America for his friends to see. They hesitated to believe he had done the job all alone with untutored labour. But so it was. Even Europeans from neighbouring missions now admitted that Chilembwe's organizing ability was above that of the average African working under them.[67]

The opening of Chilembwe's church in Chiradzulu in 1913. Photographed by M.M. Chisuse (Mogg Collection)

A Missionary in his own Land

Chilembwe regarded himself as a missionary in his own land. In 1910 the Federated Missions held a conference at Mvera, then the headquarters of the Dutch Reformed Church Mission. Chilembwe was invited to attend. This Mvera Conference was attended by the representatives of Livingstonia and Blantyre Missions, the Dutch Reformed Mission, the Zambezi Industrial Mission, the Nyasa Industrial Mission, the Baptist Industrial Mission and the South Africa General Mission, who were to form a Federated Board of Missions. This would consult over such things as education, Bible translation and other matters of common interest. The other missionaries might have hoped at this conference to persuade Chilembwe to adopt a common policy about instructing proselytes.

---

[65] John Chilembwe - H.E. Peters Mlelemba 26.3.1914.
[66] An African photographer, a member of the African Chamber of Commerce, an organization of African businessmen. He was joint secretary of the organization together with H.E. Peters Mlelemba.
[67] D.D. Phiri, *Let Us Die for Africa*, Blantyre: Central Africana, 1999, p. 22.

But he declined the invitation. In private conversation with leading African members of Blantyre mission, he would bluntly say he could not join an organization of foreign missionaries.[68] As a fulltime missionary, Chilembwe was at his mission station most of the time. He gladly received other missionaries, who visited him as a fellow missionary of the so-called smaller churches around his mission. Other Europeans, both official and civilian, generally treated white missionaries of these churches as rudely as they treated Chilembwe. Thus Captain Charles Thornburn of Thondwe was to say before the Chilembwe Commission of Inquiry "Mr Hollis of the Church of Christ came to my place to trade, and I told him to clear out. I do not think a man of that kind should be allowed in the country. I cannot see how a native can be expected to look up to such a man. He is quite a low-grade man. We have plenty of missions."[69] Heads of these smaller missions, like Chilembwe, were often accused by the large missions of trespassing on their domains. This might be one of the factors contributing to the good relationship between Chilembwe and these missionaries, since they shared the same problems. An interchange of visits often took place between missionaries such as Rev John Chorley of Chipande station of the Zambezi Industrial Mission and Chilembwe; they visited him more frequently than he visited them. On such occasions he would gladly take them around the mission and show them what he was doing.

They would oblige by taking photographs of his magnificent chapel. But he would never seriously consider any suggestion of a merger with them. He maintained friendly relations with fellow missionaries such as Father Swelsen of Nguludi. Chilembwe personally got on well with both the Bishop and the Priest. Father Swelsen recalls some of his interaction with Chilembwe. "I visited Chilembwe several times in going around our schools, I spoke to him, but I did not know his particular teaching."[70] This chitchat between the pastor and the priest often took place in front of a steaming teapot. Chilembwe would not send away his guests empty-bellied if he could help it, no matter what their status. By 1913 PIM was fully established.

---

[68] *Ibid.*, p. 27.
[69] *Ibid.*, p. 24.
[70] Fr Swenson's testimony before the Commission, see D.D. Phiri, *Let Us Die for Africa*, p. 25.

Chapter Two

CHILEMBWE'S APPROACH TO CONVERSION

FOR ANY CHURCH TO GET STARTED, CONVERSION BECOMES THE MOST IMPORtant aspect of its activities. This was not different with John Chilembwe's church. As a fully ordained pastor and missionary, he faced the challenge of witnessing and winning to Christ souls who later were to form his congregation. For Voetius conversion is the immediate goal of mission; in other words, in terms of the content of mission, conversion is what missionaries could expect to work for first and foremost.[1] Conversion has, however, been understood in very different ways by different groups of missionaries and at different times. Chilembwe's approach to conversion can be understood in three ways. These three approaches include the Pietistic understanding of conversion, the Social Gospel approach and the Christianization approach.

Rev John Chilembwe and Rev John Chorley

---

[1] J.J. Kritzinger, P.G.J. Meiring, W.A. Saayman, *On Being Witness*, Johannesburg: Orion 1994, p. 27.

The Pietistic Approach to Conversion

As far as the modern Protestant mission movement is concerned, conversion as goal of mission will always be inextricably linked to the theology and practice of the Pietists, especially the Moravian missionaries. Von Zinzendorf commissioned them with the words "Go then in Jesus' name and see if among the Moors souls can be found who will allow themselves to be led to the saviour".[2] It was for this understanding of conversion as "winning souls for the lamb" that the Moravians become famous. Conversion for the Pietists hinged on the conscious personal decision of the individual after a sometimes fierce penitential struggle. Chilembwe's effort in witnessing to people started as early as the period in which he interpreted for Booth. In his own time, Chilembwe went out to witness in the villages though it shows that sometimes he had problems with people responding to his preaching. He did not take this as an excuse to stop ministering to people for he confidently said 'but they will not hear now'. One of his opponents was his own elder brother James Chimpele. When Chilembwe came back from the United States as a missionary and an ordained Baptist pastor, he witnessed to Chimpele about his faith in Christ. Chimpele submitted and was baptized.[3] The first person that Chilembwe witnessed to after his return from USA was his own sister Awanjilang'wa, who later adopted the Christian name Mary. The first baptism service that he conducted had only one candidate, his sister, showing that the first baptized member of PIM was a woman. Chilembwe made sure that the members of his household received the light of the gospel. The next baptism included other relatives like his mother Nyangu and Ngupangwa, Chilembwe's sister and the mother of Stephen Nkulichi. Stephen Nkulichi was hanged during Chilembwe uprising and Morris Chilembwe was shot.[4] Conversions like these contributed to the establishment of PIM. Closer to the period of the uprising Chilembwe's Pietistic approach showed again very clearly when he sent Peter Kalemba to start PIM work in the central region. This mission work needed the conversion of individuals who would become members of this church. Being assisted by Anderson Nyangu, Kalemba shared his faith with Duncan and Salatiyele Nthambala and William Njawayawa who all lived in the area of T/A Kalumbu in Lilongwe district. The second group of converts to PIM in Lilongwe (then Mangoni) included Aaron Kamkalamba from Nyanje, and J. Kokha from Chikhanda. The list of converts increased, later Chiphaka, once a member of Nkhoma Mission, was converted. Chiphaka was instrumental in the conversion of Harrison Matapila and later his brother Joseph, and Aziri Kafulatira, all

---

[2] *Ibid.*, p. 27.
[3] The date of his baptism is not known.
[4] Interview Mrs Chilumpha, PIM, 14.8.2000.

members of Nkhoma Mission.[5] It was through this vividly Pietistic approach to conversion that PIM in Lilongwe was established.

Some of the earliest convents of PIM with John Chilembwe in black suit. Left to right: Morris Chilembwe, John Chilembwe, and Stephen Nkulichi. Seated: Awanjilang'wa, Chilembwe's sister, the first baptized member of PIM, Chilembwe's mother Nyangu and Ngupangwa, his sister and the mother of Stephen Mkulichi. (David Stuart Mogg Collection)

It can be seen that the conversion of the people who formed the earliest PIM membership did not involve any kind of assembly or crusade, but rather individual contact. This contact resulted in a personal confession and decision of an individual to accept the faith and be willing to be baptized. This is a characteristic of the Pietistic approach to conversion.

This pietistic approach is in the Lausanne Covenant expressed as the solemn undertaking of more than 2000 evangelical delegates in 1974 to work for the evangelization of the whole world. They stated that in the church's mission of sacrificial service, evangelism is primary[6]; and evangelism means 'the salvation of the unreached', brought about through reconciliation with God. All this, says John Stott, is undergirded by the theological conviction that (social-political) liberation and (eternal) salvation are two distinct works of God. In such

---

[5] Hanny Longwe, "Identity by Dissociation: The First Group to Secede from Chilembwe's Church: A History of Peter Kalemba and the Achewa Providence Industrial Mission", MA, University of Malawi, 2000, p. 32.
[6] Kritzinger/Meiring/Sayman, *On Being Witness*, p. 28.

understanding, the church's mission of sacrificial service evangelism is primary; and evangelism means the salvation of the unreached.

The Social Gospel Perspective

A very different understanding of conversion is to be found in the Social Gospel movement, which gained prominence in the USA especially since the beginning of the twentieth century. Being aware of the social evils such as poverty, disease, ignorance, oppression etc, Social Gospellers felt that all Christian missionary reserves should go into fighting these evils in order to make the world a better place, more in line with the ideals of the kingdom of God. It terms of the practice of mission, the Social Gospel required education, uplift and development. Evangelization would (hopefully) be the end result of all this, but certainly was no immediate priority. The idea of devising an evangelistic campaign to bring about the conversion of people therefore occupied a very low position on the list of priorities of Social Gospellers. What had to be ascertained were the educational, medical and developmental needs of people and the campaigns to be undertaken were to fulfill those needs.[7]

Chilembwe's approach to evangelism includes an aspect of the Social Gospel perspective. His ambition was to develop a community that would live a good life, not very much different from the life of the whites of his time. This caused him to encourage cotton and coffee farming within his 93 acre mission land. With its cotton, the PIM had no greater success than many of the other planters of the area. But the fact that it was planted at all was a measure of the mission's aspirations. Indeed by 1905, Cheek and Chilembwe had experimented with coffee, tea, pepper and rubber, as well as cotton. Chilembwe was preaching to his congregations that they must be prepared to work with their hands in the new society, and was obviously exerting all his energies to emulate the white Industrial Missions.

While a detailed economic history of the mission does not seem possible, there is some evidence that although the PIM had fewer resources to fall back on than the European missions or estates, they tried the industrial approach. It managed to struggle along in face of climatic and economic difficulties. Furthermore, it had certain advantages over the European missions: it had means of subsistence culture, a staff which, on the whole, was brought up in that tradition, and fewer supporters abroad to persuade that their subscriptions were producing quick results. The figures that exist for the mission's growth suggest that for all the initial enthusiasm of its founders, its development in terms of actual membership was small in the early years. Chilembwe and his American Negro helpers seem to have concentrated at this time on building up the permanent stock of the mission rather than going for quick, initial

---

[7] Kritzinger/Meiring/Sayman, *On Being Witness*, p. 29.

enrolments that would fade away hastily.⁸ These methods represent a Social Gospel perspective wherein the evangelistic campaign to bring about conversion of people occupied a low position on the list of priorities. Hence the emphasis was on encouraging people to work with their own hands for the uplift and development of their society.

Rev Dr Daniel Sharpe Malekebu continued this very attitude. He introduced farming when he reopened PIM in 1926. He purchased more than a thousand acres of land at Mambala in Thyolo district, where farming was done using tractors alongside manual work. The land was so vast that Mr Stephen Saidi, a resident there, described it in this way: "The size of this mission land is about 80000 acres or 80000 yards but I should say acres."⁹ It is said that on this land were grown pineapples, bananas, sugarcane, beans, *mpiru* (mustard seed) and maize, which was the main crop grown. The harvests from this farm were used to feed people during church gatherings, and some were sold for the mission's income. Land was a crucial issue in Thyolo district following the government order that the land at Chigumula be vacated, so all the people had to leave the place. Seeking permission to occupy the land at Mambata, PIM members approached Malekebu, who assigned them a portion of the land within the farm. One of them had this to say, "When the colonial government was claiming land at Chigumula in Blantyre, some PIM members went to Malekebu to ask for help. Malekebu was not happy with the move taken by the government. He therefore opened up a section of Mambala farm to be inhabited by PIM members who were in need of land to cultivate. He made Mambala some kind of a PIM village. Among these people who moved from Chigumula to Mambala were the Nakoma family."¹⁰ Some people's needs such as employment and land to cultivate were met in joining the Mambala farm. As the developmental needs of the people were essential and one of the priorities of Social Gospellers, the Mambala farm brought a fulfillment of this Social approach to evangelism. Some people who joined Mambala farm as workers, but were non Christians, later became part of the Christian community and joined PIM.

As the Social Gospel required education, uplift and development, there was one element in Chilembwe's teaching at this time which, if it was by no means absent from the other missions, did not seem to have the same note of urgency for them as it did for Chilembwe. This was the training and development of African women. This does not mean that Chilembwe had in mind a woman's movement for political emancipation like Mrs Pankhurst's in the Great Britain

---

⁸ *Ibid.*, p. 141. Shepperson and Price comment that if this was fine it suggests that Chilembwe, unlike his old master, Booth, was not over ambitious at first, and contented himself with building on small but secure foundations.
⁹ Interview Mr Stephen Saidi, Mambala, PIM land, 12.12.1998.
¹⁰ Interview Mebo Nakoma-Mambala, Thyolo, 9.12.1998.

of that day.[11] His ideas were simpler and far more difficult to realize: to pull the African women of Nyasaland out of the tribal state and to model them on the contemporary European woman, as a progressive ideal.

Mrs Chilembwe and two women of PIM from Chilembwe's own album.
(Courtesy Mr W. Sanderson)

His concepts had all the shade of the European female respectability of the time: Correct deportment, 'proper' style of dressing, a 'decent' manner of arranging the hair, and faithful church membership, a veritable Bantu "Angel in the House." In fact existing photographs of the female members of his flock, and of the standards of dress of his own wife, stress the character of his feminist ideal far better than any verbal description.

A quotation from a letter Chilembwe wrote to the Foreign Mission Board Secretary of the National Baptist Convention in 1912 illustrates further his interests in the development of women. Chilembwe did not want women to be ignorant and oppressed. Again he took a Social Gospellers perspective that all Christian missionary reserves should go into fighting these evils in order to make the world a better place, more in line with the ideals of the kingdom of God. He writes:

> Brother Jordan, what about the mothers of the race—shall I forget them? God forbid! There is a special work to do. I lay the needs of our benighted wives and mothers before you and upon the great Baptist family and Christian ladies who love Christ and believe that an African woman has a soul to be saved please allow me to plead that more may

---

[11] G. Shepperson and T. Price, *Independent African*, p. 178.

be done for the women. I feel safe in saying that I am doing good to my countrymen, as it is true everywhere the men are developing faster than the women. But there can be no healthy progress if such is the case. We believe there is an urgent need for special work to be done among the wives of the people, whom you are privileged by God's grace to bring out of darkness into light, because an African woman, like her American sister, does not exert an influence for good or evil on her husband. The ordinary African woman in her heathen state is ignorant, uninteresting and unlovable. I almost despair when I think of her ignorance, her utter lack of ambition. I believe and pray that God may rule someone to lay the foundation for the future of the race. It is sad to see a young mother, little more than a girl, with an infant on her back and know that she is thrust into responsibility for which she is quite unfit, and that at a time when she should be taken care of, and she ought to have been left to the joys of young womanhood as my little wife, one night after my prayer she said when she heard my cry that the women and girls are very difficult to work amongst. She said, 'change your cry and say that the women of Africa for Christ's cause and kingdom, there is nothing too hard for the Lord; the gospel that transforms and uplifts is sufficient for her needs' – amen, that ours is the privilege of bringing that gospel to her. Please help us. Mrs Chilembwe needs good friends to help her in her undertaking. She needs to teach our young women that God has a purpose in creating man, male and female, and that women have work to do that man cannot do. She is teaching day school and taking the sewing department and also visiting her sisters in her surroundings with her Bible in hand. She is seeking to prevent early marriage among our girls, telling them that marriage has meant too little among our parents for generations, and telling them that it is not thus that happy homes are made and a strong race reared. The world will not go forward as it should till women have been taught and have learned to take the place God has ordained for them as man's helpmeet, his equal, not his slave.[12]

Chilembwe's ambition to educate African women was also at the heart of his successor Malekebu. He too put emphasis on education, uplift and development, a characteristic of a Social Gospeller. Malekebu emphasized the point that the African woman had the potential to be developed and he described them as 'diamonds in the rough':

I have found in many cases even with the educated class of people it is not thoroughly understood what is meant by 'Heathen African'. If they read the 10th chapter of Romans, 14-15 that would greatly help them. In this Paul certainly explains it. Some have in mind a heathen African is a sort of wild animal or a monkey that lives in the woods, caves or tree tops. A well learned man said to me, he would be afraid to go among those heathens unless he had a gun to keep them from jumping on him. But what is a heathen African? The answer in short: as you see the picture

---

[12] G Shepperson and T. Price, *Independent African*, pp. 174-175.

of these two splendid specimens of human beings with all the attributes that go to make a human race. See closely their physical makeup, they are not dressed, never mind about that, their morals are as high as the tone of the key of G. Look at their nose, it is not flat as is usually attributed to us. Their lips are not so thick that they can not be trained and used to the glory of God. Their feet are not so large that they cannot walk to school and the house of God; their fingers are not so stiff and ankylosed that they can not be made flexible and trained to be used at a piano or domestic arts. Their brains and gray matter are not frozen and hardened that they cannot be loosened up and become able to assimilate and retain the western civilization. And I imagine their pulse rate beats seventy-two times a minute like any other human race. To make a long story short, a heathen African is simply a diamond in the rough. In his head there is a casket of locked up possibilities. Locked up in his gray matter there are acres of diamonds. Only and only the key of salvation is needed to open it. Who will send the key?"[13]

In his emphasis on the very fact that it is possible to develop African women to a higher standard in society, Malekebu refers to his wife as a polished diamond. He wrote about his own wife, Miss Flora Ethelwyn G. Zeto as a native-born African, a polished diamond in culture and refinement ...

Mrs Flora Zeto Malekebu (Polished diamond)

She was a young lady of whom he was proud. She was from Congo, Africa, and was brought to America several years ago by Miss Clara A. Howard, a returned missionary from Africa, also one of the early graduates of Spelman Seminary. She was placed in Spelman Seminary, Atlanta, and the leading school of America for the training of young colored women. She graduated from the following courses: High School, Sunday

---

[13] Daniel Malekebu, *A Plea for Africa*, unpublished, 1918, pp. 5-6.

teachers' training, Domestic Arts and from the Musical Department. Miss Zeto really excelled. In Sunday School work she was an energetic and accomplished teacher; in Domestic Arts, she could not be surpassed, in Music she fully demonstrated her ability. Malekebu wished that the church had more of these gifted young women who should have gone to elevate their sisters in darkness, to the highest development of Christian womanhood. Miss Zeto hoped to go back home to Africa to impart knowledge to her sisters in the Dark Continent. In emphasizing the importance of education for women, Malekebu lamented the negative attitude that people had towards education for women. She said, "The idea of educating African women had for many years been depressed. There had been that tendency that women should not be educated. This fact is painful but true. No nation can rise higher than its women. We have many more young women in Africa, who if they were given a chance, a half chance, would make good like Miss Zeto and others. Is it not worthy bringing many more to this country? Oh, for a man's chance; only a man's chance, given my people is what we need and for which we pray."[14]

The development of women was at the heart of Dr and Mrs Malekebu. Women were taught matters of health and how they can take care of their children and families. To encourage these women they introduced a "Baby of the Month" competition.

Malekebu and the winners of a Baby of the Month competition (Picture: PIM Pavillion)

---

[14] Ibid., pp. 6-7.

Chilembwe's Approach to Conversion

Women were taught how to feed and bath their babies. This encouraged women to take better care of their babies and it promoted cleanliness in their homes. Dr Malekebu was very much a Social Gospeller in his approach to conversion. With his medical skills he opened the first PIM hospital at Mbombwe in 1927. At first, Malekebu had problems with people who could not trust western medicine.

People had much trust in traditional medicine and usually reported to the mission hospital only when the situation was very bad. Once they had been treated there they began to have confidence in western medicine. This is a symbol of development of some kind. People began to drift away from some of their traditional beliefs and started to believe that some sicknesses had natural causes.

Traditionally, people believed in witchcraft. Often this kind of practice brought conflict between members of the family and even close neighbours. The very fact that people began to believe that some sicknesses were not the result of witchcraft shows that they were slowly being drawn closer to an understanding of Christianity. However the belief in witchcraft among many professing Christians still exists today.

Thundu tree at which PIM's first hospital was established in 1927
(Picture: PIM Pavillion)

Christianization Approach to Conversion

A third important understanding of conversion in mission history was that of conversion as the Christianizing of a people (*Volkschristianisierung*). Karl Graul, early secretary of the (Lutheran) Leipzig Mission Society, was the first proponent of the idea. The belief is that a whole people should be Christianized. Bruno Gutmann among the Chagga of Mt Kilimanjaro wanted to achieve this Christianization using the 'primal ties' of blood, neighbourhood and age group, so that the church should be structured closer to the tribal organization. In such an approach there was hardly any place for individual conversion, as birth and culture determined one's membership; but there is still an element in Chilembwe's approach that could support the Christianization approach. In Chilembwe's naming of the church as Ajawa [Yao] Providence Industrial Mission, the desire to structure the church on a tribal level is apparent. By the time the American Negro missionaries had been there for two years, Providence Industrial Mission, or PIM became the more popular title. The more restrictive prefix, 'Ajawa', had been dropped. Chilembwe was now preaching in the *lingua franca* of the Shire Highlands, Nyanja; and his appeal was clearly being made to the widest circle of Africans that he could find. The corporate feeling that was growing up at the PIM at this time must have helped by providing Chilembwe with a firm base from which he could extend his activities. Possibly this was so because Christian conversion was never merely a religious experience; it was also a way of becoming a member of the community where people would find their identity in Christ rather than in their race or sex. The New Testament contains no example of a local church whose membership had been taken by the apostles from a single homogeneous unit, unless that expression is taken to mean no more than a group of people with a common language.

During the period that Chilembwe was preparing for the uprising, he advised a man by the name of Peter Kalemba to open PIM in the central region.[15] Kalemba faithfully did what Chilembwe told him. After the uprising, PIM was still in existence in the central region, in particular Lilongwe district. When Malekebu reopened the mission at Mbombwe, Peter Kalemba and the church in Lilongwe recognized his leadership. When Kalemba was accused of mismanaging church funds, he decided to quit PIM and join Nkhoma Synod. A group of sympathizers approached him and they decided to start their own church. They registered their church with the DC in Lilongwe as "Achewa PIM"

---

[15] Roderick J. Macdonald, "The Rev Dr Daniel Sharpe Malekebu and the Reopening of Providence Industrial Mission 1926-39: an Appreciation", in R.J. Macdonald (ed.), *From Nyasaland to Malawi*, Nairobi: East African Publishing House, 1975, pp. 215-233; John K. Parratt, "The Malekebu Case", in A.F. Walls and W.R. Schenk (eds.), *Exploring New Religious Movements: Essays in Honour of Harold W. Turner*, Elkhart: Mission Focus, 1990, pp. 119-129.

Church" on 19th October 1937, and established Nyanje as their headquarters.[16] Probably the selection of this name is the result of Kalemba's association with Chilembwe at the time when PIM was known as 'Ajawa' (Yao) PIM. They also tried to form their church on a tribal basis. The reasons behind the breaking away of the church were largely on tribal basis in one way or the other. Such statements as this were heard: *"Akumwera anali kutidyera masuku pa mutu"*.[17] This Chinyanja proverb is literally translated as "Eating *masuku* fruits on each other's heads" and means to exploit act unjustly towards someone.[18] In this context it is used to express that people from the south were taking advantage of people from the central region. This suggests that the Achewa PIM was organized on a tribal basis, wanting to do things by themselves without any outsider interfering with them. Hence they needed to have a leader from their own tribe, in this case the Chewa tribe.[19]

Church Planting

Whereas there is predominant consensus that conversion is the immediate goal of mission, the primacy of the role of church planting is more controversial. The early Dutch missiologist Voetius considered church planting to be the intermediate goal of mission, between the immediate goal of conversion and the ultimate goal of the glory and manifestation of God's grace. The planting of a mission church will of course be determined by the self-understanding of the 'sending' church and its ecclesiology.[20] Various ecclesiological understandings have developed over the twenty centuries of Christian history, of which three might apply to Chilembwe's way of church planting. These are the sacramental/euchar-istic, kerygmatic and Pentecostal understandings.

The Sacramental/Eucharistic Understanding of Church Planting

The basic tenet of this understanding of church planting in Christian mission is that what is initiated in the "mission field" is not a "new" church at all but represents the implantation of the one catholic church among a people where it

---

[16] Hany Longwe, "Identity by Dissociation: The First Group to Secede from Chilembwe's Church: A History of Peter Kalemba and the Achewa Providence Industrial Mission", MA University of Malawi, 2000, p. 49.
[17] Interview Sakhula, Kafulatira village, Lilongwe, 1998.
[18] J.C. Chakanza, *Wisdom of the People, 2000 Chinyanja Proverbs*, Blantyre: CLAIM-Kachere, 2000, p. 122.
[19] This is the same case even today with the PIM church in Soweto, South Africa. The church in Soweto struggles to keep its Malawian identity. This is done by making sure that the church is led by a Malawian. When the South African tribes grew in numbers, they began to complain that they can not be led by a foreigner, these conflicts led to the separation of the church. This shows how tribalistic the church is. PIM in Soweto is full of Malawians who are resident in South Africa. The people who are actually South Africans are the women who are married to Malawian men.
[20] Kritzinger/Meiring/Sayman, *On Being Witness*, p. 4.

does not yet exist. No missionary operating with the sacramental/eucharistic understanding of church planting therefore ever sets out to plant a new church. A Roman Catholic missionary sets out to implant the Roman Catholic Church, an Anglican missionary to implant the Anglican church and an Orthodox missionary, belonging to one of the churches in the communion of autocephalous and autonomous Orthodox churches, sets out to implant that Orthodox Church. However there are mutual differences in the practicalities of bringing about this implantation. For example, Protestant and Anglican missionaries translated the Bible and liturgical texts into the local language, whereas the Roman Catholics used Latin Bibles and a Latin liturgy up until Vatican II.[21]

This might apply to Chilembwe in the sense that after being trained and ordained by the National Baptist Convention USA Inc., Chilembwe planted the Baptist Church among a people where it did not yet exist. His naming of the church as the First African Baptist Church might support this idea. As there are mutual differences in the practicalities of bringing about this implantation, this was no exception with Chilembwe. Much as he planted a Baptist church, he used the hymns which were used by Nkhoma Synod, a purely Presbyterian church, as there was no Baptist hymnbook in the country.[22] In the same way when Malekebu reopened the mission, he used the name "National Baptist Assembly." This also shows that he did not set out to plant a new church. He left Nyasaland to USA as a member of PIM, a Baptist church and joined fellow Baptists of the National Baptist Convention Inc. On his return to Nyasaland, he was a National Baptist pastor and missionary. He re-established the National Baptist Church. The *Mission Herald* of 1948 had a column titled "Letters from the foreign fields" in which Malekebu, among other missionaries in the field, submitted his reports to the Secretary of the FMB. This supports the argument that the church in USA (the sending church) treated the churches in the field as National Baptist churches. On October 30, 1948 in the column 'Letters from the foreign fields', Malekebu wrote:

> Dear Dr Adams,
> I have just returned from Lilongwe district, nearly 300 miles from here up country, where we were nearly two weeks visiting our churches there, and had a great time. I must tell you first about our National Baptist Assembly this year.[23]

This shows that Malekebu was reporting to the National Baptist Convention of USA as a missionary of its Foreign Mission Board.

---

[21] *Ibid.*, pp. 5-6.
[22] Till today PIM still uses the Nkhoma Synod hymn book *Nyimbo za Mulungu*.
[23] *Mission Herald*, 1948, pp. 24-25.

The Kerygmatic Understanding of Church Planting

In terms of this understanding, the most important dimension in mission and church planting is the *kerygma* or proclamation of the word. The kerygmatic understanding of church planting developed along two broad lines, which can be characterized as the British-American and German schools of thought.

Church Planting according to British-American Missiologists

The two main architects of this school were Rufus Anderson, General Secretary of the (Congregational) American Board of Commissioners for Foreign Mission (ABCFM) from 1832 to 1866, and Henry Venn, General Secretary of the (low church Anglican) Church Missionary Society (CMS) from 1841 to 1872. Both men occupied administrative positions for over thirty years in two of the largest mission societies of their time. This was a time of rapid expansion of "foreign" missions, and Venn and Anderson were therefore excellently placed to do pioneering work in relation to church planting. More or less simultaneously, they came up with a remarkably similar formula for the planting of autonomous young churches. Such churches, they said, should be self-supporting, self-governing and self-propagating. (As far as the last concept is concerned, Venn used the term 'self-extending,' a term more in line with his Anglican ecclesiological understanding).

Venn, in 1888, wrote: "But above all, the system is calculated to give confidence and self-reliance to the Native Christians, and to quicken their zeal and liberality."[24] A further aspect to be noted is that self-propagation (Anderson) and self-extension (Venn) were considered essential not simply because there was a shortage of missionaries, but from the ecclesiastical perspective of mission: "to the ends of the earth and the ends of time." Venn talked about the 'euthanasia of mission' (in other words: the "mercy-killing" of mission); whereby missionaries should work themselves out of a job as quickly as possible so that they could move on to the "regions beyond."[25] The 'three selves' theory therefore undoubtedly had a theological foundation. That it was very attractive both for theological as well as administrative reasons is proven by the fact that many churches from a variety of denominational traditions subsequently adopted as the goal of their mission work the founding of self-governing, self-supporting and self-propagating churches. This understanding is not far from the "industrial" concept of mission. The way PIM started it did not entirely depend on the support from the FMB. As already stated in the early years of PIM, in particular 1900-1901, Chilembwe was alone. He governed church activities by himself, and even encouraged those he felt were his equals to be independent of the whites and govern their own activities. In the

---

[24] Kritzinger/Meiring/Sayman, *On Being Witness*, p. 8.
[25] Ibid., p. 8.

evidence of Rev Stephen Kundecha (a Presbyterian) given when the Commission of Inquiry on 8th July 1915 examined him, he states: "He [Chilembwe] repeated the same story about having a station of my own just the same as he did before."[26]

The same was also true in the time of Dr Malekebu; who encouraged self-help activities within the church. The opening of Mambala farm helped the mission to be self-sufficient in terms of finances. The church was also self-propagating, extending its influence to other areas as far as Rhodesia. This was through its members who went there in search of employment, who later planted the church there. Malekebu made a follow up of those churches for proper registration. In his letter, the Secretary for Native Affairs of Salisbury, Southern Rhodesia wrote to the Chief Secretary to the Government of Nyasaland on 6th November 1936, to inquire about this self-propagating church.

> Sir,
>
> Manjalela Jackson Milimbo
>
> 46725 Mtoko (Pass 8218 of 26.10.36)
>
> The native described above has reported to me with a pass signed by one D.S. Malekebu, stating that the holder is an evangelist of the Providence Industrial Mission, Chiradzulu, and asking that he may be afforded facilities to visit members of the church in this colony.
>
> I am to ask whether this mission has received government recognition in Nyasaland, and whether in your opinion the facilities sought should be granted.[27]

The following was the response to the letter of inquiry:

> Sir,
>
> With reference to your letter Nos. 10324/m8/9/Gen dated the 6th of November, I am directed to inform you that the Providence Industrial Mission is recognised by this government.
>
> Dr Malekebu states that Jackson Milimbo was going to Salisbury on personal business and Dr Malekebu, thinking that Jackson would feel lonely in Southern Rhodesia, gave him a letter of introduction to the mission's members there. Jackson was not sent by Dr Malekebu.[28]

This response shows that by this time this self-propagating church was already in existence in Zimbabwe.

---

[26] Kenneth R. Ross (ed), *Christianity in Malawi, A Source Book*, Gweru: Mambo, 1996, p. 153.

[27] Secretary for Native Affairs P. O. Box 393, Salisbury, Southern Rhodesia - Chief Secretary to the Government, Zomba, 6.11.1936.

[28] Chief Secretary to the Government - Secretary for Native Affairs, Salisbury, date not seen.

It is also in these 'three selves' that I see Chilembwe trusting PIM's work in Mangoni to Peter Kalemba. He advised him to go to the central region and establish PIM work there. Nothing is recorded or found anywhere showing that he was given some kind of financial or material support apart from the education that he had got from the PIM. The sending of Peter Kalemba to the central region was entirely on the understanding that he would be self-reliant. When Kalemba reached the central region, he shared his faith with other people. He was totally involved in a church-planting project. It is again from this point that one can see that PIM in Lilongwe was an entirely a self-supporting, self-governing and self-propagating church: a pure understanding of church planting according to British-American missiologists.

Church Planting according to German Missiologists

The classical German missionaries and missiologists set as the goal of mission the planting of autonomous, national churches ("*Selbstständige Volkskirchen*"). The main difference from the preceding school of thought is that the Germans ascribed to the indigenous culture a very important role in the planting and development of the younger churches. This tradition developed around the middle of the nineteenth century, very much in reaction to the earlier German emphasis on mission exemplified by Zinzendorf and the Pietists, of the conversion of individuals (winning souls for the lamb). Gustav Warneck, father of modern Protestant missiology, who blended individual conversion with national Christianization, extended it.

As time went by, the autonomous part of the concept received less and less emphasis and the national part more and more. This came out especially clearly in the work of the outstanding missionaries, Bruno Gutmann and Christian Keyser. Gutmann was a Leipzig missionary among the Chagga people living near Mount Kilimanjaro in Tanzania.

There is not much in Chilembwe's approach in this understanding of church planting according to German missiologists. The only example in this approach is Chilembwe's effort to establish the church on tribal basis, i.e. the naming of the church as Ajawa Providence Industrial Mission.

Pentecostal Understanding of Church Planting

Among early Pentecostals, ecclesiology in general and church planting in particular were of low priority. The all-consuming passion was for the preaching of the gospel throughout the whole world as preparation for the second coming of Christ.

Pentecostal missionaries therefore set out to their "mission fields" to accomplish one task and one task only: the evangelization of the world (understood as personal salvation) in preparation for the imminent return of Christ. One must add to this the fact that there were not many ecclesiological traditions the missionaries could take with them. Later, as it became clear that Pentecostal mission was going to become a long-term project, the need for a coherent ecclesiology became pressing.[29] Then most Pentecostals adopted the 'three-selves' concept.

This understanding of church planting is applicable to Chilembwe when one looks at his zeal in preaching the word of God wherever opportunities permitted him to do so. There were occasions on which Chilembwe would preach the word not with the intention of church planting, but rather to share the gospel with others. Possibly such behaviour could be part of what he meant by: 'I was called to bring light to my people.' This was his primary objective in planting the Providence Industrial Mission. One occasion when he preached the word without the intention of planting a church was during one of his hunting trips into Mozambique. While there he ended up preaching, and commented that he had come back from the hunting trip with nothing to please men but he was glad that he had preached the word there. This represents the early Pentecostal understanding where ecclesiology in general and church planting in particular was a very low priority. The PIM stands out very well in the kerygmatic understanding of church planting.

---

[29] Kritzinger/Meiring/Sayman, *On Being Witness*, p. 12.

Chapter Three

EXPANSION OF PIM BEYOND MBOMBWE

AS A SELF-SUPPORTING, SELF-GOVERNING AND SELF-PROPAGATING CHURCH, the PIM church grew to such an extent that the government took note. This resulted in the government stopping the growth of the church. This growth was in terms of schools. Obviously mission schools were inseparable from the church. For example, school would start classes with prayers according to the liturgy of the church itself. This kind of practice in one way or the other influenced the pupils, and many later became members of that particular church. Hence the expansion of PIM schools was actually the expansion of PIM church work. When the church was fully established, many people began to note that its agenda was not so different from those of other churches. Though it was described as a small church, it attracted disproportionate attention in the way of potential converts. The church began to expand into areas beyond Mbombwe. The local leaders played a very important role in these various stations. Although there were these churches developing from the outstations, the membership list was still kept at Mbombwe.[1] No formal crusades were conducted in order to plant these churches. The approach to individual conversion played a very important role in the establishment of these outstations. It is from this that one can see that the establishment and expansion of the PIM had its foundations rooted in a simple premise of organization.

The Church at Migowi

Migowi is the name of a trading centre in Phalombe district, some seventy kilometers from Mulanje *boma*. The name is derived from the river that passes through it with its source on Michesi Mountain. To the east of Migowi is Mauzi hill, which forms the boundary with Mozambique and to the west is Machemba hill. Today Migowi is the district headquarters for Phalombe. When the Providence Industrial Mission was established at Mbombwe, it attracted some members from Migowi area. As to how these people were attracted to the church at Mbombwe is not yet known. However with the establishment of the PIM School at Mbombwe, some people might have been attracted. The other

---

[1] This is probably the same practice today where the membership list for all PIM Christians is still kept at Mbombwe in one register and every baptized member is issued with a membership card with a number that is kept in PIM files at Mbombwe.

possible reason might be that Chilembwe used to pass through this area on his hunting trips to Mozambique.[2] Possibly he had some contacts with the people of this area who were then attracted to the church at Mbombwe. Chilembwe's first contact with the people of Migowi was through the father of David Kaduya. Kaduya senior was a hunter by profession. During his hunting trips he often met Chilembwe. Upon learning that Chilembwe had a school, Kaduya senior sent his son David to Mbombwe to be enrolled at PIM. It was through David that PIM found its way to Migowi.[3] David's father, however, never joined a PIM Church.

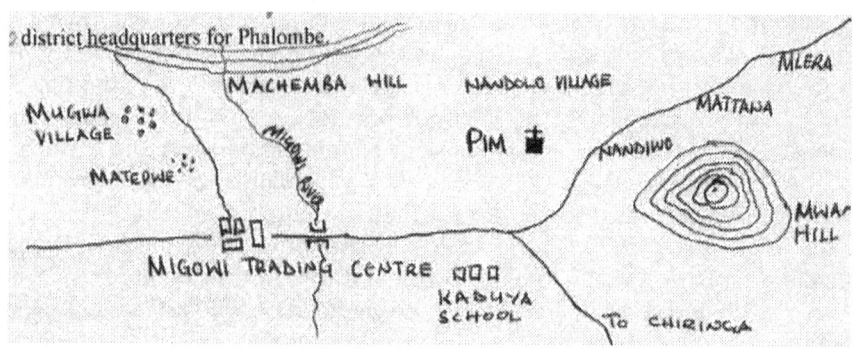

Map showing earliest centre of PIM at Migowi

Whatever established the contact, the fact remains that three prominent local leaders emerged from Migowi, who later became influential leaders of the church: David Kaduya, Benjamin Kaduya and Roland Namwera.[4] All three came from Kaduya village, in T/A Nkhumba. These were the first people to plant the PIM Church at Migowi in 1905. James Mandeule and Wylie Chigamba joined them later. These five became the pillars of the church at Migowi. The church was originally established at Chingazi, a distance of one and a half kilometer from the present PIM Church, and a distance of two kilometres from Migowi trading centre. Migowi was at the heart of Chilembwe. This was the first station away from PIM headquarters at Mbombwe. One interviewee noted: "The place we are now and our gardens was the place that Chilembwe used to plant cotton. Chilembwe had a great interest in this land."[5] The church at Migowi grew and branches were established in other areas.

---

[2] Interview Mr Palasa, 17 10 1996.
[3] George Nasolo, field research, 13-16 March, 2001.
[4] David and Benjamin Kaduya were brothers.
[5] Interview Mr Palasa, 10.10.1994.

These churches include Thabwa. This church seems to have originated from the church at Kaduya which was later named Mt Hermon Baptist Church by Dr Malekebu. During the period when PIM was silenced, Roland Namwera played a very important role in reviving this church. At the time when Malekebu retired, and some pastors broke away from PIM to form the Independent Baptist Convention of Malawi, they used Mt Hermon as their headquarters. The church at Mauzi was a local branch that originated from the church at Migowi; it is found twenty kilometres east of the church at Migowi. This church was established through the influence of the Kaduyas and Namwera to accommodate those Christians who would feel that the church at Migowi was far from their homes. This church acted as a home cell for Christians living around Mauzi and in Mozambique, as Mauzi is just on the boundary of Mozambique and Malawi. Today this church is found in Mulanje Section One according to PIM's administration, with its headquarters at St James Baptist Church at Chiringa in Phalombe district. The other churches were at Machea and Mankhokwe.[6] These churches were established before 1915.[7] This then shows that in Mulanje alone there were five or more PIM centres before the uprising.[8]

During the uprising the church at Migowi was greatly affected. Some of its local leaders were either killed or imprisoned. These include David Kaduya (killed), Benjamin Kaduya (hanged); Roland Namwera and Wylie Chigamba were imprisoned for five years in Zomba. When Roland Namwera was released from prison, he continued the work they started. Together with his wife, they were influential in reviving the PIM churches. At the time, the wife at times would go to Zomba on foot to provide food for her husband. She was also influential in providing food to those on the run during the rising, particularly those who hid in the caves of Machemba hill. The Namweras faced resistance from village headman Garinet Kaduya,[9] who discouraged people from joining PIM as it was a church of war (*mpingo wa nkhondo*). Garinet Kaduya encouraged his relatives, the Kaduya family, who were prominent members of PIM, to defect from PIM and join CCAP. This did not stop Namwera from preaching the gospel. He went as far as Thabwa, Mauzi, Machea and Mankhokwe reviving PIM churches. All the meetings were held at night. Village headman Garinet Kaduya demolished the PIM shelter, where Christians used to gather right at Mwananyani. Still this did not stop Namwera from leading the church. Despite all this discouragement, PIM Christians stood by

---

[6] Interview Mr Palasa, 10.10.1994.
[7] Interview Mr Palasa, 10.10.1994. At the time of the research the churches at Machea and Mankhokwe lacked information, however it is said that Roland Namwera and Rev Wylie Pilgrim Chigamba influenced the reviving of these churches within Mulanje district.
[8] This argument is based on the fact that this was the only information that was known to me at the time of the research.
[9] Interview Gogo Salewa, 14.10.1994.

their faith and were not shaken by the threats that came from village headman Garinet Kaduya. The church at Migowi survived the period of silence till 1926,[10] the time when PIM was officially reopened. Although the original location of the PIM church in Migowi was at Chingazi, it was then transferred to the present location near Mwananyani hill in 1940, with its leaders Roland Namwera, James Mandeule, Mr Chiopsya, Mr Mtenthiwa, Alice Kaduya, Lucy Kaduya and Fredrick Kaduya who later went to Zimbabwe in search of employment.[11] Before the church was transferred to Mwananyani, people were still meeting in the house of Roland Namwera at Chingazi. "The church at Mwananyani came out of the house of Roland Namwera and was built where it is now."[12] The church near Mwananyani hill is situated about a kilometer from Migowi trading centre. The church building was actually erected at the place where Benjamin Kaduya's house was located. As Gogo Salewa puts it: "Benjamin Kaduya's house was at the same place where the church is now built. The *thundu* tree which is there used to be the place where he kept his doves."[13] The church was built just fifty metres from the grave of Mores Chimpele Chilembwe. At the grave is the following inscription, "In memory of our beloved leader Mores Chilembwe who died in February 1915 for our freedom".[14] When PIM was reopened in 1926, the church at Migowi continued growing and opened centres at Nyezerera, Chitokoto and Mankhanamba. These churches form the earliest centres of PIM before 1940 in Mulanje district.[15]

In the late 1940s, the church at Migowi (Mwananyani) used a new name and has since been known as Mt Cleveland Ohio Baptist Church. This name was given by some of the visiting pastors of the National Baptist Convention USA Inc.[16] This name is still maintained today. Today Mt Cleveland Ohio

---

[10] Some PIM members showed interest to open the church, these were Mkulichi, Chambo and Ntambo. This was in 1924. They were not allowed till they received an official statement from the FMB. However they were allowed to worship publicly till the time PIM was officially reopened by Dr Malekebu in 1926.
[11] Interview Gogo Salewa, 14.10.1994.
[12] Interview Gogo Salewa, 14.10.1994.
[13] Interview Gogo Salewa, 14.10.1994.
[14] The inscription was written in 1977, when the former head of state of Malawi Dr Kamuzu Banda visited Mattawa and instructed that these graves be taken care of and the grave at Mwananyani was taken care of at the time when Rev Ronald Mbule was the pastor in charge of that area.
[15] With the partition of Mulanje district into two districts namely, Mulanje and Phalombe, most of these churches are found in Phalombe district. Despite the demarcation, PIM still recognizes its churches as in Mulanje district. This is so because PIM in each district is divided into sections. Mulanje having nine sections includes those in Phalombe, hence the churches in Phalombe are known as churches in Mulanje section 1,2,3 etc.
[16] Interview Mr Madulira, Migowi, 20.10.1998. This was probably one way of honouring the visitors or possibly they had intentions to adopt it and support it as is the case with other churches such as the one in Soweto, which was named First Institutional Baptist Church of Soweto when it

Baptist Church is the headquarters of the PIM churches in Mulanje Section 3, with more than eighteen churches under it. Between 1920 and 1940, the church at Migowi was very zealous in its evangelistic campaigns under the leadership of Roland Namwera. It reached the extent that PIM was known as "A Choonadi" (People of the Truth).[17] The local leadership had the responsibility of ensuring that Christians were taken care of, and that the church met their needs. This was particularly so in times of funerals and festivities. As there was only one ordained pastor, Dr Malekebu, during this period, the local leaders had all the responsibilities that an ordained pastor was supposed to have except administering Holy Communion and baptism.[18] The church usually had the presence of an ordained pastor once a year. It was at this occasion that those who were awaiting baptism were baptized. Holy Communion was also celebrated at this time in the presence of the pastor. It is from this situation that one can see that the church at Migowi was self-extending without the presence of the missionary pastor. All functions were under local leadership. The pastor's duty was just to baptize the already converted believers in order for them to be accepted into full membership.[19]

The Church at Boloweza

Boloweza village is found in the area of T/A Mwambo in Zomba district. Damson Boloweza, one of Chilembwe's deacons, first established the PIM church in Zomba at Boloweza village. A Yao by tribe, he used to go to PIM at Mbombwe for worship.[20] He then became one of the members who were close to Chilembwe and was elected deacon.[21] In 1908, he got permission from Chilembwe to open a PIM church at his own village. His family and relatives formed the membership during the early days when the church was being started.

Before the establishment of the church at Boloweza village, Damson Boloweza used to have several people who aspired to join PIM in a baptism class. This baptismal class involved Bible study and instructions on how they were to handle themselves during baptism to ease the work of the pastor

---

was adopted by First Institutional Baptist Church of Arizona in the USA Recently when the BM and E Baptist of Texas USA sponsored a PIM church at Sadzi in Zomba it was named BM and E Baptist, Texas.

[17] Interview Gogo Salewa, Nandolo village, 24.8.1996.

[18] In PIM, different from other Baptists, only ordained pastors are allowed to administer Holy Communion and baptism, however other activities can be done by a local leader, i.e. preaching, either at church or funerals or at any other occasion.

[19] The situation today is no longer the same as there are now more pastors than before. Still the local leaders have a big responsibility as one pastor could be assigned to so many churches that he can not visit all of them in a month.

[20] As to how Boloweza was converted to PIM Christianity is not known.

[21] Interview Daniel Wasiya, PIM, August, 2000.

conducting the service. In these instructions they were also taught some of the norms that the church would expect from them once they were baptized. In this class they were introduced to the basic understanding of the Bible and the church's stand on baptism, organization and church discipline.[22] When it was time for the baptismal service at PIM, those people attending classes would walk on foot all the way from Boloweza village in Zomba to Mbombwe led by their leader, Damson. When the church was established at Boloweza, every first Sunday of the month, Christians walked to Mbombwe for Holy Communion. First Sundays of the month used to be a time of festivity when Christians from different local congregations used to gather together for worship. During these gatherings a cow was killed and usually the service would start at eleven o'clock in the morning or even at twelve noon.[23] This was to give time for people to eat before the Sunday service. These gatherings acted as a uniting force for all PIM members: they would gather together as a fellowship of believers. This is also portrayed in the very fact that the church kept one membership list at Mbombwe. This shows that although the church had branches outside Mbombwe, they were not independent, as they would take directives from their headquarters.

During the 15 years of ministry, Chilembwe did not ordain any pastor; however he ordained many deacons from these outstations, some of whom served in the executive committee at the headquarters. David Kaduya a deacon in the church at Migowi, served in the main committee at the headquarters, as did Damson Boloweza from Boloweza village. This practice still continues today where some deacons from the outstations serve in the mission's main committee as the executive committee members of the church. During these occasions people could start gathering on Thursday and have several meetings from Friday evening to Sunday afternoon. This type of gathering continued even when PIM was reopened in 1926. PIM members used to address each other as 'brother' or 'sister'.[24] Whenever a PIM member was walking in the dark and wanted to ask for accommodation from a fellow member of PIM, he was easily recognized by a fellow member when he or she knocked at the door and shouted 'Excuse me brother!'[25] Although churches in the outstations were

---

[22] Interview Daniel Wasiya, PIM, August, 2000.
[23] Interview D. Komiha, PIM, August 2000.
[24] The term sister was not commonly used according to the knowledge of the researcher.
[25] Gogo Lucy Naluso Mugwa, December, 2000. Gogo Lucy Naluso recalls an incident in the early 1940s on her way from one of the PIM meetings at Nkhulambe. She attended that meeting and walked a long distance without her husband. Though the area was bushy and not safe to travel alone, as a deacon Gogo Lucy Naluso Mugwa made an effort to go and attend the meeting even without the company of her husband. Together with her little baby girl Esther at the back they set off for the meeting. On her way back darkness overtook them. On the road they met some men, three in number. They asked her name and the sex of the baby she was carrying on her back. She told them her name and that the baby she was carrying was a girl. The men said that since you are carrying a baby girl your life is spared; otherwise we could have killed you. Find a shelter

operating through local leadership they were not totally independent from the headquarters. They respected the directives from Mbombwe. This shows that PIM was centralized in terms of its administration. This type of church government is still in operation today.

The Church at Wallani

The church at Boloweza was growing and membership was increasing so rapidly that it attracted other members of the community. One person who was attracted to PIM Christianity from a distant village was Khwangwala Mpaseakuphe Wallani of Wallani village, T/A Mwambo in 1909, when the church was almost one year old at Boloweza village. This village is of about 12 km from Boloweza village. Mpaseakuphe Wallani joined PIM Christianity at Boloweza village and was baptized at PIM Mbombwe by Rev John Chilembwe.[26] Mpaseakuphe Wallani decided to take the church to his home village. After getting permission from the local leadership at Boloweza, Wallani established the church at his home place in 1913. The church was growing so fast that by 1914 membership was already over a hundred.[27] The 1915 Rising disturbed this development, affecting also some of the prominent members of the church in Zomba district. The people affected included Damson Boloweza, Khwangwala Mpaseakuphe Wallani and also some members of the Church of Christ such as Symon Kadewere. During the uprising, the colonial government soldiers from Zomba visited Wallani village and Boloweza village to investigate the possibility of PIM members being involved in the uprising. The church was completely destroyed and thus closed down.

The Church at Chinkhwangwa

During the uprising, Wallani and his friend Phambalawo, both prominent members of the church at Wallani village, went into hiding. They covered themselves in a beer basket (*ntanga wa mowa*) at Bakali village in T/A Mwambo in Zomba district. Fearing the threat from the soldiers, people helped in hunting Wallani and Phambalawo. They found Symon Kadewere, a brother to Wallani, a member of the Church of Christ at Namiwawa.[28] He was mistaken for Khwangwala Wallani, was taken to Zomba Prison and was hanged. When the real Khwangwala Wallani heard this, he fled to Mozambique, on the

---

somewhere and proceed with your journey tomorrow morning, in case you will meet some angry people who will not spare your life. Gogo Lucy Mugwa then went to a nearby house belonging to a member of the Providence Industrial Mission. They took time to open the door for her until she shouted 'excuse me brother!'

[26] Interview Nkhondo Wallani, Wallani village, T/A Mwambo, August 2000.
[27] Ibid.
[28] Ibid.

Phalombe side beside Mauzi hill, which makes the boundary between Malawi and Mozambique. He stayed there for eight years.[29]

When he returned, he stayed at Chinkhwangwa village in T/A Nkhumba in Phalombe district. He called his wife from Zomba. There he opened a PIM church in 1923; it was named Mt. Olivett Baptist Church. Khwangwala Mpaseakuphe Wallani died at Chinkhwangwa village.[30] His body was then taken to Likangala in Zomba and was buried at Wallani village in T/A Mwambo in Zomba district. The church that he established at Chinkhwangwa is still operational and maintains the same name. It is among the churches in Mulanje section 4 according to PIM's administration.

The Church at Magomero

PIM members who worked on Bruce Estates started the churches in Magomero area. These churches also had a big following. They managed to organize themselves and built shelters for worship in Bruce Estate. One of these was at Nawani village and another at Lieje village. In 1909, PIM churches on Bruce Estate were burned and 179 Christians were mistreated.[31] If by 1909 PIM membership at Magomero was not less than 179 people, it means then that the church started in this area earlier than 1909.[32]

In June 1913, two hundred workers on the Bruce Estates approached their manager, William Jervis Livingstone, to plead for permission to build again a prayer house of the PIM at Nawani village on plantation land. The request was refused but the prayer house was built. When the plantation workers threatened to strike and leave the estate, Livingstone sacked their leader Lifeyu, and burnt down the prayer house in front of the congregation.[33] If two hundred workers were member of PIM it shows that the Magomero area was a fertile ground for the PIM church. It also shows that, though the church faced some hardships in trying to secure places for worship, it was still growing in terms of membership.

In another incident, a prayer house at Mpotola's village was pulled down with the connivance of Catholics in the area. A third school of the PIM at Nanchengwa was reputedly destroyed on orders from the *boma* after complaints from Catholic catechists about its proximity to a Catholic school.[34] This kind of incidents indicates that there were conflicts between these

---

[29] Ibid.
[30] The year of his death was not known to the interviewee.
[31] M.B.K. Chipuliko, "A Brief History of Rev John Chilembwe", presentation, Chilembwe day, 15.1.1995. The people in the area suffered from the *thangata* system which was very extensive under the manager of Bruce Estate, William Jervis Livingstone.
[32] The actual year when the church at Magomero started is not known.
[33] Evidence given by A.L. Bruce in case 77. 510/1/3 file MNA.
[34] Interview Ben Mononga, Namuthokoni village, Chiradzulu, Malekebu's Kapitao at Mambala farm, his father was a worker in Chilembwe's garden in 1914, March 2001.

churches. It seems the *boma* people favoured the Catholics, and the Bruce Estates tolerated them within the plantation area.

Most members of these churches were involved in the Rising. Some were in the forefront leading the group that went to kill the white settlers at Magomero. Such individuals include Moses Linya whose name also appears on the membership list of the early PIM. Another one was Linjesi Khomelera who was Livingstone's servant and was in the forefront of the murder of his master. Today there are 21 churches in the Magomero area and, according to PIM's administration; these churches are in Zomba section 1.

The Church at Chiringa

The church at Chiringa goes back to the period when the church was banned in 1915 and its members scattered and gathered in secret for worship. At the time when Leonard Muocha[35] was attending school at Nambwale, he used to worship with PIM Christians who gathered secretly in the house of Wiskes Matengo. This house was not very far from Muocha village. Muocha was later baptized by Malekebu in 1930, walking on foot from Muocha village in Phalombe district to Ulumba in Zomba district, a distance of about 80 km. The church at St Paul Nkome in Chiringa is close to what used to be Muocha village, and came out of the house of Wiskes Matengo in 1922. This church is located just four kilometres from the Mozambique border. The second oldest centre of PIM at Chiringa is St James Baptist Church established in the late 1930s by Dr Malekebu.[36] Today there are eighteen churches that developed from the earliest centre of PIM. In PIM administration these churches are found in Mulanje section one.

---

[35] The former Chairman of PIM, the successor of Dr Malekebu, third from Chilembwe in leading PIM. See Patrick Makondesa, *Moyo ndi Utumiki wa Mbusa ndi Mayi Muocha a Providence Industrial Mission*, Blantyre: CLAIM-Kachere 2000.

[36] Some people argue that the first PIM Church in Chiringa is St James Baptist whereas others argue it is St Paul Nkome. I would suggest that the Church at St Paul Nkome was the first as it came out of the house of Wiskes Matengo who was also on the list of John Chilembwe Christians in November 1914. Wiskes Matengo and Yokoniya Matengo (brothers) were still active throughout the period when the Church was banned. Hence the church at St Paul Nkome stands a better chance for being the first PIM Church at Chiringa.

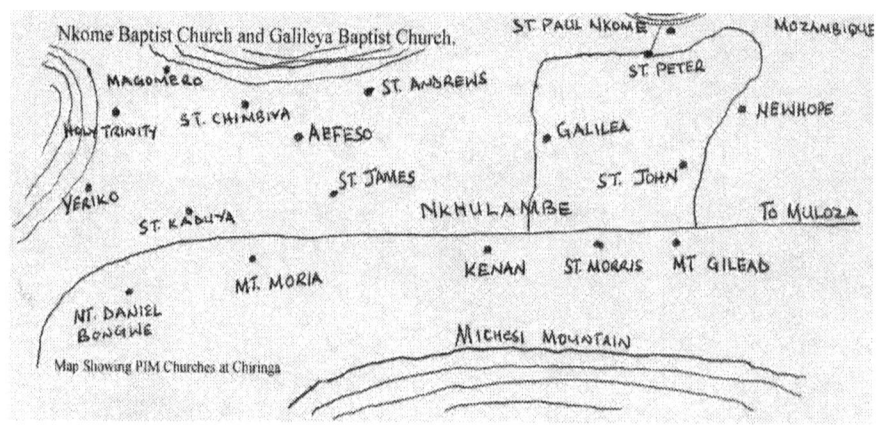

Map showing PIM churches at Chiringa

The churches include St James Baptist Church (the current PIM headquarters in Mulanje section one); Aefeso Baptist Church, Mt Daniel Baptist Church (Nkuthuwa village); Mt Moria Baptist Church (Bobo village); Yeriko Baptist Church; St Kaduya Baptist Church (Kaliati village); St Andrews Baptist Church; Magomero Baptist Church; St Chimbiya Baptist Church; Holy Trinity Baptist Church (Bwanali village); Kenani Baptist Church (Nkhulambe); St Morris Baptist Church (Nakonaka village); Mt Gilead Baptist Church; St John Baptist Church; New Hope Baptist Church (Yohane village), St Peter Baptist Church; St Paul Nkome Baptist Church and Galileya Baptist Church.

The Church at Thabwa

The Church at Thabwa traces its origins to Migowi, through the preaching of such local leaders as David Kaduya, Wylie Chigamba, Roland Namwera and Lucy Kaduya. After the uprising, this church was revived by Roland Namwera. The church at Thabwa is found in the area of Chief Kadewere in T/A Chikumbu in Mulanje district and is known as Mt Hermon Baptist Church.[37] Dr Malekebu further developed this church. He started laying the foundation for the construction of the church at almost the same time as the New Jerusalem

---

[37] Today this Church forms a National Headquarters for Independent Baptist Convention which came out of PIM under the leadership of Dr Daniel Malekebu influenced by the three pastors of PIM Mang'anda, Bulaimu and Nandolo. See Patrick Makondesa, The Beginnings of the Independent Baptist Convention, MA Module, Department of TRS, University of Malawi, Zomba, 2000.

Temple at Mbombwe and St John at Mphanda in Lilongwe district. This was between 1928 and 1933.[38]

The Church at Nasiyaya

Nasiyaya is a village that is found five kilometers east of Migowi trading center. This village is at a distance of six kilometers from the PIM church at Migowi. B. Mabutawo was the man behind the establishment of this church. He did not join PIM as a result of preaching. He heard news of Chilembwe's protest against the government's oppressive rule. Having been one of the victims of this oppressive system through forced labour of carrying timber from Phalombe to Mulanje he was interested to hear more about this protesting. He therefore left for PIM Chiradzulu in October 1914. His aim was to meet Chilembwe and discuss further about this protest. While there, he was convinced and became a member. When he was baptized he started a church at his home village and named it Betania Baptist Church. Although this church was just a few kilometers from the church at Migowi, it was not a branch, but existed independently from Migowi church. However they worked together with the church at Migowi as members of the same PIM family. This church still exists today, and treats the Migowi church as headquarters for Mulanje section 3.

The Church in Lilongwe

The first one to hear the word of God from Chilembwe in the central region was Peter Kalemba. He was working in one of the shops in Blantyre. When he heard about Chilembwe, he left Blantyre for Chiradzulu. He joined Chilembwe and was baptized by him. Peter Kalemba[39] was one of the prominent figures who brought PIM Christianity to the central region. He was a man of God and a good preacher.[40] He was born in 1889 and was Chilembwe's student.[41] Chilembwe taught that without shedding of blood there is no freedom. When there was war in Tanganyika, the whites took local villagers to join the war. John Chilembwe called the congregation and addressed this issue. On 12th December 1914, at the time Chilembwe wrote the letter to Governor Alfred Sharp, Peter Kalemba was still at PIM, Mbombwe.[42] This letter raised the concerns of Chilembwe towards the oppression brought by the white settlers. When things were crucial, Chilembwe's concern was about his church and his

---

[38] Interview Mr Palasa, Migowi, 14.10.1996.
[39] Hany Longwe has it that Peter Kalemba's real name was Lawrence and his father's name was Mkufu. He was of the Mlelemba clan most probably from Mulanje district. He first attended school at Blantyre Mission and was later encouraged by his father to join a school which was run by an educated African.
[40] Interview Billiat Kaphaidyani, Mitundu, Mlongoti village, T/A Chiseka, Lilongwe, 2 May, 1999.
[41] Interview Mr Sakhula, Lilongwe, 3.5.1999.
[42] Interview Billiat Kaphaidyani, Mitundu, 2.5.1999.

people. He began to prepare for the future church. When Chilembwe got the response from the Governor, he advised Peter Kalemba to leave immediately for the central region and open PIM there. This was done in order to keep the seed of the church alive. If the church in the southern region were to be completely destroyed, PIM would still exist in the central region. When he reached the central region, Kalemba immediately began making disciples. Many received the teaching of PIM. The church was established at Kalemba's village, today known as Nyanja headquarters.[43] The first converts of Peter Kalemba were the following: Anderson Nyangu, the first Chief Kalumbu, Chief Nyangu, Nkomba, Nkhosa, Fanwell Senzani and Andrew Dzamalala (Secretary of Peter Kalemba). Additional disciples in Lilongwe included Henry Kafulatira, Joseph Matapila, Kaname, Chikumba, Lumwira, Kamkalamba, Chonde, and Chikumba. These were the people who are regarded as the first converts of Kalemba. They supported him in the establishment of PIM in the central region, in particular Lilongwe district.[44]

In 1926, when Malekebu officially reopened PIM, Peter Kalemba had already reached as far as Salima, Mchinji, Dedza, Ntcheu and Mzimba.[45] In Dedza district the following were prominent followers of Kalemba who helped PIM work in Dedza: Nyanda, Kaludzu senior and Isaac Msuzi. During the 1915 uprising, the church in the central region was affected, though its leaders were not killed. However they suffered torture or ill treatment. When the government made inquiries, Peter Kalemba was found to be a disciple of John Chilembwe.[46] He had part of his ear chopped off and was sent back home to the central region. Others were imprisoned. Kalemba left for the central region and reached Kalumbu village.

In Dedza he strengthened Msuzi, and Kachiwanda, and entrusted them with the responsibilities of the church there while he took care of the church in Lilongwe. The centre in Dedza was at Chipira where the church started.[47] The church in Dedza continued growing. When the PIM was reopened, the church in Dedza sent their candidate Kaludzu, to be trained as a pastor at PIM headquarters.

In 1928 Kalemba received a message that Malekebu would visit the central region to baptize. Kalemba himself could not baptize, as he was not an ordained minister. At the time of this baptism service, Kalemba was in charge of PIM in the central region, though not ordained as a pastor. The church was

---

[43] Interview Billiat Kaphaidyani and Kafulatira, Kafulatira village, 3.5.1999.
[44] Ibid.
[45] Interview Sakhula, 3.5.1999. It seems Kalemba established PIM churches in these areas though they were organized in a small way. From Sakhula's explanation, some of these churches were families and with the death of some members of the family the churches died. However there are some churches which exists till today and are still under PIM, in Ntcheu, Salima and Dedza.
[46] Interview Sakhula, Lilongwe, 3.5.1999.
[47] Ibid.

totally in the hands of a layman. When Malekebu came, he baptized 350 people in one day. These were candidates that had been instructed by Peter Kalemba. The baptismal service took place at Kalumbu village.[48]

In 1928, there was a church building project launched at PIM in Mbombwe where the foundation of the New Jerusalem Temple was being laid. Christians in the central region contributed financially; in this sense the outstation supported the main station. This was part of the general appeal that the church made to all of its outstations.

In 1930, Malekebu made a second missionary visit to the central region and baptized many people as well. In about the same year, some women[49] brought forward the idea that there was a need to buy a bicycle for Peter Kalemba for his church work in the area, and church money was used to buy a bicycle for him. After some time, some sort of jealousy arose. People turned against Kalemba and accused him of mismanaging church funds by buying his own bicycle, despite the fact that these were the same people who had originally supported the idea. This plan of turning against Kalemba was led by Fanwell Senzani, Nkhosa and Chikumba. When Malekebu made a third missionary visit to the central region in 1932, it was reported to him that Peter Kalemba had bought a bicycle using church money. The case was heard at Chivuluvulu near Damphwi in Dedza district, and it led to Peter Kalemba being excommunicated from PIM.[50] Malekebu then sent Willie Mbamela and Wilfred Mtambo to take the bicycle to PIM at Mbombwe. This move caused conflicts within the church in Lilongwe. The Christians reacted furiously. They felt it an injustice that church money contributed by the people of the central region should go south to the PIM headquarters. Some argued against the removal of Peter Kalemba, their leader in the central region.

When Peter Kalemba was excommunicated, he joined CCAP Nkhoma Synod.[51] Some of the church members organized themselves and called Peter Kalemba from CCAP and formed their own independent church The leaders who instigated this idea were Henry Kafulatira, an evangelist for Peter Kalemba, Kokha, Skefa Kaphala, and Kankalamba of Nyanje near Nanjiri. In Dedza Aaron Nkuka was leading Kalemba's group. They named their church Achewa PIM. Peter Kalemba was then ordained as a pastor by Kaugulu of the Seventh Day Baptists.[52] Dr Malekebu's action in excommunicating is a clear example of the PIM's centralized administration. All directives are from the core to the periphery. The buying of a bicycle was a good idea, but the fact that it did not follow the right channel proved to be a wrong move. At the time that this event

---

[48] Interview Sakhula, 3.5.1999.
[49] The names of women who raised the idea were not mentioned to the researcher.
[50] Interview Sakhula, Lilongwe, 3.5.1999.
[51] Interview Sakhula, Lilongwe, 3.5.1999.
[52] Interview Sakhula, Lilongwe, 3.5.1999.

took place, there was a great need of money at the main station as there was the big project of constructing the New Jerusalem Temple. Therefore any use of money in any other way would be considered a serious offence. Kalemba's excommunication can also be looked at from a different angle by considering how it was relayed to Malekebu. As this was reported out of jealousy, it is likely the evidence was biased and incomplete, provoking such a cruel reaction from Malekebu.

Despite these conflicts, the church in Lilongwe was still growing and reaching out to other areas. In 1933 the foundation of the church at Mphanda was started.[53] According to Ephraim Billiat Kaphaidyani, the foundation of Mphanda church building was laid from 1930 to 1932. When the foundation was being laid, Peter Kalemba was still a leader in the central region under Malekebu. After the foundation was laid, it took a long time for the church building to be erected. This was probably due to financial problems emanating from the main station at Mbombwe, as this project was launched by them with the assistance from local leadership at Mphanda. The purpose of building Mphanda Church was to make it the PIM centre in the central region.[54] The first proposed area for this church was at Nkhosa village; later it was decided that the church be built at Nyangu's village. Chief Nyangu offered 33 acres of land.[55] There was a long break between laying the foundations of the building and the construction of the whole church. However development was an ongoing process at Mphanda. A primary school was started under the leadership of Chiwaula. When Sakhula was the head deacon for the central region, he introduced the idea of making bricks for the church building. "My lorry worked at Mphanda, it carried stones from Bisai to Mphanda. We managed to build three ovens of bricks".[56] When Malekebu visited the central region, he had a meeting at Tsambe at St John Baptist Church. This caused some conflicts as people expected him to be at Mphanda. Malekebu said he had ceased working at Mphanda, possibly as a result of the conflicts with the Achewa PIM.[57] These kind of conflicts led the other members of the church to go against the Achewa PIM who were intervening with PIM premises at Mphanda. Chief Nalikore intervened and claimed Mphanda Church as belonging to PIM. Since Mphanda Church was on the boundaries of Nyangu and Nalikore village, the area was declared to be in Nalikore village and no longer Nyangu's. The place is still known today by the name Nalikore. Chief

---

[53] Interview Sakhula, Lilongwe, 3.5.1999.
[54] Interview C. Chipungu, Mphanda, Lilongwe, 15.12.1998.
[55] Interview C. Chipungu, Mphanda, Lilongwe, 15.12.1998.
[56] Interview Sakhula, Lilongwe, 3.5.1999.
[57] Nyangu was influential at Mphanda. He decided to join Achewa PIM and offer the land where PIM was standing to Achewa PIM but later came back to PIM and was influential in the construction of the PIM Church at Mphanda.

Nalikore was a PIM member at Mphanda Church.[58] The church at Mphanda was still growing some time in late 1940s[59] when it received a visitor from USA, Dr C.C. Adams, the Secretary of the Foreign Mission Board of the National Baptist Convention of USA Inc. Many people mistook him for Chilembwe.[60]. They held the idea that Chilembwe did not die, but that after escaping from Nyasaland he went to America, and came back as C.C. Adams. What made people think that was the way he spoke, and his preaching was not so different from Chilembwe's ideas.[61]

The Bell at Matapila

The church at Chamadenga village and the church at Matapila village were led by Feliati Dirawo Kaunde[62] and his wife Velina who instructed their children never to leave PIM, the church started by their grandparent Joseph Matapila of Matapila village at Mazengera.[63] The churches that existed during the time of Kalemba and still remain PIM after formation of the Achewa PIM are the churches at Chipamphale village; Malemia village; Nampala village; Kachala village; Nkwende village; Chiudzira village; Kwankwera village; Dunde village and Mwatibu village.

---

[58] Interview C. Chipungu, 15.12.1998.
[59] The exact year would be probably in 1949. Interview Billiat Kaphaidyani, 2.5.1999.
[60] The PIM churches in Lilongwe that existed during the time of Peter Kalemba and still exist today as PIM are the following: St John Baptist at Tsambe; Kasamba Baptist at Nkhosa village; Chitedze Baptist at Kasenda village.
[61] Interview Billiat Kaphaidyani, Mitundu, 2.5.1999.
[62] Feliati Dirawo Kaunde died on 20.3.2001 at the time when this chapter was being worked on He was laid to rest on 22 March, 2001 at Matapila in T/A Mazengera in Lilongwe district. At the time of his death he left his wife Velina, twelve children and forty two grandchildren. The burial service was conducted outside his PIM Church at Matapila with the Chairman of PIM Rev Macford B. Chipuliko preaching on the subject 'Know your enemy'. At the burial site the Director of Christian Education and Evangelism Rev Addison T. Mabuwa preached on the subject 'Arise and go for this is not your resting place'.
[63] Interview Melissa Kaunde, January 2001.

The PIM church at Matapila

All these churches had their centre at Mphanda. Sakhula, Kalumbu and Nyangu built the school at Mphanda. It had four blocks with four rooms. It had standard one, two, three and four. Since there was no further development, some of the land was lost to the surrounding local villagers. Mphanda Church is proud of producing a branch at Nkhosa village that later bred the first PIM Chewa pastor, Rev Kakhobwe of Nkhosa village, whom Malekebu ordained in the late 1940s. The church in the central region was at the heart of Dr Daniel Malekebu as he often reported to the Foreign Mission Board of the National Baptist Convention of USA Inc about the progress made 'up country.'[64]

The Church in Ntcheu

The church in Ntcheu was under Wilson Kusita, a Ngoni convert to PIM in 1908. He looked after a PIM school near Ntcheu *boma*. Clair Njilima, a brother of Duncan Njilima, who owned a store in the district, assisted Kusita in church affairs. Duncan's store in Ntcheu was run by Clair and contained, according to the DC, £300 worth of goods.[65] Both Clair Njilima and Wilson Kusita were influential leaders of PIM in Ntcheu district. In 1913, Kusita became an itinerant Watchtower preacher in Ntcheu district under the influence of Kamwana, and opened schools in Liwonde district. He was executed after the rising, having returned to his PIM allegiance after October 1914.[66] By January

---

[64] See "A Letter from Dr Daniel Malekebu to Dr Adams, Secretary of the Foreign Mission Board of the National Baptist Convention of USA, Inc", *Mission Herald*, November-December, 1948, p. 25.
[65] S1/68/19 MNA, Zomba.
[66] NCN 4/1/1 and S10/1/6, MNA, Zomba.

1915 he was already at PIM, Mbombwe. After leaving Ntcheu he wrote to Elliot Achirwa, Kamwana's representative:

> The people will not be saved by you but here it is possible that we will be saved (because) that John Chilembwe is a real American. Here I am with the people that I know and I am not afraid.[67]

By the end of December 1914 there were tell tale signs in Chilembwe's letter; he had begun speaking of Africans as 'my people' and ending with undisguised eschatological proclamations whose meaning could not be mistaken by readers of the Bible. Chilembwe wrote to Kusita to encourage him:

> Preach the gospel trusting our heavenly father will help us. Strengthen all weak brethren. Preach the kingdom of God is at hand.[68]

Chilembwe's words of encouragement to Kusita were that of an overseer encouraging one in charge of a church in the out station. This shows Kusita was totally in charge of the PIM church in Ntcheu, and as it seems was in frequent contact with headquarters. Another prominent member of the Ntcheu church was Kamenya who was found on the baptized list of PIM members as number 911, and on the Ntcheu list of those people imprisoned in the Ntcheu district as PIM followers as number 104. This shows that the PIM church in Ntcheu was already active by the period of the rising.

The Church in Harare

Natives of Nyasaland who were members of PIM established the church in Harare, Zimbabwe. It was not established as a result of any crusade or large gathering, but through labour migration. The people who left Nyasaland for Zimbabwe, had no intention of going there as missionaries. They went there in search of employment.[69] As they had left Nyasaland with PIM Christianity, they began to organize themselves and met in their houses as PIM Christians. As a house fellowship began to expand, other people started joining them. With the intermarriages between them and Zimbabweans, the church was growing and becoming part of the people of Zimbabwe. At the very beginning, this church was frequently joined by those who came from Nyasaland in search of employment. Since the church was already full of people who came from Nyasaland, most newcomers from Nyasaland felt at home there.

---

[67] Kusita - Achirwa, 16 December 1914, NCN 4/1/1, MNA, Zomba.
[68] John Chilembwe - Kusita, 22 December 1914, NCN 4/2/1, MNA, Zomba.
[69] The names of the first members of PIM in Zimbabwe were not identified during the time of the research, however those who followed include Manjalela and Jackson Milimbo both from Chiradzulu.

Picture of the church in Harare, Zimbabwe

At about the same time as the foundation of the New Jerusalem Baptist Temple at Mbombwe was being laid, the foundation of the first PIM church in Zimbabwe was also being constructed. This was also the same period that the foundation of the church at Mphanda was being laid. In 1933, construction of the church was completed at Mbale, Harare.

The letter from the Secretary for Native Affairs to the Chief Secretary to the Government of Nyasaland inquiring about Jackson Milimbo's affiliation to PIM in Nyasaland shows that by 1936, PIM was already established as a church in Zimbabwe. The response from the Nyasaland government showed that Dr Malekebu had the knowledge of Milimbo as a PIM Christian who sought permission from the church at Mbombwe recommending him to the church in Zimbabwe.

The correspondence shows that the government of Nyasaland recognized PIM as a church and saw no reason why its member be should excluded from serving PIM in Zimbabwe. When the church in Zimbabwe was growing and its building completed, Dr Malekebu thought it wise to seek the official recognition of the government of Southern Rhodesia. In return the government of Southern Rhodesia, after being approached by Malekebu, wrote to the government of Nyasaland seeking information concerning whether PIM is recognized by the government or not.[70]

Secretary for Native Affairs,
P.O. Box 393, Salisbury,
Southern Rhodesia.
15th January 1937.

---

[70] As to whether the recognition of the church was granted in the very same year or the year after, is not known. However the church continued to operate without problems since that time till today.

The Chief Secretary to the Government,
The Secretariat,
Zomba,
Nyasaland.
Sir,
This Government has been approached by one D.S. Malekebu, who describes himself as Principal of the Providence Industrial Mission, and gives his address as Chiradzulu, Nyasaland, for recognition of his Church in this Territory.

As this particular Mission appears to be an American institution without European supervision in South Africa, I should be grateful for any information you may be able to supply regarding the activities of the Chiradzulu institution, and advice as to whether the mission is recognized by the Government of Nyasaland.

I have the honour to be,
Sir,
Your obedient servant,
(Signed)
Secretary for Native Affairs.

The Church in South Africa

The beginning of the church in South Africa was not very much different from the church in Zimbabwe, as it was also started as a result of labour migration. In the early 1930s, two PIM members went to South Africa in search of employment. Their names were Moses Kanenkha and Isaac Mangani. They went there to work in the mines and settled in Orlando township in Soweto. Later they began to communicate with Malekebu introducing the idea that they would like to open PIM there. In the late 1930s they started to gather in the house of Moses Kanenkha.[71] This marked the beginning of PIM in South Africa. The group was growing. Mostly it was the natives of Nyasaland that joined them. In the early 1940s, Malekebu visited them and made a proper registration of the church with the government of South Africa. The church extended its work to Messina and Chiawelo in Soweto.[72] The church at Chiawelo was growing and membership increased. The people then decided to find a place for them to meet comfortably. They secured a classroom at a

---

[71] Interview Ms Chambata, daughter of the late Rev Isaac Chambata, South Africa, 20.2.1998.
[72] Interview Rev Farasia Phiri, Chiawelo, Soweto, South Africa, December 1997.

government school in Chiawelo, Soweto.[73] The church at Messina was a result of the influence of the local South African born S.R. Khuzwayo.[74]

This development shows that PIM ministry was at its peak in the 1930s. During this period there was both rapid expansion of the church in terms of influence and extensive church building projects, which were totally in the hands of local leadership.

---

[73] Interview Rev Farasia Phiri, Chiawelo, Soweto, South Africa, 7.2.1998. Also see Patrick Makondesa, *PIM in Soweto: A Question of Identity*, Occasional paper, Colloquium, Department of Theology and Religious Studies, 1998.

[74] Interview Rev Muocha, 12/4/1996. S.R. Khuzwayo was later ordained by Malekebu and went to minister at Messina and in 1950 Dr Malekebu sent Rev Isaac Chambata to South Africa to look after the Church at Mapetla. The arrival of Rev Chambata brought a lot of changes in the PIM Church of South Africa.

CHAPTER FOUR

PIM Expansion through an Institutional Approach to Mission

Historically, the modern missionary movement (Latourette's "Great Century") was a movement from the west towards Asia and Africa. The missionaries brought the best that they had to these foreign shores. Christian churches all over the Third World were therefore the beneficiaries of a variety of typical western cultural institutions.[1]

Schools

The first area to receive attention was that of education. The missionaries came from a book-culture and couldn't conceive of a mission without teaching people to read, and giving them the Bible and other literature. This necessitated the opening of schools. Mission work became primarily a teaching activity, and to enroll in a mission school was tantamount to becoming a Christian.[2] In Transkei, the Christians were called the "school people."[3] The teacher-evangelists became the founders not only of the African church; but from this early beginning developed the present educational system of modern African states. Literacy training made it possible for people to read and study the Bible, even in their own language.[4]

In Malawi, the history of mission education can be traced from 1875, when the Free Church of Scotland missionaries arrived at Cape Maclear to establish Livingstonia Mission. There, Dr Robert Laws opened the first School where he taught boys and girls the alphabet and other elementary subjects.[5] After the establishment of the station at Cape Maclear in 1875, other missionaries began to come to Malawi to establish their own mission stations. From 1875, when the mission was first opened, to 1929, education was a mission responsibility.

---

[1] Kritzinger/Meiring/Sayman, *On Being Witness*, p. 143.
[2] Ibid. p. 143.
[3] This would be similar to a Malawian concept "Wosapita kutchalichi" literary translated as "the one who does not go to Church" This concept means the one who is not educated. This then shows that education and church go hand in hand. School and church were treated as one.
[4] Kritzinger/Meiring/Sayman, *On Being Witness*, p. 143.
[5] Soon Wiliam Koyi from South Africa became the head of the school.

There were no government schools in the country and African education was left completely in the hands of the missionaries.[6]

The general view held by all the missions in the country was that education and Christianity were inextricably linked, but education was to be subservient to Christianity. Such being the case, the aims of education were to be interpreted with the mind and in the spirit of Christ, and followed up, in all its manifold implications, for the individual and for the community. It was felt that education was not to be external to the primary plan of the Christian mission, but at the very centre of it.[7]

Just as other churches would do, Providence Industrial Mission at Mbombwe started to work on the construction of a little church and school house on a self help basis. At the end of 1900, Rev John Chilembwe and a few Christians of the PIM had managed to complete a school building to accommodate not less than a hundred pupils. John Chilembwe wrote to the *Central African Times* of the Shire Highlands at the end of the year regarding his proposed school work:

> By giving the children of Africa good training they will be able to possess an indomitable spirit and firm dependence upon God's helping and sustaining hand. And make observations, which will be of greatest use to different tribes of African sons, who only need the quickening and enlightening influence of the gospel of Christ to lift them from this state of degradation, and make them suitable members of the great human family.[8]

At the end of 1900, at the PIM boarding school, there were 100 pupils, a mud church, and 15 pupils were baptized.[9] Chilembwe's purpose for education was the development of the students both spiritually and socially. He used the school as a pulpit for his Christian and social ideologies. Mr Maynard Gibson Mbela, who entered the Providence Industrial Mission in 1904 and passed into Chilembwe's class (Standard III) in 1907, expressed the following views:

> Chilembwe taught us a good deal about planters and white settlers. He complained about the planters who were cruel to their African tenants, stopped them from collecting firewood and cutting trees from their estates, etc. Many of the tenants were Christians in his Church. Indeed the Europeans did not seem to like him because they used to send detectives to his mission to find out what he was doing.[10]

---

[6] Kelvin N. Banda, *A Brief History of Education in Malawi*, Blantyre: Dzuka, 1982, p. ix.
[7] Ibid., p. 49.
[8] *Central African Times*, 8.12.1900, p. 10 in: Shepperson and Price, *Independent African*, p. 127.
[9] M.B.K. Chipuliko, "A Brief History of Rev John Chilembwe", Chilembwe Day Celebration, 1995, p. 1.
[10] Information from Maynard Gibson Mbela in: Shepperson and Price, *Independent African*, p. 146.

Though the government census for 1911 did not mention the PIM amongst its statistics, though it included the other, smaller white missions, this was reflected in the contemporary literature of the National Baptist Convention where the stock of the PIM at this time appears as: 1 missionary, 5 churches, 800 members, 7 native helpers, 625 pupils, superintendent, Rev John Chilembwe.[11]

In the year after the two Americans Negro missionaries had left the PIM, in 1906 and before 1913, Chilembwe had been strengthening the schools of his mission. He could report to the Foreign Mission Board headquarters in 1912 a total of 906 Africans under his teachers, an increase of nearly 300 on the figures he had given them two years before:

Foreign Mission Board Headquarters, New York as of 1940

This is about the number of scholars they teach as follows: Nankundi school, W. Kusita, 168, 8 miles from the main station; Matili school, D. Boloweza, 190, 15 miles; Ndunde school, T. Nowazi, 82, (6) miles; Thumbwe school, T. Ngokwe, 120, 10 miles; Malika school; A. Jamali [who became Chilembwe's secretary during the period of the 1915 Rising], 60, 2 miles; Sangano school, H Chese, 86, 3 miles. The main school, 200, teachers, S.L. Nkulichi and I.Z. Chilembwe.[12]

---

[11] Journal of the Thirtieth Annual Session of the National Baptist Convention, 14-19 September 1910, Nashville Tennessee, p. 59, in: Shepperson and Price, p. 166.
[12] Journal of the Thirty-second session of the National Baptist Convention, 11-16 September 1912, p. 119-122 in: Shepperson and Price, *Independent African*, p. 171. This report did not indicate any school activity in the earliest centers of the PIM. Probably there were no schools operating in these areas at the time. This can further be proved by the very fact that most students from these areas attended a boarding school at Mbombwe, the PIM headquarters.

Chilembwe realized how immature his staff were. This is indicated in a 1912 report which he sent to his American Negro headquarters, which casts light not only on the level of his teachers at this time but also on his desire to improve standards amongst them:

> Please note these teachers are still under instruction three months during each vacation. I am trying to give them the art of teaching the Bible by various helps while engaged in their teaching. My desire is that each teacher should be properly fitted and an expert in Bible teaching, as in our other branches. I hope to see in this country and in the confines of our work, some young men to be qualified in the preliminary steps to the ministry of the church in this land, possessing (a) certificate as a teacher or schoolmaster to be a qualified native pastor.[13]

For Chilembwe, the school was a step to the development of a native ministry of the church. The school was a means of getting converts who would be well versed in biblical teaching, as he clearly states "I am trying to give them the art of teaching the Bible." Knowing that opening of more schools was a means to evangelism, the PIM was ambitious enough to start a lot more of them. By 1912 a marked change had come into the official note. After giving a list of PIM schools the District Commissioner went on to notice the PIM's ambition to start more of them. But, he added, "they have been severely repressed." He commented in a warning fashion:

> This mission requires careful supervision and should not be allowed to spread.[14]

In a letter addressed to the Resident in Chiradzulu dated 12th January 1914, Chilembwe wrote the following:

> Regarding to your request concerning the establishment of the Providence Industrial Mission Schools, PIM was opened on Feb. 1900. After good conversation on the subject finally I was allowed to open my mission at Chiradzulu sub-district and after wards I had opened out stations until about 1912. I was called by the Resident, Chiradzulu, and asked to report the number of outstations.

---

[13] *Ibid.*, p. 172. It seems Chilembwe trained his personnel both as teachers and evangelists. His desire was to make these teachers become qualified pastors, however there is no evidence that Chilembwe ordained anybody as a pastor but many were ordained as deacons. These deacons were in charge of outstation churches. Chilembwe's report to the American Negro headquarters indicates that he desired to train more people into the church ministry. Hence the teachers were the right candidates to take this task. They were to undergo instructions for a period of three months during each vacation though it is not known for how many sessions of vacations would make one into a qualified native pastor. Much as there is nowhere stated that Chilembwe ordained anyone into the church ministry, this serves as evidence that he did assign others to the work of the ministry in other branches of the church in order to properly equip each teacher in Bible teaching. I think Chilembwe had in mind some people he entrusted with responsibility in the outstations, as he describes it was a preliminary step to the ministry of the church.
[14] *Ibid.*, p. 173.

I reported 7 including the main station school and I was told not to open anymore than that. And the list of our schools as follows:

- Sangano School opened Sept 1907
- Ndunde School opened Sept. 1908
- Nankundi School opened Oct 1909
- Thumbwe School opened Sept 1908
- Chingoli School opened   Aug 1908
- Matiti School opened Sept 1911

This school was built under the request of the village headman and their children. Reply to Mtepela's village Kanyenda's. I heard something about this school that it had been built by the boys of the village on Dec and had seen one of our teachers who was reported to me but it was not settled how we can supply material.

As I did not seen the headman of the village and hear whether they have reported to the *boma* or not, I did not supply books.

Yours respectfully,

(sd) JOHN CHILEMBWE[15]

Chilembwe's response to the Resident at Chiradzulu, clearly indicates that schools were in high demand. Village headmen and their subjects pressed for mission education. In the case of the school at Mtepela, the village headman and his subjects, through self help, managed to build a school identified with the PIM, even before discussion with PIM's authority. Hunger for education instigated much of PIM's expansion. That people identified their schools with PIM was reason enough to assume that they were PIM aspirants. With time, most people who attended these schools ended up being PIM members. The established schools became fertile ground for the ministry of the church.[16]

The PIM offered a boarding school as early as 1900. Many people walked to the PIM for education and later returned to their home villages and introduced PIM churches into their areas. Such people included David Kaduya, Peter Kalemba, and Damson Boloweza.

David Kaduya was one of the students at the PIM boarding school. His conversion to PIM Christianity followed. After some four to five years at PIM, David Kaduya became a committed Christian and a strong Chilembwe supporter. He soon attained the position of a deacon in the PIM church in Mbombwe. He then introduced PIM Christianity at his home village Kaduya at Migowi in Phalombe district, convincing his sisters Alice and Lucy, brothers

---

[15] John Chilembwe - Resident, Chiradzulu, 12.1.1914.
[16] Today, all the areas mentioned, where schools were existing are the PIM's strongholds; a clear indication that these schools played an important role in the conversion of individuals to PIM.

Fredrick and Benjamin, who all joined PIM. With time others joined them such as Wylie Chigamba, Mandeule, Chiopsya and Roland Namwera. This is a vivid example of how the PIM expanded through the Institutional Approach to mission. Students who came for an education at Mbombwe, went back to their homes not with a school but with a church.

Similarly to the father of David Kaduya, the father of Peter Kalemba played a role in PIM expansion by sending his son to the boarding school at Mbombwe. Peter Kalemba for several years attended school at Blantyre mission.[17] His father, then living at Chikumbu village in Mulanje district, encouraged him to join a school that was run by an educated African, Chilembwe, at Chiradzulu. After his schooling Kalemba was employed in one of the shops in Chiradzulu. During that time, he attended church at the mission and was amongst the baptized members of the PIM.[18] In November 1914 Peter Kalemba was advised by Chilembwe to take the PIM church to the central region. Since the PIM school at Chiradzulu taught its students to higher standards, people at Kalumbu in Lilongwe respected and envied Kalemba because he was educated and knowledgeable beyond their expectation. Kalemba was welcomed in the area as a model of success for all Africans. He soon began witnessing about his faith. Soon he had a large following confessing their faith PIM Christian. The respect that Kalemba received due to his PIM education, was reason enough for some to follow him and receive PIM Christianity in Lilongwe.[19] PIM expansion through the institutional approach to mission was further affected in this way. Kalemba went to PIM for education and went away not with a school but a church.

There is a great probability that there might be a lot more people that did not start churches wherever they came from, but were nevertheless converted to PIM Christianity through their enrollment in PIM schools. Such people include Dr Daniel Malekebu, who was one of the first students to be enrolled. He lied to his parents, stating that he was enrolled by force. At the school, he was identified as the most intelligent boy. While at school, he was involved in different activities, including scripture reading during the morning assembly. After some time he was converted to Christianity and later became the successor of Chilembwe.[20]

Ruth Malekebu, a sister to Daniel, after visiting her brother Daniel at PIM and noting that life at school was quite different from the village followed her brother to the PIM for an education. She saw her fellow girls going to classes and admired them. She went home to seek permission from her parents to be

---

[17] Hany Longwe's findings, "Beginning of PIM's Churches in Mangoni", undated document.
[18] A list of the baptized member believers of the First African Baptist Church standing membership. Kalemba's name is number 284 page 9 of the list. Dated November 1914.
[19] Interview Kaphaidyani, 2.5.1999.
[20] Daniel Malekebu, "My Life and My Work", unpublished, 1940.

enrolled at the mission school. At first, the parents resisted but later gave in, and she was allowed to go and register her name. She proved to be one of the best female students. She was then baptized and after her education she was made one of the teachers at the PIM School. Later she married I.M. Lawrence. Ida Chilembwe, who also came for schooling at the PIM, was later converted to Christianity and then married John Chilembwe.

Cidreck Namasiku of Mpaso village, Chiradzulu came to the PIM as a student, then married a daughter of Andrew Mkulichi. (Mkulichi, being a member of PIM and Chilembwe's relative, followed his wife and joined PIM Christianity). Namasiku became a strong member of PIM and accompanied Chilembwe to most of the outstation meetings.[21] Wallace Kampingo of Chimpesa village went to the PIM as a student and was then baptized, Endson Nasolo of Ntipasanjo village, Chiradzulu went to the PIM for schooling. When Chilembwe introduced literacy education at the PIM, he registered. One of the subjects taught every day at the school was religious education. These lessons converted him and he decided to join PIM as a church member; he was then influential in the conversion of his own relatives and was chosen as one of the deacons. Richard Chiwayula of M'bwana village, Chiradzulu came to the PIM school, later deciding to join PIM as a church member. Simon Makhole of Nazombe village, Phalombe, went to PIM as one of the students at the boarding school, was later converted and became a PIM member. Daglous Mankhokwe of Chaweza village in Zomba, heard about a boarding school at PIM through some PIM members of Boloweza village. He went to PIM as a student, later joining the PIM as a Christian. Bannet Kadangwe of Chikalasa village in Zomba, heard about PIM School from his friend Daglous Mankhokwe. He followed a friend and joined school at PIM. He was then baptized and became a PIM member. Khwangwala Wallani of Bakali village, influenced by Damson Boloweza, went to the PIM as a student, later becoming a member of the PIM taking a branch from Boloweza village to Wallani village. Isaac Chambo of Nkwaila village, Chiradzulu, heard that there was a school at PIM Mbombwe run by an educated African. He had interest to enroll in this school, and was later converted through the Bible lessons that were taught in class.[22] Richard Chiwayula, of M'bwana village (T/A Kadewere) in Chiradzulu district followed his brother Jackson, who married Nasolo's daughter at Mtipasonjo village, in enrolling at the literacy school at the PIM. He attended classes up to a sub-standard. He was entrusted to read scripture during the morning assembly before classes started, which made him popular amongst his fellow students. With this background, he later decided to join the PIM as a member and was baptized. He became a dedicated member and was

---

[21] George Nasolo, field research, March 2001.
[22] George Nasolo, field research, March 2001.

appointed a church monitor and a financial officer for the building of the church at Mbombwe.[23]

Airon M'bwana was converted to PIM indirectly through education at PIM. The Chiwayula brothers, whose education became renowned in their village as a result of visits to their parents from PIM boarding school, influenced Airon. What attracted him most was the way the Chiwayula brothers shared the gospel with the people of their village. To him, there was no difference with the way the white missionaries ministered to the natives. On one occasion he accompanied the Chiwayula brothers to PIM, not to be enrolled, but to be baptized. Another person who was not directly converted through attending school at the PIM was Simon Makole. Through admiration and influence of some PIM members who attended school at PIM, he decided to join them and went for baptism. He was influenced by David Kaduya of T/A Nkhumba who shared boundaries with T/A Nazombe where Simon Makole came from. G. Kunjirima of Nyezerera village, T/A Nkhumba, Phalombe district, followed his brother Duncan Kunjirima who went to PIM for school, was converted and proved to know more than at the time he was not at school. G. Kunjirima asked permission from his parents to go to the PIM and join his brother at school. He was enrolled in the literacy class, and proved to be an outstanding candidate; his intelligence meant Chilembwe did not want to lose him. He convinced him to join the PIM. He was then baptized. Bannet Kadangwe of Makowa village, T/A Kadewere, in Chiradzulu heard from some of the students at the PIM School. He decided to become one of the students, so he registered his name and was soon given scriptures to read in the morning assembly. This motivated him to join the church and he was baptized. He then influenced Daniel Mangulama, his nephew, who went to the PIM school and was later converted to Christianity, becoming an influential member of the PIM and later one of those imprisoned at Zomba Prison. Moses Linya of Nyezerera village, Chikowi in Zomba was sent to the PIM School by his parents. Frank Chambo went to the PIM School. He was enlisted among those who were to lead in the reading of scriptures during morning assemblies. This cultivated an element of Christianity within him and he decided to join the church as a full member. He became influential in the conversion of some of his relatives, including his own wife, Ellina Mkwaira, who was a cousin to him from the father's side.[24]

The New Social Centre

Providence Industrial Station was progressing very fast. It soon became the new social centre in Chiradzulu and the mission influence extended to other parts of the country, particularly over the southern region of Malawi. When the mission was destroyed, during the 1915 uprising, the church was at its peak in terms of

---

[23] George Nasolo, field research, March 2001.
[24] George Nasolo, field research, March 2001.

its educational influence. All the work was destroyed and the Mission remained in ruins. When Dr and Mrs Malekebu came from the USA, as missionaries of the Foreign Mission Board of the National Baptist Convention, they revived PIM schools and immediately reintroduced the boarding school. Malekebu viewed education as the key to success of any development in the areas of health, agriculture and economy. He pleaded with the Afro-Americans to support mission work in Africa, particularly in the area of educational development. With the changes in educational policies in Nyasaland, he did not support the idea that education should be secularized. Education should not solely be placed in the hands of the government; it would not be safe for a heathen African. He therefore made enormous efforts to encourage the Afro-Americans to build in Nyasaland an institution like the Tuskegee Institute in the USA, and saw a great beginning for Tuskegee in Nyasaland at the PIM. To him education was also a means to Christian values, which he prioritized above anything else. From what he wrote one can see that Malekebu used an Institutional Approach to mission as a means of expansion of church work. He wrote to the Afro-Americans the following:

> The Christian and non-Christian African can occupy any amount of land and develop as much as he is able to do, and raise what he wants to the best of his ability for himself and his children's children. The land belongs to him; nobody will interfere with him. The chiefs who are known as "native authorities," the same as a paramount chief, who are in charge of a certain area can invite any mission head to put up and build school in his area. He will give a tract of land for the schoolhouse and enough land for agricultural demonstration. Any village headman has the power to do this. This shows how the people of Nyasaland appreciate Christianity and education today, both high and low.[25]

With deep interest in the expansion of the church and its activities Malekebu showed interest to acquire more land for this purpose. He recalls the time when a European had offered him the opportunity to buy a very big area of land. It seemed Malekebu had an interest to acquire the land but there was no means to do that. This is what Malekebu wrote:

> A European had in 1938, 5000 acres of land, very fine land, with brick buildings that could easily be turned into a fine hospital, school buildings, and dwelling houses. It has very fine water supply, splendid agricultural land that would mean so much to a mission in the future if properly supported and developed. He particularly wanted to sell it to me, because he was very deeply interested in what he saw we were trying to do at Chiradzulu. The price per acre is anywhere from seven shillings and six pence to twenty shillings.[26]

---

[25] Daniel Malekebu, "A Plea for Africa", unpublished, p. 7.
[26] Ibid., p. 8.

In his plea to the Afro-Americans Malekebu believed that the slave trade was to a certain extent a divine plan that would enable some Afro-Americans to support the church in their motherland. He believed the Afro-Americans had a greater responsibility in bringing the light of the gospel to fellow brothers and sisters in Africa. This argument can further be understood from what he wrote:

> I cannot believe that the coming of my people from Africa to this great land of opportunity, as cruel as the methods seem to have been, was a mere accident. But I believe it was divine providence, that the brothers who remained behind might receive the light from his brother across the Atlantic. The fathers who are almost all gone felt this and blazed the way.[27]

He however cautioned the Afro-Americans that before they began to either send missionaries to Africa or put in any effort as a way of assisting the people of Africa, they must have a real picture of what Africa was all about. It seemed the Afro-Americans had a wrong picture of Africa. They believed cannibalism existed in Africa that their lives would be at risk because of wild animals and a lot of diseases. Hence Malekebu saw it necessary that before they made any decision on Africa they should have a thorough knowledge of it:

> But before the Afro-American of today can help Africa, he must study Africa and the changes that have and are taking place. The African jungle idea must be eliminated, the giving of children to crocodiles, the fear of the African eating missionaries, the fear of African fevers must be replaced by real knowledge of the facts that Africa is waiting to hear from America. Africa is waiting to see his American brother coming in to put over a big religious, educational and health program. Africa is talking college!![28]

Malekebu believed that civilization of Africa depended on the quality of education she could receive. He saw the need for the training of native Africans in different fields with emphasis on agriculture and economics. He was convinced that Africa could not develop alone. The continent needed a certain force from outside to keep it moving. He believed that if an African could receive good training, he would be able to develop his continent. Though Africa is large, he still believed that it was possible to develop her:

> Since Africa is so large we should have one college in East Central Africa (Nyasaland) and in the Union where agriculture should be greatly emphasised and economics. As the college will be a training centre for teachers, preachers and health workers, Africa will not be too large to civilise as some people in America say she will civilise herself. The importance of these matters is only too obvious to dwell on. When Jesus was here, he helped people to help themselves, so must our friends help

---

[27] Ibid., p. 10.
[28] Ibid., p. 12.

us to help ourselves. What country or what nation can go forward without leaders or prophets of her own?[29]

He acknowledges to have said all those things with a deep sense of appreciation for what his own denomination was doing and also for what others had done already in the past, which in his opinion was not enough. He emphasized that the Afro-Americans should remember that they were trying to do mission work among other denominations that were doing their best in Africa, and had been doing so for many years. Some had large printing presses for making and printing literature in some of the African languages, enlarging the standards in education, building hospitals for the people and other things.

Malekebu emphasized education to the Afro-Americans as a means to evangelism and church expansion. He suggested the principles upon which church work should be built in Africa. He looked at Africa as a young country from a missionary point of view. Africa found herself caught in the net of world economic difficulties, spiritual breakdown and secularism before she had a chance to stand on her feet. Government in some places took the lead in education, where formerly missions had been doing it for years. It meant government taking great steps in establishing government schools, in which religious teaching would probably not be included. He believed this may perhaps do well in developed countries. He was of the view that the teaching of religion in mission schools was a good idea when one looks at the background of the children that went to school. The only way they would get the restraining influences of Christianity was at the mission school and mission stations. In Nyasaland, however, with exception of Jeans Training Centre, all education was in the hands of missions and Government gave grants in aid to them. He communicated to the Afro Americans that the paramount thought of any Mission Board should be to build up a Christian community. Around this could come education and all its branches; agriculture, health and home making industries in all its forms. He emphasized that mission work in Africa should be built on clear knowledge of African life. This, he claimed, was what they had been trying to do and seemingly with some success.[30]

However, he noted that Africans' burdens are made heavier in the sense that they lack the resources to run such institutions, hence the need for the help of the Afro-Americans. He argued that the African workers found it hard because the local membership was not able to carry all the financial responsibilities of the church alone. The local church was very anxious and willing to do its best for the kingdom of God. He challenged the church in the USA to study the economic condition of the people in different sections of the field. He was sure that after this study, the church would find out that the people of east Africa and south Africa were getting for their labor six to twenty

---

[29] Ibid., p. 15.
[30] Ibid., p. 16-17.

four cents or less per day. In other places where there were few or no Europeans at all, the people had no way of making money. Bearing in mind that the world was developing, in Malekebu's view it became hard for Africans; and yet in a wonderful way, they went on happily, cheerfully pushing the work forward, but with an anxious ear set toward across the Atlantic listening to hear what their friends and brothers would do by way of helping them in the good work of the Lord.

What made it even harder were the demands of the new era: from the early 1920s, changes had been taking place in education all over Africa. The British territories established what was known as Education Departments headed by a Director of Education. They had a code and educational rules that were supposed to be followed by all missions in order to receive grants-in-aid from the government. These manifold requirement: included that missions must have men and women of a certain grade, from abroad, devoting their entire time to the work of education as teachers and managers. African teachers must be of a certain grade, and supervisors of mission schools had to be well trained and qualified. Schools must be graded according to the code and prove their efficiency. School buildings must be of a type and construction meeting the government requirements. At a glance, one could see this African worker deeply interested in the kingdom of God and in the elevation of his people who were financially poor. He was anxious to put over a big programme for God and the denomination. The local church was trying hard to meet the requirements of the government. However Malekebu expresses his disappointment as to the response of the parent body in the USA. He expresses it in this way:

> The church in America says in so many ways: "Africa is too big, we cannot civilize it all." Others are saying "we have Africa right here in America" and still others are saying, "I lost nothing in Africa." When the African worker makes an appeal to the home church that is supposed to support the work, others say, "well he is at home," still others say, "he is a native." The work is at a stand still mainly due to the fact that it lacks proper help from the home base. The teachers leave because there is no money to pay them; they are men of families and must be supported. The mission fails to get grant in aid from the government as is due the mission because it is quite impossible to come up to the requirements under these conditions. These are the things the church in America should know and think over.[31]

Government's Recognition of PIM Schools

After a detailed study of the educational system in Malawi in 1924, the Phelps Stoke Commission led by Dr Thomas Jesse Jones commented that Malawi had

---

[31] Ibid., p. 19.

great resources that had not been adequately developed, that the unique type of mission education provided for the Africans without the aid of the government was undoubtedly effective. Since many parents did not care to educate their children, absenteeism at school was great. With poor attendance, schools were not able to achieve their goals as expected. The commission pointed out the inability of the colonial government of Nyasaland to organize and correlate the splendid educational work of the mission with the various phases of colonial life. In 1924 the commission visited many of the mission schools. In their report they recommended that there was need for the establishment of a Department of Education headed by the director, and that working with the department, there should be an Advisory Board on Native Education consisting of representatives of government, the settlers and the missionaries—with African representation provided. Government officers should pay friendly visits to mission schools. It was amidst such recommendations that the colonial government of Nyasaland began to think about the possibility of creating education as a department of its own, a new phase.[32]

As the government was to take charge of education in Nyasaland, there were several dialogues between the government educational department and the mission schools concerning the fulfillment of some requirements. Immediately after the government's introduction of an education department, PIM registered its schools. The government educational director made a visit to the PIM School around 1927, and sent a copy of his inspection notes that carried names of teachers, and places where they were educated. After the Director's visit, correspondence between the Director of Education and the PIM Principal, Dr Daniel Malekebu, followed. The church was further advised to send the qualifications of each teacher. The inspection notes dated 2 August 1927 were as follows:

Table 1. Table Showing Qualification of each PIM Teacher

Name of Teacher	Qualifications, if any	Present standard	Where educated
Friday Mkulichi		III	PIM
Zan Musa	Cook	V	SDA
Kettle Chilewe		III	ZIM
J Chinangwa		III	PIM
Nampatiwa	Gardener carpenter	IV	Scotland Mission
Mr A.R. Lawrence	Common sewing	V	PIM
John M. Lawrence		III	7th Day Adventist
Alexander Likangala		III	ZIM

---

[32] Kelvin N. Banda, *A Brief History of Education in Malawi*, Blantyre: Dzuka, 1982, p. 69-70.

Office Mapeleka		III	ZIM
B Strachan Skin not sent		IV	
Joscan Kaojole	Only carpenter		

The Education department was making every effort to try to improve the standard of teachers. On 10th August 1927 the Director of Education organized an English Essay Competition and encouraged native teachers to join. The purpose of the competition was twofold, as indicated in his letter to Dr Malekebu, who was in charge of the school at the PIM: "To encourage the study of the English language among Native teachers, and to induce teachers to investigate all possible methods by means of which they can improve their schools for the benefit of the village community."[33] The subject they were asked to work on was 'How can I ensure that my school shall have the best possible effect upon the health and progress of the local community?'[34]

The essay addressed developmental issues not different from Malekebu's ideas of establishing an education system that would help the development of a native. PIM sent seven essays for the English competition and the Director of Education confirmed receipt of them.[35] Out of the forty-one Native teachers that entered the competition, a teacher from the PIM won the third prize, not a mean achievement. The first prize went to Yolam Kamwendo of the Southeast Africa Union of the Seventh-day Adventist Mission, Malamulo; second prize to William Steere Lipande of UMCA, Likoma; and third prize went to two people. John Asharoff of the Church of Scotland Mission, Blantyre; and E. Strachan Skin from Providence Industrial Mission. Amongst the contributing teachers were some deserving honourable mention, according to B. Gaunt, the Director of Education. Such people included Ruth Lawrence of PIM, Mateyu B. Jere of Livingstonia Mission, Ekwendeni; L. Godfrey Kalea of Overtoun Institution, Livingstonia; James Douglas Mtigha of Overtoun Institution; and John Sikazure of Livingstonia Mission, Karonga.[36] The third prizewinner from the Providence Industrial Mission received his prize via the head of his institution according to

---

[33] A letter from the Director of Education, Nyasaland Protectorate to Dr Malekebu, Providence Industrial Mission, 10.8.

[34] The conditions attached to this essay competition were as follows: 1. Competitors must be certified to be at present employed as Native Teachers in schools in the Nyasaland Protectorate. 2. All essays must be forwarded to R.F. Gaunt, c/o Education Office, Zomba, through the European In-charge of the school in which the competitor is employed, and must be mailed in time to reach Zomba before December 31 1927. 3. Essays must be written on one side of the paper only, and should not exceed 750 words. 4. At the head of the paper competitors should write clearly their own name and the name of their school. There shall be no age limit, but the age of the competitor should be stated. 5. Mr Gaunt who will obtain the assistance of two other judges shall examine the essays. 6. There shall be one prize of one Guinea and consolation prizes of 7/6 and 5/- each.

[35] A letter from the Director of Education, Nyasaland Protectorate to Rev D.S. Malekebu, PIM, 29.12.1927.

[36] B. Gaunt - Malekebu, 31.1.1928.

a letter from the Director of Education to the head of the Providence Industrial Mission:

> I enclose a circular letter with regard to the English Essay competition from which you will see that the third prize has been awarded to E. Strachan Skin of your mission. I attach a postal order for 5/- and should be grateful if you would give the prize to E. Strachan Skin together with my congratulations on the essay submitted by him.[37]

The government still wanted teachers in mission schools to be well qualified and wrote to the PIM requesting a list of those to be included in the register of licensed teachers. If the licensed teacher qualified for a teaching certificate, or was granted an honorary teaching certificate, his name would be transferred from the register of Licensed Teachers to the Register of Certificated Teachers.[38] The educational department also under Rule 8(v) of the Education Ordinance, demanded that a copy of the education rules to be kept in each registered school, of which the PIM received four copies. This shows that by 1927, the PIM School was already a school registered by the government and was also among the grant-aided schools. The following letter shows the amount that the PIM School received from the Education Department as a grant:

> I have the honour to forward herewith cheque for £4.10.0 in payment of: Grants in accordance with Rule 22(b) for 2 teachers at £2-5-0. Per head being grant for ¾ year at rate of £3 per annum.
>
> Two teachers at £2-5-0 = £4.10.0
>
> Owing to pressure of work it is regretted that it is impossible to send full lists of teachers to whom passes have been awarded but this will be done as soon as possible in 1928.[39]

The full lists of teachers that the PIM sent to the educational department which are referred to in the above statement were sent to the Education Department on 10th December 1927. The list included the following persons who were teachers at PIM: Amon Mussa, Timothy Chinangwa, E. Strachan Skin, John M. Lawrence, Kettle Chilewe and Youngson Mampatiwa.[40] The school at PIM was running smoothly. Communication with the Department of Education was frequent and by 31st December 1927, Providence Industrial Mission submitted the following general and statistical report as required by the Director of Education:

---

[37] B. Gaunt - Malekebu, 1.2.1928.
[38] Director of Education - Providence Industrial Mission, 27.9.1927.
[39] R.W. McKinnon Director of Education to PIM 2.1.1928.
[40] Providence Industrial Mission to the Education Department, 10./10./1927. Malekebu acknowledged receipt of this letter in his letter to the Education Department 6.1.1928.

Reference to your letter No. 26/70/27. 3rd February 1926 beg to give the following information regarding our work for year ending 31st December 1927.

Total number of schools	Number on Roll	
1	Boys	Girls
	282	122
Total Expenditure for 1927 Educational Work		£567-6-2

The year 1927 marked the real beginning of our work. We had classes in English from primer 1 up to standard V. Advance classes had their school in the morning, the lessons covered reading, writing, moral lessons, simple Arithmetic, dictation, story telling, both oral and writing, and hygiene.

In agriculture both theory and practice. To the general school we could only give theory due to the differences in time for school and hoeing. But pupils were requested to put into practice information given them, and for what we can understand the results may be good.

The pupils in the lower class (vernacular) besides lessons prescribed for them, were given general lectures and simple lectures in hygiene. From the industrial point of view we were very much handicapped due to lack of space for real work. Mrs Malekebu however organised women and girls into sewing classes. During the year each class was required to keep the school building clean as part of their industrial work. The school was required also to keep the campus, roads, and paths in good order. At the close of the school, pupils were requested and asked to put into practice what they were taught and learned while in school, by keeping their yards and paths in their villages clean from one house to another. The attendance for the year was very good as we emphasize importance of attending school daily. The school closed with regular school closing exercises; one day for lower classes and one day for the advanced classes during which three prizes were given, in order to encourage the pupils; 1 for scholarship 6/, 1 for daily attendance 6/- and 1 for spelling match 5/-.

A dormitory has been built (not quite complete) for boys 60 x 20 ft one side (4 rooms) will be occupied by two teachers. The other side will house about 20 boys with a dining room and study hall 20 x 20 ft.[41]

---

[41] Providence Industrial Mission to Education Department, 15.2.1928.

Dr Malekebu's Interest in South Africa

Malekebu was interested in the expansion of church work to places outside Nyasaland even as far as Cape Town. He recommended the work done by a local African from Cape Town in trying to establish a church, and deeded it to the Foreign Mission Board of the National Baptist Convention of USA Inc., which seemed to have been neglected. He made an effort to visit this church in Cape Town, undertaking sole responsibility for its upkeep. Similarly, he saw education at this institution as the key to success in church work and proposed some response in the area of education from the FMB of NBC Inc.[42]

Dr and Mrs Malekebu visited the church at Cape Town during their first visit to Nyasaland in 1921. At his time they faced some problems with the colonial government of Nyasaland, forcing them to return to clear up some issues. They visited a church at Cape Town that had no pastor and was affiliated to the Foreign Mission Board of the National Baptist Convention of USA Inc. Malekebu recalls that some years back a coloured lady in Cape Town bought a piece of land at the foot of the beautiful Table Mountain overlooking the city. As Malekebu described it, it was one of the most beautiful spots in Cape Town. This land was deeded to the Foreign Mission Board of the National Baptist Convention of USA Inc. Dr Murf built on this spot a two-storey house and left a church foundation that was never completed up to the time when the Malekebus visited the place. A splendid congregation was built up. In 1921, the Malekebus spent seven months at this congregation. The Malekebus claim that after years without a pastor, people were almost discouraged. Some joined other churches, but with deacon Daniels and others who remained, the church continued. During these seven months they were engaged in preaching and ministering to this congregation. Their stay at the station proved to be of great importance. Malekebu expresses it in this way: "In a very gratifying way the church took on a new life, some of the members returned, many souls were converted and added to the church."[43]

In 1938, the Malekebus made a second visit to the church in Cape Town. They only stayed there for a few weeks ministering to the church. Through Dr Malekebu the congregation at Cape Town requested the Foreign Mission Board of the National Baptist Convention of USA Inc to send them a pastor to take charge of the work and built it up. The church in Cape Town was made up of a coloured congregation. The deacon Daniels who had held the church intact was by then an elderly man and could not continue with the work as he had used to. As a way of compelling the Foreign Mission Board to resume work at this station, he cited a very good job that was done by the Secretary of the FMB, Dr J.E. East, who erected a school structure at this place some years back:

---

[42] Daniel Malekebu, "My Life and My Work", unpublished, 1940.
[43] Ibid., p. 24.

At Shiloh Baptist Church, Arundel Street, at the foot of the Table Mountain, overlooking the beautiful Table Bay, you are able to see every ship coming in and going out. It is a fine and healthful place. In and around Cape Town are many places where the church draws and where its influence is felt. Then the school at Middle Drift where the late Dr J.E. East worked almost a miracle. This school should not have been left or rather allowed to remain so long without a strong man to continue the work where the late Dr East left off. I think with a strong group of workers at Middle Drift enlarging the work toward college, for that is the demand of the day, we would have and must have a trained ministry.[44]

Tuskegee Institute in Nyasaland

Education was a primary focus of Malekebu's church work and he cried out for something similar to the Tuskegee Institute. Tuskegee Institute was a powerful school of thought represented by Booker T. Washington, a former Virginian slave who had been freed when a young boy by the civil war, and had acquired sufficient education and training to found the Tuskegee Normal and Industrial Institute in Alabama in 1881. This soon achieved fame both in the United States and overseas, as a school for accommodating Negroes to the changed circumstances of the post-civil war America. Booker T. Washington's ideas were simple, practical and persuasive: Let the Negro work his way to the top from the bottom upwards; let him first learn properly the humblest jobs (farmer, mechanic, domestic servant) before aspiring to the higher positions in business and politics.

In 1939 Dr Malekebu was invited by President W.H. Dinkins and the Board of Trustees of Selma University, Selma, Alabama, to deliver the commencement address.

He went there on May 29, 1940. At this time the honorary degree of Doctor of Divinity was conferred upon him. He visited Tuskegee Institute afterwards. It was a revelation on his part to see this great institution. He was very much impressed and expressed his feelings that no wonder government officials, educators and missionaries from all over the world made trips to the great school. In his opinion, he emphasized that Africa needs a Tuskegee. He pleaded with the Americans to help him make one. He expressed the view that for many years, Africa had been the field for exploitation and abuse of the African people by foreign nations. However he acknowledged that many times the good friends of Africans had expressed in public, as well as through the press, their disapproval of such acts, and that much had been done to change conditions for the better. The Africans certainly appreciated this.

Malekebu was convinced that Schools like the Tuskegee Institute in central Africa and elsewhere, would put the people on the upward march, just as

---

[44] Ibid., p. 26.

Tuskegee had done in America for the Afro-Americans as well as the world. He pleaded with the Americans that he saw a great beginning for a Tuskegee in Nyasaland:

> I am asking all Afro-Americans and all the friends of the African people in America to help us put over a program that will go down in history and for the advancement of my people in Africa.[45]

Malekebu's ambitious programme of education contributed to the expansion and development of the PIM. The school at the PIM taught agriculture as one of the subjects. Agricultural activities were introduced, and farming was a priority. At one time Chilembwe had introduced cotton farming at Migowi.[46] Malekebu's idea of building a Tuskegee Institute in Nyasaland was only very partially implemented through these agricultural activities. Many people who attended the PIM school eventually became members of PIM. One such man was Kafadala Mzima, who walked all the way from Mzimba to PIM on foot, the journey taking one month. While in Zimbabwe his father had told him that he should enroll at the PIM boarding school. After completing his education, Kafadala Mzima was ordained a pastor by Dr Malekebu.

At the time he was writing the document "My Vision", Malekebu had formulated his plans for education. Thus in 1926 they were not only carrying on religious work, but a school was also opened at the main station, where Dr and Mrs Malekebu were two of the teachers. People were anxious for education. They started teaching the beginners in the vernacular, and when they advanced they taught them in English. They carried on like this for many years, until some of their students passed government teacher's examinations as to be second grade and others third grade certificated teachers. As schools increased, these teachers became useful to the mission. At the main station, they had three schools: village, central, and station school. Wherever a church was established they opened a school for the people. By 1940, at the time he was writing the "Plea for Africans," they had thirty-five day schools. More chiefs and village headmen begged for schools all over the country, but the mission was not able to meet the demand for lack of funds and teachers.[47] From this, one would see that the establishment of centres of learning helped in the expansion of PIM work as many people were attracted to these institutions, hence Malekebu's ambition to establish a school wherever a church was planted. When chiefs and local villagers requested a school, the school was established and the church followed. Such situations include the school at Milepa. This school was established at the request of the village headman. Later

---

[45] Daniel Malekebu, "My Life and My Work", unpublished, 1940.
[46] Interview Palasa, 14.10.1996. As to whether this type of farming contributed to church expansion in terms of conversion or some people joining PIM is not yet established.
[47] Daniel Malekebu, "My Vision", p. 6.

on the church was established and built close to the school blocks.[48] This contributed to the expansion of the PIM work.

Agriculture

The Nyasaland African Farmers Association

In his own writing to the Afro-Americans, Malekebu stated that Nyasaland was an agricultural country. There were no gold mines, no copper, no diamonds, nor silver as in other parts of Africa. People raised maize, peas and beans of all kinds. Some had cattle, pigs, goats and chicken. Tobacco, cotton and tea were the cash crops. To enhance agricultural activities, the church formed an organization known as 'The Nyasaland African Farmers Association,' with the purpose of stimulating interest among farmers, as well as helping in soil conservation—in order to raise better crops for home and market. The government permitted Africans to grow tobacco and cotton, which was previously allocated to Europeans only. Consequently many Africans could make a profit. Like everything else, after a time both tobacco and cotton reduced in value and people could hardly make six shillings to pay their hut tax. When it was time to sell, the buyers made a lot of excuses as to why they could not give a good market price for the produce. Some would say it was not properly cured, others that they had plenty on hand that they had not sold from previous years.[49] These excuses and the failure to sell produce made Dr Malekebu suggest that there must be an organization to help farmers in caring for and selling their produce. This organization was to enable people to present their views to the government on any matter affecting them. It was also suggested that a letter be sent to the government to appoint an agriculturist (European instructor) who would teach the people how to grow and cure tobacco so that the buyer would no longer be able to find fault. The government sent Europeans and some African inspectors and aides who went from place to place in those areas where tobacco was grown to help the people of the areas. Many people who were not PIM members developed an interest in joining this organization. As these activities were done in PIM churches, some people showed interest not only in this organization but also in the church. Many became members of PIM, contributing to its expansion. Malekebu introduced market places where people could sell their produce and other things. This encouraged some people to join PIM by virtue of the desire to be close to Dr Malekebu: the educator, teacher, and builder of the PIM.[50] Malekebu himself writes:

---

[48] This school was handed over to the government in 1995 by Rev R.T. Mbule, in the presence of Rev W.D. Manyika, Aaron Wallani, George Nasolo and Patrick Makondesa.
[49] These Africans sold their produce to the white farmers.
[50] Interview D. Komiha, August, 2000.

The mission has grown very rapidly in the last half of the half century. Christian influence has been greatly felt throughout the country, not only by preaching, but improving conditions. In the backward areas where there were no good roads, today automobiles can pass through without any trouble. Across streams and rivers bridges have been made that the people can cross without endangering life. In places where one thought of a mere wilderness, we have gone and cleared forests and built up a clean community with a nice and beautiful little brick church, school house and other houses for teachers and evangelists around the church. These houses are white washed with natural white sand or blue and red. It makes a new environment for the people, but still you are in Africa.

Where there was no market, we started one where the people come and sell whatever they may have among themselves. Old people who were too old to walk to town, sell their maize or cassava or potatoes or chickens and now they are doing it at their nearby market. These markets have helped greatly in interesting the people to take more interest in agriculture. They have served many people in finding food in time of famine. Some one said, (a village headman) that "Dr Malekebu has done a great work in this country; but the greatest of his work is the making of a market" because this man was able to get food to fill his stomach in time of famine.[51]

Malekebu put the teaching of agriculture into practice by buying 800 acres of land at Mambala in Thyolo district.[52] Mambala farm turned into another area where people would come from different places to be employed. Most people who came for employment on this farm became PIM members; such as the parents of Sadi Mpeleya[53] who came from Mozambique and worked at the mission farm at Mambala in 1931.[54] When the colonial government was claiming land at Chigumula in Blantyre, all the residents were asked to vacate the place because the land was sold to white settlers. Therefore the black community that settled in these areas was asked to move out. However there was also another story that the father of Sadi Mpeleya slapped a white man. This led to the removal of all the black community around that area.[55] Some PIM members[56] went to Malekebu to ask if they could be accommodated at Mambala farm. Dr Malekebu separated part of the farm area to house those people who were in need. In response to the church opening up a section of Mambala farm to PIM members who were in need, an influx of others joined them, in pretence of being PIM members, who later joined the church. However some people who joined Mambala farm at that time remained non-

---

[51] Daniel Malekebu, "My Vision, East Central and South Africa of To-Day", p. 12, unpublished.
[52] Ibid., p. 8.
[53] Sadi Mpeleya himself was baptized in 1945 and became PIM member following his parents.
[54] Interview Sadi Mpeleya, Mambala, Thyolo, 9.12.1998.
[55] Interview Sadi Mpeleya, Mambala, Thyolo, 9.12.1998.
[56] Such people include the Nakoma family, Masuku family and the Goodson family.

PIM members, such as Stephen Saidi who commented, "It was difficult to have access to the PIM area for Malekebu wanted PIM members only to acquire land at the estate."[57] The people who secured land at Mambala were encouraged to plant mango trees, which could help them during famine or droughts.[58] Some entered the PIM land at Mambala through the corruption of Mr Mononga, who was in charge of Mambala farm. After some time these people were converted to PIM. When Malekebu learnt about this he did not chase the accused away. This attitude contributed to their joining of the church as they saw Malekebu as a good man. One of them said "Malekebu was a good man in the sense that he could listen to the grievances of the people:[59] When the church bought the land at Mambala, people who were originally the inhabitants of this place began to move away from the area. Their reasoning was that the PIM liked fighting so to dissociate themselves from them they just decided to move out of the area. Some would not even register their children to attend the PIM school that was introduced in the area. After understanding the functions of the church in the area they began to come back and later joined PIM.[60] So the introduction of agricultural activities and the opening of PIM land contributed to the growth of PIM.

Hospital

Another institutional area in which churches became involved is that of health. It came naturally to missionaries to help people physically when they thought they had the ability. Western standards of hygiene and western medicine were introduced soon with great effect. The people found that many of their ailments could be cured in (seemingly) miraculous ways.[61] Better-equipped dispensaries replaced the earliest medicine box of the missionaries when the people flocked to the mission stations.

---

[57] Interview Stephen Saidi, 12.12.1998.
[58] Interview Gese Masuku, Mambala Farm, Thyolo, 11.12.1998.
[59] Interview Justin Goodson, Mambala Farm, Thyolo, 10.12.1998.
[60] Interview Esnala Likungwa, Mambala farm, Thyolo, 12.12.1998.
[61] Kritzinger/Meiring/Sayman, *On Being Witness*, p. 144.

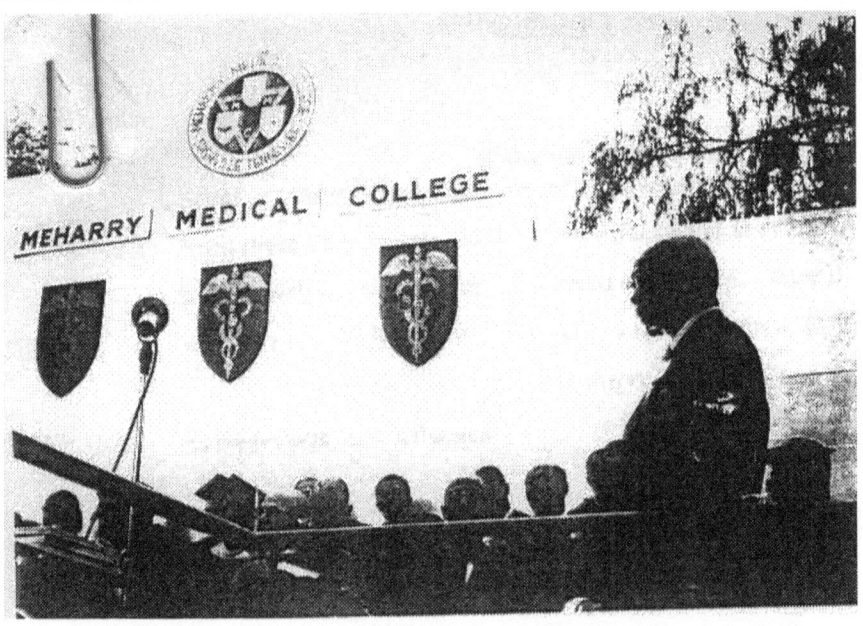

Malekebu giving a speech at Meharry Medical College during one of his visits

The Providence Industrial Mission was not different from any other church in the area of health. The early leadership of PIM believed that western medicine could be of great importance to mission work. This was emphasized, too, by the fact that Chilembwe sent one of his scholars in 1911 to the Henry Henderson Institute of the Blantyre mission for hospital training. At the end of this course, he was to return to the PIM to work for Chilembwe's mission.[62] Chilembwe's sending of a PIM School student shows how ambitious he was in promoting scientific medicine among Africans. Though there is no information as to how this situation continued, there is still evidence that health was a church concern at the early period of PIM's establishment. What Chilembwe desired to have at his church at Mbombwe was later fulfilled through Dr Daniel Malekebu, a medical Doctor graduated from Meharry Medical College.

The James E. East Hospital

When the PIM was reopened in 1926, a first hospital was established in 1927 under a *thundu* tree at Mbombwe. Construction of the hospital was done some time later, in 1940. After the completion of the first hospital building, Dr Malekebu had this to say:

---

[62] Shepperson and Price, *Independent African*, p. 172.

> No mission work is complete without a hospital. Today there stands one. It has a thatched roof and 16 brick beds, two wards for women and two for men. With very little means at our disposal, the hospital has done a great work. Thousands of people have been treated. In order to help the women in the villages to appreciate the services of a doctor, five women were trained who would be helping other women in maternity cases. This had proven to be of untold value. For more than thirteen years in this work, we had only two deaths in our school family.[63]

Child Welfare

As part of the hospital activity, in 1928 a Child Welfare Unit was organized. Child mortality was very high, so they thought something could be done to help the women care for their babies and improve home life as well. Dr and Mrs Malekebu called a special meeting of married women in the district, Christians and non-Christians, with their babies. Mrs Malekebu would take water, soap and a towel, and bath one or two of these babies while mothers looked on to see how it was done. After a while she would have one of the women do it, while she observed, to see if the lesson had been taken in. They were told to do this in their villages. They were shown when and how to feed their babies; when and how to put them to sleep. They were told not to feed their babies with solid food before time. The women saw life as they had never seen it before. In the villages, inspections had to be made to make sure that these instructions were put into practice. After a few months PIM put on a baby show at the mission, for which the district commissioner and his wife were invited to be judges. Any mother whose baby showed by cleanliness and physical appearance that it had been well cared for and well fed, received a prize. There were first and second prizes. The judges had a hard time finding who should get the prizes. Finally they did and they had to give a third prize. They started this as an annual affair. This resulted in Child Welfare Societies in some of the missions from this beginning.[64] Such activities drew many women into PIM membership.[65]

Malekebu was convinced that medical work was part and parcel of Jesus' ministry, as he would go about healing the sick. Therefore the church has the responsibility to take care of those that are suffering. Malekebu gives some kind of a theological argument to back up his medical work:

---

[63] Daniel Malekebu, The History of my Life and my Work, unpublished, 1940, p. 18.
[64] Ibid. p. 19.
[65] From the sources I got this information it seems many women were interested in these functions as it involved both PIM and non PIM members which had no doubt contributed to some women becoming frequent attenders of these functions that led them later into the PIM church. (Source from Mrs Chilumpha, Mbombwe, Chiradzulu).

> Human suffering has always been with man and perhaps will continue to the end of time. The great teacher came to the world to save man from his sins and fit him for the life to come. Certainly, He was equally interested and showed his deep sympathy toward those who were in any way suffering with physical maladies and pains and went about to heal the sick and suffering. The people went and followed Him everywhere. Nothing perhaps made him more popular among men than when he was healing the sick. This work continued with his followers (Disciples), as he had commanded them; heal the sick (Matt. 10:9), cleanse the lepers, raise the dead, cast out devils; freely you have received freely give.

He noted that modern missions were no exception to Jesus' ministry of healing. He cited an example of his own mission being actively engaged in helping suffering humanity through scientific medicine for so many years. Situated in Chiradzulu, one of the smallest districts and one of the most thickly populated districts in Malawi, the PIM hospital proved to be very small. It had only two wards for women, two wards for men, sixteen brick beds, a drug room, examination and treatment room. Small as it was, the hospital had an impact on the surrounding community. People began to get used to the scientific medicine and visited the hospital in their large numbers. Malekebu had this to say:

> Thousands and thousands of people have been treated every year in our hospital. One of the worst enemies of the people in Africa is witchcraft. Women bring their children when there is no hope for recovery. Men and women are sent to the hospital when life is given up, because someone has told them "the sick person has been bewitched and cannot live. Since he is going to die let us take him to the mission hospital". It is at this time with this sick person, the miracle must be performed.
>
> After the few days treatment the patient is improving. In a few weeks he is better and well again. The news now is the person who was said to be witched and could not live, is now well. How and why? Because the medicine at mission hospital and the Doctor there cured him. So the Doctor and his "white man's medicine" is greater than the witchcraft. It is at this point that the scientific medicine and teaching of hygiene and physiology are slowly, but actively and definitely combating and shortening the power of witchcraft and fear of witchcraft today."[66]

As many people began to consider the mission hospital as something valuable to their health, it became too small to accommodate them. Malekebu saw the need to enlarge the hospital and increase its services; and in 1938, work on a new building, 60 x 20 ft, was begun. It was hoped that after completion it would serve as the hospital for women and the old one for men. He therefore requested funds from the Foreign Mission Board of the National Baptist

---

[66] Daniel Malekebu, "My Vision", pp. 5-6.

Convention of USA Inc to complete the building and to buy equipment. He needed $10,000.00 to complete the hospital and $5,000 for equipment.[67]

He also created a wish list of the immediate needs of PIM.[68] For the hospital, the following terms were listed:
1. The old hospital roofing material (Zinc)- Five thousand dollars ($5,000.00)
2. To complete the new hospital building- Twenty five thousand dollars ($25,000.00)
    (a) 16 hospital beds to replace brick beds in the old hospital $29.95 each
    (b) 26 beds for the new hospital- $29.95 each
3. 100 sheets; 100 pillowcases; 100 bath towels: 50 wash clothes bandages, all sizes gauze.
4. 1 microscope and slides
5. 12 Doctors' white coats
6. 20 gowns; 20 operating rubber gloves; knives; needles; syringes; glaseptic syringe and case; 4 syringes, 10 o.k. syringes of 30m; 4 syringes, 5 c.c. 2 nasal sprays; rubber sheets.

As a medical doctor and a pastor, the welfare of the people was at the heart of Dr Malekebu. He noted that if the health of the people were neglected, then the uplift of the people in Africa would be incomplete. He therefore proposed to build a leper colony. In his booklet, 'My Vision', Malekebu addressed issues of health.

He expressed concern that besides other diseases there were also many cases of leprosy. According to the statistics that he got there were 6000 known cases of leprosy in the country in 1938. His main concern was that if this disease were not checked, it could spread and double in number by 1950. What made matters worse was that there was no proper care or special means of segregation or isolation. This endangered the lives of people in Nyasaland, which was only 47,949 square miles, with a population of about 1,600,000 in 1938.

In August 1943, Malekebu had a chance to visit the Leprosarium at the U.S. Marine hospital at Carville. The officials showed him different departments of the institution. This further strengthened his desire to establish a Leper Colony.

Malekebu acknowledged that of the 800 acres of land at Mambala in Thyolo district on which the teaching of agriculture was carried out, 60 acres were reserved for the Leper Colony. However finances were a limiting factor to this ambitious project, preventing the programme's materialization.

---

[67] Daniel Malekebu, "My Vision", p. 6.
[68] The other needs that were listed were connected to education, agriculture and evangelistic work. These include: for education: Library Bibles, Religious books, History, Art, Science and magazines; Evangelistic work support for fifty (50) evangelists at $25.00 per month, agriculture 1 tractor, six cultivators $4.25, 1 station wagon and printing press. All that Malekebu requested was provided except the printing press.

The hospital proved to be one of the most important facilities that the mission offered to the people of Chiradzulu and surrounding areas. It provided employment to some; and in the process, some of them joined the church. Others who came for treatment admired the life led by the people who were living around the PIM campus at Mbombwe and decided to imitate such lifestyles, thereby finding themselves associated with PIM members who later convinced them to join the church. The school, the hospital and the agricultural activities such as the farmers' association and the Mambala farm contributed to the expansion of PIM in terms of its influence, growth and development.

CHAPTER FIVE

MEMBERSHIP IN PIM CHURCH

The Visible and the Invisible Church

THE CHURCH CONSISTS OF THOSE WHO ARE PARTAKERS OF CHRIST AND OF THE blessings of salvation that are in Him. The Reformed conception is that Christ, by the operation of the Holy Spirit, unites people with himself; endows them with true faith; and thus constitutes the church as his body, the *communo fidelium or sanctorum*.[1] Catholics define the church as the congregation of all the faithful who, being baptized, profess the same faith, partake of the same sacraments and are governed by their lawful pastors under one visible head on earth.[2] Catholics teach that the visible church is first; then comes the invisible, the former giving birth to the latter. This means that the church is a *mater fidelium* (mother of believers) before it is a *communio fidelium* (community of believers).[3] It is Christ that leads men to the church, the church that leads men to Christ. All the emphasis falls not on the invisible as the *communio fidelium* but on the visible church as the *mater fidelium*.[4] Calvin says that the church as invisible is the bearer of divine gifts and powers, transforming mankind into the kingdom of God. As visible, the church is constituted of people confessing a common faith, observing common customs, and using visible means of grace.[5] For both Luther and Calvin, the church was simply the community of the saints, that is, the community of those who believe in and are sanctified in Christ; and who are joined to Him as their head. This is also the position taken in the Reformed confessional standards. The invisible church is the church as God sees it, a church containing only believers, while the visible church is the church as man sees it. This means that the church of God is simultaneously both visible and invisible, as it exists on earth. The visible church embodies its institutionalized form. The church can be understood in two different dimensions and therefore church membership should also be understood very clearly in this context. Those who are in Christ are the church, part of the visible body of Christ they belong to, or even if they are not part of the visible body of Christ. God alone knows the identity of those who are in Christ for

---

[1] Ibid., p. 553.
[2] Ibid., p. 562.
[3] Ibid., p. 563.
[4] Ibid., p. 553.
[5] Ibid., p. 563.

certain, although there are clear signs of being in Christ which we are encouraged to look for. Paul assesses the situation in 2 Timothy 2:19.

> God's solid foundation stands firm, sealed with this inscription. "The Lord knows those who are his and everyone who confesses the name of the Lord must turn away from wickedness."

The membership that is described in PIM is that of the visible church. PIM as a local church carries some characteristics of how the local church in the New Testament accepted its membership. Basic to right action with regard to church membership is the truth that the local church is a fellowship of believers. The New Testament teaching and practice point us to at least four fundamental conclusions.

1. The early church was a fellowship of believers

The whole emphasis of the apostolic preaching was on the necessity of a personal and individual response to the message of the gospel as it was preached. When the crowds in Jerusalem on the day of Pentecost asked, 'What shall we do?' they were told:

> Repent and be baptised, every one of you, in the name of Jesus Christ for the forgiveness of your sins. And you will receive the gifts of the Holy Spirit. The promise is for you and your children and for all who are far off for all whom the Lord our God will call (Acts 2:38-39).

The mention of children is not a reference to their immediate inclusion in the church as members but a promise that the gospel will save them, as they believe it even as it will save others who have not yet heard it. Men and women were urged to repent and to turn to God [Acts 3:9] and receive the forgiveness of their sins through Christ [Acts 16:31]. The early church was synonymous with those who 'believed and turned to the Lord' [Acts 11:21], and in whom there was 'the evidence of the grace of God' [Acts 11:23]. The terms used to describe Christians in the Acts of the Apostles all point to and demand a personal response to the gospel.[6]

2. The early church was a fellowship of believers who professed their faith through baptism

In the early church baptism of always followed faith; it never preceded it. On the day of Pentecost, after listening to Peter's proclamation of the gospel, 'those who accepted his message were baptized' [Acts 2:41]. When the Ethiopian put his faith in Jesus as the Messiah and Saviour, the first question he asked on seeing water was, 'Look, here is water. Why shouldn't I be baptized?' [Acts 8:37]. Paul's immediate action after his conversion, upon receiving back his

---

[6] Ibid., p. 564.

sight, was to be baptized [Acts 9:18]. He plainly knew this to be Christian practice, and it may have been part of the instructions given to him by the Lord Jesus, either directly or through Ananias. The same was true for Cornelius. It is significant that it was when Peter saw the evidence of re-birth, both in Cornelius and the members of his household, that he concluded that baptism should take place [Acts 10:47-48]. Even though it was in the early hours of the morning, the Philippian jailer and his family professed their faith by means of baptism [Acts 16:33]. Everything in Acts points to this as the established pattern. More importantly, however, than the narratives from the book of Acts, is the Lord Jesus Christ's command to his disciples to 'make disciples of all nations, baptizing them in the name of the Father and of the Son and of the Holy Spirit' [Matt 28:19], and his words recorded in Mark 16:16, 'Whoever believes and is baptized will be saved, but whoever does not believe will be condemned.' Here baptism clearly follows faith, and is seen as the badge of discipleship. Whatever views we take of Mark's longer ending, it relates our Lord Jesus Christ's instruction, which regulated early church practice.

3. Believers' baptism and church membership were synonymous in the early church and New Testament period

The apostles and first disciples formed the embryonic church. On the day of Pentecost those who were baptized on repentance and profession of faith in Christ 'were added to their number that day' [Acts 2:41], and 'they devoted themselves to the apostles' teaching and to the fellowship, to the breaking of bread and to prayer' [Acts 2:42]. The stress was on 'believers' being together [Acts 2:44], and as people entered into salvation they became part of the church [Acts 2:47]. When the early believers confessed their faith in Christ through baptism, they were automatically regarded and received as part of the visible community of believers where they lived.[7]

4. The New Testament descriptions of members of a local church demand and take for granted the existence and profession of personal faith in Christ

Paul describes the Corinthians as being part of the church because they 'call on the name of our Lord Jesus Christ' [1 Corinthians 1:2]; the Ephesians as 'the faithful in Christ Jesus' [Eph.1:1] or 'believers who are in Christ Jesus'; the Philippians as those in whom God has begun his good work of regeneration [Phil 1:6]; the Colossians as 'the holy and faithful brothers in Christ' [Col 1:2]; and the Thessalonians as those "who turned to God from idols to serve the living and true God, and to wait for his son from heaven" [1 Thess 1:9-10]. Peter writes of church members as having come to Christ 'the living stone' to become themselves living stones in God's building or temple, the church [1

---

[7] Ibid., p. 49.

Peter 2:4-5]. In accordance with the New Testament prerequisite, church membership should be restricted to those who make this profession of faith, and ideally to those who confirm it by believer's baptism.

Admittance into PIM Church Membership.

From these four conclusions drawn from the New Testament method of accepting an individual into church membership, one can deduce how important and necessary baptism is in identifying a member of the local church this principle of baptism forming a very important role in accepting people into church membership was also true of people who registered with PIM.

Believers' baptism as the usual procedure was used to accept individuals as PIM members. An individual was not regarded as a PIM Christian untill baptism had been administered. Just as in other churches, PIM believes that Christian baptism is rooted in the ministry of Jesus of Nazareth, in his death and in his resurrection. It believes in incorporation into Christ, who is the crucified and risen Lord. It believes in entry into the new covenant between God and God's people. PIM believes that in baptism, its members participate in the life, death and resurrection of Jesus Christ. By baptism, Christians are immersed in the liberating death of Christ where their sins are buried, where the old Adam is crucified with Christ, and where the power of sin is broken. Thus, those baptized are no longer slaves to sin, but free. Fully identified with the death of Christ, they are buried with him and are raised here and now to a new life in the power of the resurrection of Jesus Christ, confident that they will also ultimately be one with him in a resurrection like his [Rom 6:3-11, Col 2:13, 3:1; Eph 2:5-6].

Baptism is the only to be recognized as a PIM member. However, there were many ways in which people found their way to this baptism. Many of the names mentioned below were found on the list of baptized PIM members of November 1914.[8]

Membership through Relations

An individual could join PIM through the influence of his or her relations. Relatives, friends and neighbours would play an important role in the conversion of an individual. Through such interactions an individual would be convinced of PIM church membership and would be baptized. Such individuals include Andrew Mkulichi, born at Michiru in Blantyre where his parents earlier settled from Chiradzulu district. His mother was a sister to John Chilembwe. When his uncle Rev John Chilembwe came from America and

---

[8] The list of about 2300 baptized members of PIM was found in the PIM old offices. The other list was in Malekebu's own handwriting, the names written in an exercise book. If one visits the PIM Pavilion today at Mbombwe, one will find this old hardcover displayed.

started a Baptist church, known as Providence Industrial Mission, or the First African Baptist Church, the Mkulichi family went back to their original home, Chiradzulu. They established their village at Mbombwe, just close to the mission station. He joined his uncle and was baptized. With time, he became part of the church committee.[9]

Another example is Awanjilang'wa Chilembwe She was born at Sangano area some years after the birth of John Chilembwe. She was Chilembwe's sister. She stayed with her parents who settled at Michiru until 1900. When her brother came back from the USA and opened PIM, she left Michiru and stayed with him. She was the first person to be converted and be baptized by him.[10] She worked with her sister in-law Ida Chilembwe in establishing women's groups and helped to conduct home craft lessons. Another person was Samuel Chiwayula, born at M'bwana village in T/A Kadewere in Chiradzulu district. Samuel used to visit his brother at Ntipasanjo village where he married. He would sometimes accompany his brother when going to PIM for prayers. Little by little he was influenced by the teachings of the church, decided to be baptized and became a PIM member. He was later chosen as a church monitor.[11] Another person that joined PIM through the influence of relatives was the famous David Kaduya of the Chilembwe rising, who later started a PIM church in Migowi. The church that was started by Kaduya is presently known as Mt Cleveland Ohio Baptist Church.

Yet another person to join PIM through relations was Daniel Mgunda, born at Bakali village in T/A Mwambo in Zomba district. He was a Mang'anja by tribe. He joined PIM following his brother Phwambwala Wallani, who had a strong influence on the people of his village. He enlightened them about being free from oppression that came from the whites. He encouraged them that the freedom about which he was speaking would only be found in PIM, stressing that Chilembwe was on the side of the oppressed. This persuaded Daniel to be converted and be baptized. He became a strong member and participated in the 1915 uprising. He was among those imprisoned at Zomba prison.[12]

Antony Mangulama, born at Makowa village in T/A Kadewere in Chiradzulu district, was in a family that embraced PIM teaching. Not wanting to be isolated in religion, he followed his relatives and was baptized. He became influential in the spreading of PIM in Zomba when his family moved from Chiradzulu to T/A Mwambo in Zomba district. Moses Linya was born at Nyezerera village in T/A Chikowi in Zomba district, a Mang'anya by tribe. His parents were

---

[9] Interview Mrs Chilumpha, Mitete village, T/A Mpama, Chiradzulu, 23.3.2001.
[10] Interview Mrs Chilumpha, Mitete village, T/A Mpama, Chiradzulu, 23.3.2001.
[11] The function of the church monitor in PIM is more or less that of a church messenger. He is involved in delivering messages among Christians, and assists in communication between church members. He has to visit Christians of various areas and report to the committee about the welfare of Christians in their respective homes.
[12] Interview Nkhondo Wallani, PIM centenary celebrations, Mbombwe, 14.8.2000.

involved in the *thangata* system that was being practiced in Zomba. When the parents heard about Chilembwe protesting against the system, and the use of natives in a war that did not concern them, they were attracted and decided to join. The parents then enrolled their son at the PIM boarding school. While there he was converted and baptized. During the uprising he was among those who were imprisoned at Zomba prison and was released in 1926.[13]

Lucy Kaduya joined PIM through her brother David. She was born at Kaduya village in T/A Nkhumba in Phalombe district, a Mang'anja by tribe. When her brother brought PIM to Migowi, he tried his best to make sure that his relatives became members of the church. Among those who responded to this appeal was his sister Lucy. Alice Kaduya was also one of those that responded to David's preaching and joined PIM on the advice of her brother. Alice helped to nurse those people who were on the run during the 1915 uprising, providing them with food and shelter.[14] Changamakuti (also known as Benjamin Kaduya) was a cousin to David, their mothers being sisters. He was influenced by David to join PIM. When he was converted Changamakuti became the most influential person of the church at Migowi. He was the one who buried Morrison Chimpele Chilembwe at Mwananyani, Migowi, at the time when he was killed by the colonial forces in 1915. The church at Migowi was actually built close to his house. PIM Christians who fled from Mbombwe during the uprising found shelter in his house.[15]

Rev Wylie Pilgrim Chigamba

Wylie Pilgrim Chigamba joined PIM following his uncle David from his mother's side. When his uncle was at PIM he called Wylie to be enrolled at the PIM School, where he was converted and became a PIM member. He was among those who were imprisoned at Zomba in 1915. He was there for five years and became a PIM pastor during the time of Dr. Malekebu.[16]

---

[13] Interview Mononga, Namuthokoni village, T/A Mpama, Chiradzulu, 19.3.2001.
[14] Interview Sub T/A Kaduya village, 30.3.2001.
[15] Interview Sub T/A Kaduya village, 30.3.2001.
[16] Interview Ellefe Siyamanda, Nandolo village, 22.3.2001.

Lawrence Kaduya was a younger brother of David Kaduya. Though the father of the Kaduyas did not join Chilembwe's church, he still encouraged his children to study at PIM. This, he thought, was a great honour to his friend Rev John Chilembwe.

In light of this, Lawrence was sent to PIM's boarding school to join his brothers there. This action also had the advantage of being an escape route from the hard labour that was being practiced in the area, of being forced to carry wood from Phalombe to Mulanje *boma* on foot without getting any form of payment. While at school, just like his brothers, he joined PIM and was baptized.

G. Kunjilima was born at Chabuka village in Mulanje district and was a Lomwe by tribe. He used to stay with his brother Duncan who was running a business in Blantyre town. Duncan was a member of PIM. When Duncan went to Chiradzulu, the young brother was given the responsibility of looking after the shop in Blantyre. When he returned he spoke highly of the PIM church at Mbombwe. G. Kunjilima was very much impressed by the church. He asked to accompany his brother on one of the trips to Mbombwe and henceforth decided to enroll at the literacy school. After some time at Mbombwe, he was converted and baptized. He became very instrumental in spreading PIM in Mulanje district at Chabuka village.[17]

B. Maneya was born at Nampinga village in T/A Nkhumba in Phalombe district, a Mang'anja. B. Maneya became fearful when he learnt that his brother W. Maneya had joined a church that was protesting against white rule under the influence of David Kaduya. After seeing that his brother was prospering and that there was nothing harmful about PIM, he decided to join the church. He decided to go and enroll at PIM School by himself. He was then baptized and became an influential member of PIM at Migowi. At the time of the uprising some people from PIM, Mbombwe were accommodated in his house. I. Maneya, seeing that since his brothers had joined PIM and that there had been a tremendous development in the mode of their dressing, he decided to join also. Therefore he was baptized and became a PIM member. He played the special role of reporting to the members of the church at Migowi the occurrences at PIM, Mbombwe. He was the one to break the news at Migowi that the people at PIM, Mbombwe were preparing for the uprising.[18]

D. Mwendawamba was born at Garinet village in T/A Nkhumba in Phalombe district. His father was a good friend of Mr. Kaduya a hunter and the father to David. Upon learning that Mr. Kaduya had sent his son David to PIM School, he desired to send his son too. When David visited the village, D. Mwendawamba followed him on his way back to PIM. There he was enrolled

---

[17] This is probably one of the earliest centres of PIM. Further research could no doubt establish how the church at Chabuka village was started and how it expanded to other areas from the original place.

[18] George Nasolo, field research, March 2001.

at the PIM School, where he was soon given the responsibility of reading scriptures during the morning assembly. This attracted him to join PIM where he was then baptized and became a very influential member. During the uprising he was among those that went to Magomero to kill Livingstone.[19] At the time Mr. Kaduya sent his son David to PIM for education, Likangala asked him to talk to his friend Chilembwe to see if he could also be accepted. Since Likangala used to accompany Kaduya on his hunting trips, they developed some sort of friendship. It was out of this friendship that Kaduya talked to Chilembwe to accept Likangala into his school. Through the morning devotions at the school, he was converted and was baptized. He did not stay long at Mbombwe. He went back to Migowi and worked with the church.[20] As the parents of S. Kadangwe made their decision to join PIM, he as a child of the family had no choice but to follow his parents. He was baptized together with his parents when he was eighteen years old. At the time of the uprising he was still young and his parents took him into hiding at Machemba hills. His father was taken to prison but he was left free, owing to his youth. He had no real knowledge of the uprising, he just saw people running away.[21]

M. Zilongolola was born at Kaduya village and was related to the Kaduya family. As the Kaduya family was joining PIM, he thought it wise to do the same. At the time of the uprising, he provided shelter to those who were running away from PIM. Milliward Kaduya was a brother to David. As David's father ensured all children in his house could benefit from the education offered at PIM, Milliward was among the children that were sent to Mbombwe. There he was baptized and became a PIM member. When the uprising was imminent, David told his brothers to go back to their home at Migowi in order to have some of his family members survive the uprising. Moses Kaduya, one of the Kaduya family who was also enrolled at PIM School, followed his father's advice. He was then baptized while at school. He often left PIM and preached at his home place. At the uprising, he was advised by Kaduya to go home. He was among those who hid at Machemba hills. The other member of the Kaduya family that joined PIM under influence of Kaduya senior was Ephraim. During the time of the uprising, he used to go to the Machemba hills to deliver food to his brothers who were hiding.[22]

B. Mangasanja came from Mitawa village in T/A Nkhumba. His brother persuaded him to join PIM for reasons of fashion. Greatly impressed with the smart dressing of PIM members, Mangasanja decided to devote himself to PIM membership. He went to the church at Kaduya and enrolled his name, was later taken to PIM to be baptized. During the uprising he ran away to

---

[19] Interview Ellefe Siyamanda, Nandolo village, 22.3.2001.
[20] Interview Sub T/A Kaduya, Kaduya village, 30.3.2001.
[21] Interview S. Kadangwe, Sikita village, T/A Nkhumba, 28.3.2001.
[22] Interview Sub T/A Kaduya, Kaduya village, 30.3.2001.

Mozambique. Finally, another who joined the membership was P. Boloweza (born at Kaduya village), under the influence of his brother, Damson, who shared with him his experiences at PIM. He went there and registered his name. While there, he was converted and baptized. During the uprising he ran away to Chingondo village, in Zomba district, where he settled.[23]

Membership through Marriage

Marriage contributed to the increased membership of the Providence Industrial Mission. In these cases either the husband followed the wife or vice-versa. In some situations a man would leave his church for the sake of marrying a PIM woman whose parents refused to let her leave PIM. During the early period of PIM and in the early 1940s, some men from Blantyre would go there predominantly to seek a wife, as they believed that women of PIM were well disciplined, clean, smart and educated.[24] Jackson Chiwayula, born at M'bwana village in Kadewere in Chiradzulu district, married Nasolo's daughter at Ntipasanjo village in Mpama in the same Chiradzulu district. Mr. Nasolo, a member of PIM, did not want to lose any of his children to another church. He asked Mr. Chiwayula to leave CCAP and join PIM in order to marry his daughter. He was then baptized and became a strong member. Jackson was an excellent house builder and he was very influential in the construction of the first brick church at PIM, which was destroyed by the colonial forces in 1915. He also became a member of the church committee.[25]

Another member of PIM who joined through marriage was Mrs Fales Malangano from Chingondo village in T/A Mwambo, a Mang'anja. Fales got married to Duncan Malangano who had joined PIM through the influence of his uncle, Damson Boloweza. Malangano, a committed Christian of PIM, asked his wife to join him. Fales agreed. She was then baptized and became a PIM member, becoming influential in organizing women's auxiliary meetings.[26] Mrs D. Boloweza, Sena by tribe, born at Bangula in Nsanje district, also married into PIM. She married Damson through the *lobola* system of marriage negotiations. When Damson was converted and baptized under the influence of David Kaduya, he convinced his wife to join. The wife was then baptized and became influential in women's activities in Zomba district.[27] Similarly, Filles Nellie Kadangwe, born at Makawa village in T/A Mwambo in Zomba district, a Mang'anja by tribe, followed her husband Barnet Kadangwe and was

---

[23] Interview Mr Namakhwa, Mabuka village, 23.3.2001.
[24] Daniel Malekebu, The History of my Life and my Work, unpublished, 1940.
[25] George Nasolo, field research, March 2001.
[26] George Nasolo, field research, March 2001.
[27] George Nasolo, field research, March 2001.

baptized. Filles was known for spreading PIM Christianity in her home area. Her efforts succeeded in convincing many more women to join PIM.[28]

Esnath Mkwaira was born at Mkwaira village in T/A Mpama in Chiradzulu district, a daughter of village headman Mkwaira. She got married to Isaac Chambo and thus joined PIM. She worked together with Mrs Ida Chilembwe in running sewing classes. She also joined the literacy school and was entrusted to read scriptures during women's meetings.[29] Ellina Mkwaira, a sister to Esnath, was married to Frank Chambo, a brother to Isaac. She also followed her husband to PIM and was baptized by Rev John Chilembwe. Ellina was talented at singing hymns during women's meetings. She was noted to be very competent in many things that were happening in the church and in women's meetings.[30]

Cidreck Namasiku joined PIM by following his wife, Stephen Mkulichi's daughter. He was born at Mpaso village about four kilometers to the eastern side of PIM, a Lomwe by tribe. Since the Mkulichis were strong members of PIM and related to the Chilembwe family, they influenced Cedrick to join. He was then baptized and became a strong member of PIM. Later he became Chilembwe's companion in most of his outstation meetings.[31]

Membership through Personal Witness

Membership through personal witness involves those who joined PIM through meeting PIM individuals who shared their faith with them. Such people included Mrs S Zilongolola, born at Kaduya village in T/A Nkhumba, who was a Mang'anja by tribe. David Kaduya first approached her when he started a PIM church at Migowi. He shared his faith with her and encouraged her to join. When Mrs Zilongolola was convinced of the faith and showed interest to join PIM, she approached her husband so that they could both join PIM. She then requested that Kaduya meet her husband personally. David arranged to meet Mr. Zilongolola and shared his faith with the family, who were converted to PIM. They were taken to PIM at Mbombwe to be baptized. They became PIM members at the outstation church at Migowi. She was then selected second to Mrs Kaduya, who was leading women's activities at the church in Migowi. She was involved in organizing women's meetings at Migowi when Ida Chilembwe would visit Migowi to encourage women to have home craft classes in their own local stations.[32]

Another who joined PIM through personal witness was J. Siyamanda, born at Chabuka village in T/A Nazombe in Phalombe district, a Lomwe. In one of

---

[28] Interview Nkhondo Wallani, Wallani village, T/A Mwambo, March 2001.
[29] Interview Mrs Chilumpha, Mitete village, T/A Mpama, Chiradzulu district, 23.3.2001.
[30] Interview Mrs Chilumpha, Mitete village, T/A Mpama, Chiradzulu district, 23.3.2001.
[31] Interview Mononga, Namuthokoni village, T/A Mpama, Chiradzulu, 24.3.2001.
[32] Interview Ellefe Siyamanda, Nandolo village, Migowi, 22 March, 2001.

his business trips at Phalombe, Siyamanda met Bwanaisa, who shared his faith with him and encouraged him to join PIM. He further encouraged him that if he had any doubts they should arrange to go to PIM at Mbombwe together so that he may see for himself. They went to PIM, and Siyamanda did not hesitate; he asked for baptism immediately. He became a PIM member and was meeting with the church at Migowi, very far away from his home. He remained a strong PIM member and during the uprising he was among those who were imprisoned and ill treated at Mulanje *boma*, and the one who witnessed that the body that was brought to the *boma* was not Chilembwe's.

Another member was Napiyo, born at Namtari village in T/A Nkhumba. He came from a family of two and joined PIM through personal witness. His parents were often taken to work at Mulanje *boma* when there was the plan to plant tea in the area. They were working the whole day without pay. One day Napiyo met Damson Boloweza, a PIM Christian. Boloweza preached to him and encouraged him that what was happening in Mulanje was not in line with biblical teaching. He told him that if he was interested in knowing more about it, they should arrange a visit to PIM. At the time they visited PIM, Napiyo was baptized.[33] Damson Boloweza had a friend by the name of Biziwick Mwachande, born at Matope village in sub T/A Kaduya, a Mang'anja by tribe. When Mwachande visited his friend Boloweza at Kaduya village, Damson told him about his faith and encouraged him to join PIM. Mwachande argued that an African could not start a church and be confident enough that he was belonging to a particular denomination. After a thorough explanation from his friend, he was converted and was later baptized at Migowi during Chilembwe's visit to that particular outstation. Mwachande was baptized at an outstation church, which contrasts with the others were baptized at Mbombwe. He became a strong member and accommodated those who were on the run during the 1915 uprising.[34]

Another one was Morrison Malekebu,[35] born at Mandanda village in T/A Nkhumba in Phalombe district. Morrison met a man called Chikumba, a student of PIM, who preached his faith to Morrison, and told him how good PIM was compared to other churches. He encouraged Morrison to become a member of a church where he could have an opportunity to read scriptures. He told him about his own experiences at PIM School where he could be asked to read scriptures during morning assemblies. When Malekebu learnt about this he was very much attracted. He then accompanied Chikumba to PIM at Mbombwe. Morrison enrolled at a PIM school and was later baptized. He was

---

[33] Interview Mr Namakhwa, T/A Mabuka, Mulanje district, March, 2001.
[34] Interview Sub T/A Kaduya village, 30.3.2001.
[35] Morrison Malekebu was no relative of Dr Malekebu, Chilembwe's successor.

given the responsibility to be a church monitor. During the time of the uprising he was among those that hid at Fort Lister.[36]

Membership through Self-motivation

Membership through self-motivation involved those that joined PIM not as a result of being preached to, but through self-interest in what they heard about PIM. These people were actually interested in things like an African starting a church that seemed to be progressing; news of Chilembwe's protest against the government's oppressive rule; and the standard of education that was being offered at PIM. Mr B. Mabutawo was among those that joined PIM through self-motivation. He was born at Nasiyaya village in the present Sub T/A Kaduya, a Lomwe by tribe. He was one of the victims forced to carry timber without payment from Phalombe to Mulanje *boma*. When he heard about an African who was courageous enough to protest against the system, he made up his mind to join him at Chiradzulu. He went to PIM to meet Rev John Chilembwe and was convinced about joining the church. When he was baptized he started a PIM church at his home village and named it Betania Baptist Church. At the time of the uprising, he accommodated some of those who were on the run from PIM in Chiradzulu. The church that he started is still in existence today.[37]

Another self-motivated member was R. Bonongwe born at Manase village in T/A Nkhumba in Phalombe district. He heard that Chilembwe desired to set the African free from colonial oppression. He visited Changamakuti at Kaduya village to get the correct information about Chilembwe. When Changamakuti explained to him about PIM, he went there by himself and met Chilembwe. While at PIM he was baptized, becoming a dedicated Christian and being given the responsibility of a deacon. During the uprising, he was among those that went to Mandala to get ammunition. B. Kamfumu born at Matepwe village in T/A Nkhumba in Phalombe district, was another of the forced timber carries. When he heard of an African who started a church at Chiradzulu, he was attracted by that fact, as then Christianity was white dominated in terms of leadership. The fact that Chilembwe was against *thangata* and other oppressive activities, made Kamfumu convert and be baptized with the purpose of helping in the protest. During the uprising, he was among those that were arrested and imprisoned at Mulanje *boma*.

Another who joined PIM through self-motivation was J. Namalemba. He was born at Chamasowa village in T/A Nkhumba in Phalombe district, also a Lomwe. He was a nephew to village headman Chamasowa. His uncle suffered the ill treatment of the colonial government because he was very passive regarding whatever they instructed him to do as a chief. This pained Namalemba. When he heard that Chilembwe was preaching against the

---

[36] Interview Mr Namakhwa, T/A Mabuka, Mulanje district, March 2001.
[37] Interview Sub T/A Kaduya, Kaduya village, 30.3.2001.

thangata system he decided to join him. He went to PIM by himself. He explained to Chilembwe his concerns and ambitions. Chilembwe's response made Namalemba want to be converted. He was then baptized and joined PIM. He was among the fighters during the 1915 uprising.

Another was T. Nazombe, born at Chabuka village in T/A Nazombe in Mulanje district. His parents were among those who suffered ill treatment from the white settlers at Fort Lister. When the *boma* was being established at Mulanje, they were forced to go and work there without any payment. The rumour that Chilembwe wanted the Africans to be free from the evil of the white settlers made him want to leave his parents for PIM. There he was converted and baptized. He became a strong member of PIM and was among those who were imprisoned at Mulanje *boma*. Another one was A. Muripa, who was born at Mandeule I village in T/A Nkhumba in Phalombe district. When he heard about Chilembwe protesting against forced labour he went to PIM to meet him, seeking help. His intention was to seek assistance from Chilembwe to liberate the people of his area from such practices. Chilembwe's response to him was that such practices would only come to an end if the people took their time to pray. Muripa was encouraged to join PIM and was then baptized.[38] J. Namizinga also joined PIM through self-motivation. He was born at Chiumbuzo village in T/A Nkhumba in Phalombe district. When he heard about Chilembwe's letter to the government protesting against the oppressive system, he decided to join him. He went to PIM to see Chilembwe. He was then baptized. During the uprising he was among those that went to Magomero to kill the white settlers there.

In some cases the self-motivation came about as a result of seeking revenge after being ill-treated or humiliated. These included Y. Sokonombwe of Mgona village in T/A Nkhumba, who was furious about it and desired revenge on his oppressors. When he heard about the impending uprising at PIM, he went there to meet its leaders. While there, he was baptized and became a member of PIM. During the uprising he was among those who fled to Mozambique.[39] Another one was Duncan Kunjirima of Chabuka village in Mulanje district, a Lomwe of the Khokhola type. He was a hard worker who owned an estate and a large herd of cattle. He was similarly ill treated. A man who commanded respect of fellow Africans being treated in that way was an insult. When he heard that at Chiradzulu there was an African who had started his own church and was against the white settlers' oppression, he decided to join him. He went to PIM and met Rev John Chilembwe. He was then converted and baptized. He became a prominent PIM member who even supported Chilembwe financially. He was among the people who led the uprising in 1915. He was a leader of

---

[38] Interview Sub T/A Kaduya, Kaduya village, 30.3.2001.
[39] Interview Sub T/A Kaduya, Kaduya village, 30.3.2001.

one of the groups that was assigned to go to Mandala in Blantyre. He was then tried, proven guilty and hanged in Zomba.[40]

L. Kachamba of Bwanaisa village had relatives who suffered similar ill treatment. When he heard from Bwanaisa that there was an African who was totally against this practice, he was very much impressed and wanted to fight for his relatives. He went to PIM with that motive. There he was warmly welcomed. Seeing the type of welcome he received, he decided to join the church. He was then baptized and became a PIM member. He was among those that were imprisoned at Mulanje *boma* during the uprising.[41]

Another member was Abraham Seyani, a Mang'anja, born at Nambazo village in T/A Kadewere in Chiradzulu district. His village was near Mwanje estate owned by Conforzi. His father and other relatives were involved in the *thangata* system practiced at the estate. When he heard that the PIM leader was protesting against such practice, he decided to join the church.[42] Also, there was Daglous Mankhokwe, born at Chaweza village in T/A Mwambo in Zomba district. He was sad about the way people were ill treated by the white settlers in Zomba. When he heard of an African who had studied in America and had started an African church, he was attracted and decided to join. When he arrived at PIM he was impressed with what he saw and wanted to be part of those who were already members. He was baptized and became a PIM member. He was one of the victims in Zomba during the 1915 uprising.[43]

K. Mazanga was born at Ramose village in T/A Mwambo in Zomba district. Mazanga heard that there was an African pastor at Chiradzulu who had started a church; he was surprised an African could lead a church. He had a desire to see that for himself. He went to Chiradzulu at PIM. When he arrived there, he found that there was also a school at the same place. Impressed, he enrolled for school and was given the task of reading scriptures during morning assembly. This cultivated his interest in the things of God and he decided to become a member of the church. Since he proved to be a good preacher, he was sent to help Phwambwala Wallani in establishing a church at Mwambo in Zomba. Mazanga was one of those that were imprisoned at Zomba during the 1915 uprising.[44]

W. Mangasanja of Matawa village in T/A Nkhumba in Phalombe district also belongs to those reacting against mistreatment. His intention was to be part of those people who were protesting against the system. When he arrived at PIM he was baptized. Mangasanja was one of those who were imprisoned at Mulanje *boma* during the 1915 uprising.[45]

---

[40] George Nasolo, field research, March 2001.
[41] Interview Mr Namakhwa, Mabuka village, Mulanje district, March 2001.
[42] Interview Effe Magombo, Namulu village, T/A Kadewere, Chiradzulu, 23.3.2001.
[43] Interview Nkhondo Wallani, PIM centenary celebrations, 14.8.2000.
[44] George Nasolo, field research, March 2001.
[45] Interview Ephraim Kaduya, Sub T/A Kaduya, Kaduya village, 30 3 2001.

Membership through Admiration

This involved those who joined PIM because of admiring those who were already members. Some of them admired those who were enrolled at the PIM School and wanted to follow them. Others admired how well PIM members dressed, J. Zilongolola born at Nambazo in Phalombe district. When his brother—one of PIM's first converts—visited his home at Nambazo, Zilongolola, he was attracted to the mode of dressing, an expression of modernization that his brother had acquired during the period he was at PIM. When his brother returned to PIM, Zilongolola followed him and was enrolled at a PIM school. He was then baptized and became a PIM member.[46] N. Kwalanyiwa settled at Manase village in T/A Nkhumba. He originally came from Mozambique. His settlement at Manase was near the house of Mr Bonongwe. The mode of dress that Mr Bonongwe acquired from PIM attracted Mr Kwalanyiwa, who asked him where he acquired this style. Bonongwe took him to the church at Kaduya. When he saw how the people were dressing at the church, he was further attracted and decided to join. Kwalanyiwa became a prominent member of PIM and offered refuge to those people who were running from PIM during the uprising.[47]

S. Zilongolola was another one who came from Kaduya village. Kaduya, who completely changed the mode of dress at the time he joined PIM, attracted Zilongolola. He then enrolled at PIM School. Later he was baptized and became a PIM member. Another person was J. Namalombe born at Nampinga village in T/A Nkhumba. He was one of the people that were influenced by Kaduya's way of living. As Kaduya developed a good life and knowledge of dressing and treating others fairly, Namalombe was attracted. He admired Kaduya's mode of living. One day he accompanied him on his way to PIM, and was baptized. He did not stay long there, and went back to his home where he was influential in strengthening the church at Kaduya. He played a great role in recruiting people to join the uprising.[48]

S. Mwanduza was one of those people that contributed to the conversion of people through admiration. Originally from Mozambique, he came to Malawi with his relatives and parents and settled at Mpini village. When he heard that there was a church that was started by an African, he followed the story and ended up at PIM. While he was there he enrolled at the literacy school, was baptized and became a PIM member. At school he learnt reading, writing and the proper PIM mode of dressing. When he went back home to Mpini village his relatives admired him and they were all converted to PIM. B. Chakhuta of Nyezerera village T/A Nkhumba was among those that joined PIM through admiration. He heard of an African who had started a church. He was very

---

[46] Interview Ephraim Kaduya, Sub T/A Kaduya, Kaduya village, 30.3.2001.
[47] George Nasolo, field research, March 2001.
[48] George Nasolo, field research, March 2001.

much surprised as he thought that only whites could start a church. When he went to Mbombwe he admired how things were being carried out under the supervision of a black man. He could not help but ask for membership, for which he would have to be baptized. He accepted baptism and became a PIM member. During the uprising he was among the group who went to Magomero. B. Mandawala was born at Manyamba village in Phalombe. He was influenced by the mode of dress that the Kaduya family had developed due to their connection. He made up his mind to visit PIM and was enrolled at a sub-standard. Two years later he was converted and was baptized. He was among the group that went to Magomero during the uprising.[49]

Another was Airon Mbwana of M'bwana village in T/A Kadewere in Chiradzulu district, a Yao by tribe. He was influenced by the Chiwayula brothers, who were mostly identified by their education. They came to his village and shared the gospel there. With this Airon admired them greatly and decided to follow them. While at PIM he was converted and baptized. G. Kunjilima admired the increase in knowledge that his brother Duncan had acquired while at PIM, so decided to follow him and was enrolled at literacy school himself. Being an intelligent student, Chilembwe influenced him to become a member. Ruth Malekebu, born at Ntupanyama village in T/A Kadewere admired her brother Daniel Malekebu. When she visited her brother at the school, she admired how her fellow youth were prospering there. She asked permission from her parents to allow her to enroll. After some resistance, they agreed. She was one of the best female students at the school. She was then baptized and became a PIM member, later becoming a teacher at the PIM School when the mission was reopened in 1926.

S. Ntandeni, born at Chimombo village, admired the life and education of Kaduya at Migowi. Ntandeni decided to join and was baptized right there at the church at Migowi. Harrison Kapyola was born at Bakali village in T/A Mwambo in Zomba district. Seeing the mode of dressing of Phwambwala Wallani and the members of PIM at Bakali village, he admired them and asked Wallani how he could join. He was told that he should register his name with Wallani who would take his name to the pastor at PIM for approval. Several names were taken to PIM and the people were called for baptism. This made Wallani village a centre of attraction and prayers for PIM Christians[50].

Chikopa from Maliro village, W. Maneya from Nampinga village, and A. Konini from Chamasowa village, were also among those influenced by the Kaduya family's way of dressing and behaviour since they joined PIM Christianity. They were actually baptized at the church at Migowi. They became influential members and provided refuge to some PIM members at the time of the uprising.

---

[49] George Nasolo, field research, March 2001.
[50] The church at Wallani is today known as Holy Mount Baptist Church.

Membership through Employment

This membership involves those who became PIM members after being employed either by the church or one of the PIM Christians. Most of these people were employed at Mambala farm between 1926-1940. Some of these names appear in the old hard cover partly eaten by termites in the PIM Pavilion at Mbombwe. Those that have detailed information include Ben Mononga born at Namuthokoni village, on the eastern side of PIM headquarters at Mbombwe. Chilembwe employed Ben as a houseboy. On Sundays he was not allowed to work but was encouraged to go to church. He was moved by Chilembwe's powerful preaching.[51] He was converted and became a PIM member. He was chosen to be a church monitor, who delivers messages to Christians over quite a distance. He was also chosen as a bell ringer. During the uprising he was among those who were flogged at Zomba prison.[52] Another one was Cidreck Magombo from Chikuni village in T/A Mwambo in Zomba. His parents left Chikuni village and settled at Namuthokoni village in Chiradzulu, about two and a half kilometres east of PIM. He went to PIM in search of employment. Chilembwe took him for general duties at the mission. Every morning before resuming work, prayers were conducted. Cidreck was influenced by these prayers and was then baptized.

Membership through Influence of Outstations

This membership included those who had joined PIM at the influence of the earliest churches outside Mbombwe, particularly the church at Migowi in T/A Nkhumba; at Nasiyaya village in Phalombe, the churches in Lilongwe, Ntcheu, Magomero; and the churches at Wallani and Boloweza villages in T/A Mwambo in Zomba district.[53] Such people included L. Mpotokosi, born at Kaduya village. He was a grandson of Mr Kaduya the hunter. When a PIM church was established at Kaduya village, he was among the first converts, and was very influential in the spreading of PIM Christianity in Migowi and surrounding villages. He accommodated many people in his house during the uprising. Also one converted at Migowi was B. Likakazi, born at Nandolo village, which shared a common boundary with Kaduya village. Likakazi was attracted by Kaduya's mode of dressing and showed interest in joining the PIM church. He approached the leaders of PIM at Migowi and was allowed membership. He was then baptized. He became a very strong member of PIM,

---

[51] According to Ben, he had never seen Chilembwe preaching like that.
[52] Interview Mr Mononga, Namuthokoni village, T/A Mpama, Chiradzulu district, 24.3.2001.
[53] The areas specified here are those that were in existence before 1915. The other centres that were established between 1926 and 1940 are too numerous to mention. These centres will include those at Thyolo, Lilongwe, Dedza, Zomba, Mulanje, Mozambique, Zimbabwe and other districts in the southern region of Malawi, as PIM was mostly powerful in the southern region of Malawi between 1900-1940.

also influencing his family members to join PIM. He was among those who accommodated those who were fleeing from PIM during the uprising. Another one from Migowi was John Mveka of John Village. As the village was near Kaduya village where PIM was founded, John used to attend church at Kaduya regularly and decided to join, as a full member. Sawasawa was also of Kaduya village and was influenced by the church that was established at Migowi. He had not actually been witnessed to; he just decided to join PIM. He went to the church and registered his name. He was later baptized and became a PIM member. He helped in nursing the wounds of those that were on the run from PIM and provided accommodation for them.

M. Boloweza born in the same Kaduya village being aware that all of his relatives had joined PIM, decided to follow suit. He registered his name with the church at Migowi, greatly attracted by the conduct of worship that took place at this local branch. He worked hand in hand with the other who members of PIM at Kaduya village and greatly helped with the provision of food to those running away from Mbombwe during the uprising. S. Mpwelemwe was from the same Kaduya village. He was influenced by the Kaduya family and the church that was established in their village. He once attended a church service at Migowi and was surprised that everything was done in such an impressive way. To him it was a strange thing to see a church led by an African to be organized in such a way. He was then converted and was baptized. He became a strong member at a local branch and was chosen as a deacon of the PIM church at Migowi.

M. Nanthambwe of Jimu village heard of the church that was established at Migowi. He further learned that the church was just a branch of the original church that was started by an African at Chiradzulu. He attended the church at Migowi. He was impressed with the way prayers were conducted on that day. To ensure that the church really had a headquarters somewhere, he went to PIM at Mbombwe in Chiradzulu by himself. There he was converted and baptized. Simoni Makole of Nazombe village in T/A Nazombe in Mulanje district joined in the same manner. Since Nazombe village shared a boundary with T/A Nkhumba, the news was heard that there was a church that had been started by an African at Migowi. Makole wanted to know more about the church. He went to Migowi where he met the Kaduyas and was told that what he had seen at Migowi was just a portion of the real thing at Mbombwe. He further learned that the school at Mbombwe provided a superior education; making one behave like a white man both socially and spiritually. Makole was convinced.[54]

Martin Milumba of Majanga village in T/A Mwambo in Zomba district heard about PIM at Chiradzulu through a local branch at Wallani. He was told that at the headquarters there was even a school, which was similar to those

---

[54] George Nasolo, field research, March 2001.

established by the whites. Milumba walked from Zomba to attend church not at a local branch but at PIM Mbombwe. There he was converted and baptized. Also influenced by the outstation church was Wilishe Chigamba, sister to RWPC. She used to attend services at the PIM at Migowi because it was close to their home, but she had no interest in becoming a member. With time, she got used to the services and decided to become a baptized member. The very fact that the church made a lot of outreaches in neighbouring villages made it known as Church of the Truth by some people who were not members. Wilishe Chigamba was among those who were imprisoned at Zomba in the 1915 uprising.[55]

Membership through Education

This involves those who went to PIM for school and came back to their villages as PIM members. Among these were Endson Nasolo at Ntipasanjo village in Chiradzulu, who registered at the PIM school. He enjoyed religious lessons, which were taught every day. This brought about his conversion and he was baptized. Following this, there were other members of his family who were converted when he went back to his home village. The following also received their membership through education that was offered in PIM schools: Richard Chiwayula of M'bwana village in T/A Kadewere in Chiradzulu; and Daniel Malekebu, born around 1890 in Mozambique, who with his parents migrated to Malawi and settled at Ntupanyama village in the same Kadewere village. Daniel enrolled at PIM School at the time when his parents were not in favour of education. He actually lied to them about his enrolment at the school.[56] Bannet Kadangwe, born at Makowa village in T/A Kadewere in Chiradzulu; Phwambwala Wallani of Bakali village in T/A Mwambo in Zomba district (who heard about the school from a local branch of PIM at Boloweza village in the same T/A Mwambo in Zomba district); Daniel Mangulama of Makowa village in T/A Kadewere; Frank Chambo of Mkwaira village in T/A Mpama in Chiradzulu district; and Kabanda of Chimpesa village, a Ngoni by tribe (she was one of the first female students to be enrolled at the school).

Peter Kalemba, born at Chiopsya village in T/A Mabuka in Mulanje district, a Lomwe by tribe, became influential in the establishment of the church at Mangoni, presently Lilongwe district.[57] Bwanaisa of Bwanaisa village near Fort Lister at Phalombe, heard about a PIM church in Chiradzulu; he went there and

---

[55] Gogo Salewa, Nandolo village, 14.10.1996.
[56] Daniel Malekebu, The History of my Life and my Work, unpublished, 1940.
[57] For more information on Kalemba see Hany Longwe, "Identity by Dissociation: The First Group to Secede from Chilembwe's Church: A History of Peter Kalemba and the Achewa Providence Industrial Mission", MA, University of Malawi, 2000. Kalemba's original home was Mulanje district in T/A Mabuka's area, but he married a Chewa wife in Lilongwe spent and the rest of his life in the central region.

was enrolled at a PIM school and was later baptized. He established a PIM church in his home village, which still exists today. He was imprisoned in the 1915 uprising and was released in 1927. F. Kaponya of Nsaiwa village heard about the PIM school through the church at Migowi, as did L. Nankumwa of Mvahiwa village. M. Mreko at Nyezerera village heard about the literacy education offered at PIM from the church at Migowi. During the uprising he was among those who fled into Mozambique. L. Chikumba, born at Mandanda village, was one of the first students to be enrolled at PIM due to the influence of Kaduya. He was among those that hid in the Machemba hills during the uprising. K. Makwapala and E. Chipembere, of Mlera village and Nampingo village respectively heard of the school at PIM through the church at Migowi.

These members who enrolled at PIM School were influenced mostly by the religious lessons that were taught and by the responsibility given to them in the reading of scriptures during morning assembly. In all, education became the most important thing that attracted people to the church. This even continued to the time when Dr Malekebu reopened PIM.

The Federated Missions of Nyasaland

The effect PIM had on members differed very much from that of other churches that were operating at that time. For some years there had existed a Protestant organization called the Federated Missions of Nyasaland. Its members were bound, *inter alia,* to respect each other's spheres of work and membership, and to prescribe two years' minimum training of would-be church members before baptism and confirmation. As the years passed, more and more people who had been introduced to Christianity by Blantyre mission were switching to PIM for quicker baptisms, and swifter church admission. As a result, the Blantyre missionaries began to regard PIM as an unfair competitor offering indiscriminate baptisms to untested 'believers.'[58] In 1910 the Federated Missions held a conference at Mvera, then the headquarters of the Dutch Reformed Church Mission. Rev John Chilembwe was invited to attend. The other missionaries hoped that this conference would encourage him to adopt a

---

[58] D.D. Phiri, *Let Us Die for Africa: an African Perspective on the Life and Death of John Chilembwe of Nyasaland/Malawi*, Blantyre: Central Africana, 1999, p 26. At the Mvera missionary conference in 1910, attended by the representatives of the Livingstonia and Blantyre Missions, the Dutch Reformed Mission, the Zambezi Industrial Mission, the Nyasa Industrial Mission, the Baptist Industrial Mission and the South African General Mission, all bodies agreed to form a Federated Board of Missions. This would consult over things such as education, Bible translation and other matters of common interest. Its bases of agreement were; the Holy Scriptures to be the only rule of life and faith; the apostles' creed; the two sacraments of baptism and Holy Communion; recognition of each others' church membership and church discipline: and same standard of religious knowledge for membership. It was one of these statements that the PIM seemed to breach, as it would not recognize other churches' membership and discipline.

common policy about instructing converts. But the PIM pastor declined the invitation.

By 1912 Chilembwe's members could be found as far off as the Northern Region. These were mostly people who had come into the Southern Region to seek work with Europeans. On their return home they wanted to take the Holy Sacrament at the Livingstonia Mission. The Livingstonia missionaries wrote to their Blantyre brethren inquiring if the latter were in communion with PIM. This letter from Livingstonia gave Dr Hetherwick the excuse for sending Napier as an emissary to PIM to talk about cooperation. Napier first held discussions with Chilembwe at PIM. Some days later he saw Chilembwe in Blantyre and invited him to his house, where they continued the discussions. Napier lent some books to Chilembwe that he hoped would clarify the teachings of those churches that were members of the Federated Missions of Nyasaland. "The point I urged chiefly was", Napier later testified, "that we would accept his schools as they were at the time, only he was not to extend any more".[59]

Chilembwe would not accept this. He explained that his supporters in America would not continue to back him if he sent them statistics that indicated that his work was not progressively expanding. Chilembwe was not impervious to all suggestions for co-operation. He agreed, for instance, not to receive Church of Scotland catechumens and baptize them before they had gone through their prescribed two-year course of instruction. Beyond this undertaking, however, he would not go. In private conversation with leading African members of Blantyre mission, he would bluntly say he could not join an organization of foreign missionaries.[60]

The process through which PIM accepted its members for baptism differed greatly from the churches in the Federated Missions. Any person would be baptized any time he or she had shown interest in becoming a member. This could even be seen at the time when Dr Malekebu was in charge of the church. He had a special baptismal costume so that he would not get wet when baptizing. Some people would be attracted to be baptized simply because of the costume. Those who made a decision to be baptized while the baptismal service was already in progress were not denied their chance. At times after the ceremony when some had shown interest in becoming members of PIM, baptism was administered again. This system still continues today. It is in the PIM tradition that baptism of its members does not require one to be in a class of instruction for some years or months. At the time that people show interest in being baptized and becoming members, they are just given instructions on how they should handle themselves at the time when they are being baptized.

Every member who was baptized was entered on the list of baptized believers at the church's headquarters at PIM. Every member that belonged to

---

[59] Ibid., p. 27. Napier obviously wanted to stop PIM from expanding.
[60] Ibid., p. 27.

the church at an outstation would register his or her name with the outstation and the leaders were to register the member at the headquarters. This system started as early as 1900 and continued up to 1940, being an element in the stronger emphasis the National Baptists have on centralized structures.

The Sociology of PIM

The PIM membership list (see Appendix 2) comprised people that had different occupations. These occupations largely depended on the areas they came from. A closer look at the stars against each name shows that most of PIM membership came from Mulanje or Phalombe districts. This formed the earliest PIM center outside Mbombwe and it proved to be the most successful area for PIM Christianity. Most members from this area were farmers, earned their living through growing crops and keeping domestic animals. Some were hunters, such as Benjamin Kaduya, who was nicknamed Changamakuti because of his hunting skills. His brother David Kaduya was once recruited in the army. During the uprising he used his skills to defend the PIM station at Mbombwe when he successfully expelled the enemies from the mission campus during their first attempt to attack the mission. Some of the members were fishermen and fish sellers, such as Roland Namwera, Wiskes Matengo and his brother Yokoniya Matengo. They practised their profession on Lake Chirwa, Sombani area.

From the membership list it would seem the Migowi church had a bigger membership that exceeded those of other churches, with Mbombwe coming in second. The church at Mbombwe comprised membership from the surrounding Mbombwe area and areas within Chiradzulu district. Most of these members settled in Chiradzulu through marriage. Others came to Chiradzulu in search of employment. Most of them worked in mission stations and estates. Also employed at PIM mission was Moses Piyo, a Mozambican, who was employed by Chilembwe as a garden boy. Another Mozambican was Pio Mtwere, who came with his family to settle in the Shire Highlands from Mozambique in 1903. He soon found work in Chiradzulu and as Chilembwe's gun carrier. He was then baptized and became a member. After his baptism in 1910 he became a Catholic catechist, and left PIM for Nguludi, where he worked for over 20 years.[61] Yotamu Bango was a mission messenger at PIM, and was sent to deliver a letter to the German authorities at Tunduru in Tanzania during the rising.

Those Christians within Magomero area were employees of Bruce Estates under the supervision of William Jervis Livingstone. Most of them were working in the fields. Some of them were watchmen, cooks and porters in the

---

[61] Ian Linden, *Catholics, Peasants and Chewa Resistance in Nyasaland 1889-1939*, London: Heinemann, 1974p 92.

houses of the white settlers at Bruce Estate. Among these were Linjesi Khomelera, who worked as a houseboy in the house of the estate's manager Jervis Livingstone, and Moses Linya who was the head *kapitao* on the Bruce Estates. These people were leaders of the PIM in the Magomero area. Some PIM members were traders and shop owners in Blantyre and Ntcheu. Prominent was Duncan Njilima, who owned a shop in Blantyre, a plot at Chirimba and another shop in Ntcheu district. Some of the educated Africans were also employed as teachers, including Wilson Kusita, who was in charge of a PIM school in Ntcheu. Ida Chilembwe, Chilembwe's wife, was a teacher at PIM Mbombwe and in also charge of sewing classes at the mission headquarters. Andrew Mkulichi was also a teacher at the PIM school, Mbombwe.

Those Christians that came from Zomba were mostly local farmers and a few were fishermen in the Lake Chirwa, Kachulu area. A nephew of Mpaseakuphe was a messenger at the government offices in Zomba. He was the one who leaked information from the *boma* that the intention of the *boma* people to visit PIM, Mbombwe, was not for peace or discussion as it was communicated but rather for arresting PIM leaders. Also one who was employed in the government was Peter Kalemba, who was a court clerk at Kalumbu in Lilongwe. He was an influential member of PIM in the central region, then Mangoni area.

This shows that the membership of the PIM as it was in November 1914 comprised people with different occupations and skills. Some of them were builders and carpenters. These were involved in the construction of the PIM church in 1912-1913. They comprised people of different ethnic groups. Most were Lomwe and Yao from the Southern Region of Malawi, particularly from the districts of Mulanje, Thyolo, Chiradzulu and Zomba. There were a few Ngoni from Ntcheu and some Tonga, for example Wilson Zimba, who protested while in prison camp in Zomba against the ill treatment of women who were imprisoned during the rising. Among the list were also some Chewa from the central region, such as i.e. the Nyangus and Kalemba's wife, Joseph Matapila, and the Sodoka family: the first converts of the PIM in Lilongwe.

All these people of different occupations and ethnic backgrounds were united together under the umbrella of PIM members. They would usually gather together for worship at Mbombwe during the first Sunday of the month for Holy Communion and fellowship. Those in the Magomero area, in the Bruce Estate, organized themselves as regularly gathered PIM Christians within the Bruce Estate for prayers and fellowship, which brought them together as members of one PIM family, despite their differences in ethnic background and social status. Most of these joined the rising and were at the forefront in the Magomero attack on the white settlers. As the headquarters had one register of its Christians, this added strength to the bond of fellowship for all PIM

Christians wherever they belonged. They all felt as one body through this one membership list.[62]

---

[62] A complete list of early PIM Christians whose names were registered at the PIM headquarters as of November 1914, signed by G.L. Kapitao, can be seen in appendix 2.

CHAPTER SIX

PIM's Ministry of Justice

THERE IS A THREE DIMENSIONAL UNDERSTANDING OF THE DEFINITION OF mission based on the evangelizing, serving and community strengthening dimensions of gospel work. The dimension that will be considered in this chapter is the "ministry of justice" (*dikaioma*). Verkuyl calls this ministry of justice the "*Missio politica oecumenica*," and Richard Mouw calls it "political evangelism." The ministry of the church is "wholistic." Its mission is to bring the entire gospel (the whole truth) to all people in the entire world, and to teach them to obey all of God's commandments (Matthew 28). The good news should everywhere be heard against the background of the bad news of society. The ministry of justice stands against all injustice, in whatever form, and in whatever circles, not necessarily in spectacular programmes but wherever Christians live, speak and do what is right. Naturally it will often be unpopular. Those who benefit from the unjust structures or actions will not exactly welcome intrusion into this area. It will also be an area where mistakes will be made, but if done in a spirit of humility and love the Lord blesses this prophetic ministry. It should be realized that Jesus' ministry was eminently one of carrying out justice. Much has been written in the past years about the obligation of the church to take sides, but one thing is certain: the church in its mission should be unambiguously on the side of justice. Not that it is always crystal clear on which side justice is. Often situations are so intricate, incorporating so much historical injustice on both sides of the conflict, that the church's main role will be that of mediating and reconciling. But the search for justice cannot be ignored.[1]

Each age has its main issues of injustice. There is something like a "kairos" (an appointed time) for everything. Therefore the church must concentrate on that issue. In the early days of PIM ministry the main issues were racism and *thangata*.[2] There were also some injustices that were practised within that early society by the white planters, traders and other white settlers, who were employers of native labour, and did not treat their labourers well. They were paying them unfairly, 3/- for an adult native. At times they were beaten and

---

[1] Kritzinger, Meiring, Saayman, *On Being Witness*, Johannesburg: Orion, 1994, p. 146.
[2] *Thangata* was a system where by people would be forced to work without pay. This was common during the early days in Nyasalandi. and was encouraged by the white settlers, particularly those who owned estates.

whipped by the employer, for no particular reason, without referring the case to the *boma*. Labourers were being dismissed from the work after finishing some work without the employer paying them, or often they were paid in kind instead of cash. If the labourer asked for cash payment he was beaten, then told to go away without any questioning. The settlers evicted natives as they pleased. They were holding courts of their own. The natives could be sent to the *boma* with a letter containing information about them that may or may not be true. There the *boma* accepted anything written by the white man and punished the poor native without calling the white man for his evidence personally. A white man would often beat a native if he did not take off his hat in his presence. A native often met shouts of *chotsa chipewa* (take off your hat) from the white settlers. He was given a heavy load to carry and received small pay in return. If a native was unable to lift it he was beaten. Many people died in this *tengatenga* (porterage) work. Some died on the road, and others on their arrival at their villages. Natives' land would be sold without first consulting them, leaving them stranded with no where to go.[3]

As well as these social injustices, white planters would burn PIM prayer houses after allowing them to be built in the first place. Chilembwe did not threaten them; he only sighed and said, "See the evil doings of the white planters in the country".[4] He said if the planters did not like the prayer houses to be built on their land, they should have stopped it at the first request rather than to allow them to be built and then destroy them by fire with no reason. Another form of injustice was that some of the white planters and settlers did not usually pay the prices asked for when buying fowls and goats etc and threw whatever payment they thought of at the native.

There was injustice in the way cases were handled between the native and the white settler. Usually the government was quite slack and biased towards white planters. Whenever a native was trying to defend himself against a white, the Resident (a British administrative official) would get angry and state that a white man does not lie.

During the time of war the native soldiers, referred to as *askari*, were not taken care of. When these men died in the wars in different countries, such as Somaliland, the government did not look after their relatives, not even helping their wives and children.[5] These wars had nothing to do with the natives. For example, many people were recruited in 1902 for the Jubaland war.[6] Most recruits were killed, only few of them returned from the war. The church took no action against the government on these grievances. It remained quiet. The

---

[3] George Simeon Mwase, The Real Cause for Forming a Rebellion and How the Army was Divided and now they Fought to the End, pamphlet, Chancellor College Library, p. 29.
[4] Ibid., p. 30.
[5] Interview Rev Wylie P. Chigamba, MBC, tape, 3rd March Martyrs Day programme 1983.
[6] George Simeon Mwase, The Real Cause for Forming a Rebellion and how the Army was Divided and How they Fought to the End, pamphlet, Chancellor College Library, p. 33.

pastor of PIM, Chilembwe, did not threaten either the planter or the government. There came some rumours that war had broken out between the British and the Germans. This rumour was heard sometime in August 1914.[7] This news reached John Chilembwe, who waited to hear what would happen again to his countrymen in regard to recruiting more soldiers for the war. Sometime in September 1914, he heard that the *boma* was again recruiting men of the country for the fresh war.

Probably the First Pastoral Letter in Malawi, October 1914:

The first pastoral letter in Malawi was issued in 1914 by the PIM pastor Rev John Chilembwe. This letter was to be inserted in the newspaper, for the public to read. Therefore it was written in English and was sent to the editor of *Nyasaland Times*, Blantyre, with a request for publication. The letter addressed social injustices of the government of the day, highlighting the social evils of the society, which were against the teaching of the gospel and humanity.

The Voice of African Natives in the Present War

> We understand that we have been invited to shed our innocent blood in this world's war, which is now in progress throughout the wide world. On the commencement of the war we understood that it was said indirectly that Africa had nothing to do with the civilised war. But now we find that the poor African has already been plunged into the great war.
>
> A number of our people have already shed their blood, while some are crippled for life. And an open declaration has been issued. A number of Police are marching in various villages persuading well built natives to join the war. The masses of our people are ready to put on uniforms ignorant of what they have to face or why they have to face it.
>
> We ask the Honourable government of our country which is known as Nyasaland, will there be any good prospects for natives after the end of the war? Shall we be recognised as anybody in the best interests of Civilisation and Christianity after the great struggle is ended?
>
> Because we are imposed upon more than any other nationality under the sun. Any true gentleman who will read this without the eye of prejudice will agree and recognise the fact that the natives have been loyal since the commencement of this government, and that in all departments of Nyasaland their welfare has been incomplete without us. And no time have we been ever known to betray any trust, national or otherwise, confided to us. Everybody knows that the natives have been loyal to all Nyasaland interests and Nyasaland institutions. For our part we have never allowed the Nyasaland flag to touch the ground, while honour and

---

[7] Ibid., p. 33.

credit have often gone to others. We have unreservedly stepped to the firing line in every conflict and played a patriot's part with the spirit of true gallantry. But in time of peace the government failed to help the underdog. In time of peace everything for Europeans only. And instead of honour we suffer humiliation with names contemptible. But in times of war it has been found that we are needed to share hardships and shed our blood in equality. It is true that we have no voice in this Government. It is even true that there is a spot of our blood in the cross of the Nyasaland Government.

But regarding this worldwide war, we understand that this was not a royal war, nor a war of gain for any description; it is a war of free nations against a devilish system of imperial domination and national spoliation.

If this were a war as above mentioned such as war for honour, Government gain of riches, etc, we would have been boldly told: Let the rich men, bankers, titled men, storekeepers, farmers and landlords go to war and get shot. Instead the poor Africans who have nothing to own in this present world, who in death, leave only a long line of widows and orphans in utter want and dire distress are invited to die for a cause which is not theirs. It is too late now to talk of what might or might not have been. Whatsoever be the reasons why we are invited to join in the war, the fact remains, we are invited to die for Nyasaland. We leave all for the consideration of the Government, we hope in the mercy of Almighty God, that some day things will turn out well and that Government will recognise our indispensability, and that justice will prevail.

John Chilembwe
In behalf of his country men.[8]

This letter was written some time in October 1914. Andack Jamali, one of PIM's office clerks, took the letter on the bicycle to the editor, *Nyasaland Times*, Blantyre. After a day or so, Andack went again to Blantyre to see if it was inserted and to bring the paper to PIM. The paper was brought to Rev John Chilembwe at 8:00 am. The words that were written in the paper (a letter from the editor) were as follows: "John Chilembwe your letter has been refused by the censor." And at the foot of the same, the editor noted something about the Dutch request, which was also refused by the Government somewhere in South Africa.[9] After reading this paper at 9:00 am the same morning, a runner came on bicycle from Blantyre. He said he had been sent by the Editor of Nyasaland Times, for whom he was working, to tell Rev Chilembwe to hide the paper and not to show it when *boma* officials came to inquire about it, and said, his master, the Editor, was arrested for inserting words about Rev John

---

[8] Shepperson and Price, *Independent African*, pp. 234-235.
[9] Shepperson suggests that this mention of a "Dutch request" may be a garbled reference to the South African rebellion of 1914 led by Solomon Maritz and Christiaan Rudolf de Wet.

Chilembwe. The paper was hidden as requested.[10] Chilembwe began strong teaching. He exhorted his followers to be strong and of good courage. They all read together from the twentieth chapter of Acts some warning passages from Paul of the dangers of dissension and the difficulties of unity (verses 29-32), especially when deprived of a leader - in this case Chilembwe himself. He strengthened his followers with the words "we ought to suffer persecutions..."[11]

It seems that even before the letter, the government had been already investigating Chilembwe's activities. They may have noticed something either from PIM headquarters or from PIM members who interacted with people of other churches. Mrs Kathleen Livingstone during the Chilembwe Commission of Inquiry stated that nearly two years earlier her husband had warned the Government through the Resident at Chiradzulu of seditious meetings taking place on the Chiradzulu plain. This suggests that Chilembwe's ministry of justice had begun to show an extremist trend at least two years before the rising, although it does not necessarily mean that he was talking about fighting at that time. Possibly one of his themes in preaching "the truth shall make you free" was understood differently by different people. Being warned, the Resident, Mr Wyatt, sent his cooks to Chilembwe's Sunday services to spy on him. They brought back nothing startling. Chilembwe was too shrewd to fall victim to such intelligence gathering: before he started preaching something with a political slant, he would look over the congregation. If he saw faces he had never seen before he would dwell on issues of salvation.[12]

In the middle of 1914, warning of a more serious nature reached the Government's ears. This time the Resident at Chiradzulu was Phillip Mitchell. He wrote:

> I was a few weeks in charge of an outstation of the Blantyre district of Nyasaland. One night as I was reading after dinner, a man appeared in my sitting room and whispered that he had something to tell me. He was plainly shivering with fright and began by requiring a promise that he would not be taken to the office in daylight; when others might see him, or called on to give evidence in court. His story was that one John Chilembwe, who had a church and school a few miles from the station, was plotting a general rising and murder of all Europeans. His story told, my visitor faded away, having left me with his name and village.[13]

During the same month, a Nguludi teacher called Euginio from Mwatuta's village, called upon Bishop Louis Auneau and told him in great secrecy that he had been informed by Paulos (Mwenye) of Masanjala village that Chilembwe

---

[10] According to Shepperson it seemed Chilembwe feared arrest after the affair of his anti-war letter—a fear which was not, apparently, unjustified, for the Governor Sir George Smith seems to have made plans at this time to deport him.
[11] Shepperson and Price, *Independent African*, p. 239.
[12] D.D. Phiri, *Let Us Die for Africa*, :Blantyre: Central Africana, 1999, p. 53.
[13] *Ibid.*, p. 53.

was plotting to slaughter all Europeans and their African supporters. He was also planning to set himself up as the temporal and spiritual leader of Nyasaland, and he was sharpening weapons, enlisting followers, initiating recruits, chiefly during assemblies held at night. Bishop Auneau reported this as he deemed it his duty to warn the public authority. He asked his second in command, Father Swelsen, to contact the Resident at Chiradzulu. The Resident at Chiradzulu wrote back to the Bishop and asked that his informant be sent to the Chiradzulu *boma* for questioning. The Bishop sent both Paulos and Euginio. In a rambling style Paulos told the Resident that Chilembwe had been saying Europeans were plotting to attack Africans in November 1914. Therefore Chilembwe was urging fellow Africans to attack the Europeans first. Chilembwe's men were planning to go to Zomba and make the *boma* bugles blow the alarm in the middle of the night while his men squatted outside the doors and as Europeans tried to come out, they would be slaughtered. For nearly a month Paulos was kept a virtual prisoner at Chiradzulu, making a poor impression on the Resident. Mitchell wrote to his superior, Blantyre Resident Moggridge: "He [Paulos] is sanctimonious (and typically mission youth) and a true rascal. Still, there may be some truth in the story. I am going to try and get hold of enough evidence to show that it is no use denying anything or we may put John Chilembwe on his guard."[14] When Paulos was asked where he had got the information about Chilembwe's plotting, he quoted Morrison[15] as his source. Morrison was sent for and, naturally, before the Resident he denied all the allegations and Paulos failed to pin him down on any single point.

Of all the officials who were connected with the investigation of Chilembwe, Bernard Thomas Milthorp was the most determined of all. Usually, however, Milthorp's initiative was frustrated by Moggridge. Lewis Trahene Moggridge had started his Civil Service career in Nyasaland as Chief Police Constable. Later as Resident at Chintheche, he had been responsible for the arrest and imprisonment of Elliot Kenan Kamwana. But now confronted with rumours of Chilembwe's plotting, he found his previous experience inadequate in appreciating the extent of the danger. For one thing Chilembwe was too clever for him—he did not go about blabbing his intentions like Kamwana.[16] After Moggridge heard of the Chilembwe plot his strategy was to conduct intelligence work. Apart from instructing Mitchell and later Milthorp to send out plain-clothes men to Chilembwe's mission, Moggridge also wrote to Dr Alexander Hetherwick and asked him if he had heard of the rumours. His reaction was that he did not think Chilembwe would be so stupid as to contemplate such a suicidal venture as rising against the Government and the Europeans. However Hetherwick asked his men at schools close to

---

[14] *Ibid.*, p. 54.
[15] Probably Morris Chilembwe, nephew of Rev John Chilembwe.
[16] D.D. Phiri, *Let Us Die for Africa*, p. 54.

Chilembwe's to keep their ears open and to report what they heard. On 23rd August 1914 Milthorp passed through the PIM. He did not see Chilembwe; the station looked quiet and deserted. The assistant Resident made a total of six visits to Nguludi mission for consultation with the Montfort fathers. However by this time both Eugenio and Paulos were frightened people. Although they were instructed to continue to watch over Chilembwe and his men, they brought no additional information to Nguludi. The Bishop himself, as he went about in the villages on pastoral duties, would make discrete inquiries about the rumours. Although the atmosphere appeared to him overcast with suspicion, no one would feed Bishop Auneau with information that he would find worth passing on to the Resident.

A series of letters about Chilembwe passed between Milthorp and Moggridge. On 23rd October 1914, at about the same time when Chilembwe wrote the letter to the *Nyasaland Times* headed "The Voice of African Natives in the Present War" (which I refer to as a pastoral letter), Milthorp wrote to Moggridge. "I haven't heard anything more about him, but my firm opinion is that there must be something in it and it is no good crying out when any disturbances take place—as like the old saying, there is never any smoke without fire! What I should advise is that he should be arrested and sent up to some outstation and to remain there till the war is over and also his special teachers. I should have much pleasure in arresting him."[17]

What Followed the October 1914 Letter

The *Nyasaland Times* Editor had advised Chilembwe to hide the letter. After doing so, John Chilembwe called the chiefs, headmen and eldermen of Mulanje and around Chiradzulu.[18] He explained to them what had come from the letter. They all felt sorry about it. Chilembwe did this because before sending the letter to the Editor of Nyasaland Times, he had also consulted these people. On 3rd December a meeting was called again in order to contemplate what they should do. Nothing definite was concluded. Later the same month, another meeting was arranged. At this meeting the conclusion was reached that not receiving an answer would mean death. They all said that it was better for them to die than to live and see all the troubles, especially the grief of women and children whenever a husband was killed in war.[19] To the Blantyre Resident Moggridge there was nothing treasonable in the letter, but it was very undesirable, having a lot to say about the poor African being asked to shed his blood in a European quarrel. He advised Milthorp to keep his eyes open. Moggridge's statement shows that the letter that Chilembwe wrote to the Nyasaland Times was evidence that Chilembwe was primarily interested in

---

[17] *Ibid.*, p. 55.
[18] Probably most of them formed part of his congregation.
[19] George Simeon Mwase, p. 35.

social justice, not a blood bath. Because he did not receive a reply to his Nyasaland Times letter, he wrote another direct to the Governor near the end of December 1914. A reply came at the beginning of January 1915, assuring him that the Government was interested in African welfare and that Government officials would call at the PIM shortly to discuss with him the problems he had raised. Chilembwe apparently received the reply with joy. His joy, however, was to last only for a day or two. Another letter arrived, from one of Chilembwe's followers who was working in the Secretariat in Zomba. It was from Moses Chikwana, warning Chilembwe that the officers who were coming were not for peace but intended to arrest him.

On 3rd of January 1915, a final meeting was held. They all decided "to strike a blow" or alternatively they should ask to be buried alive. Chilembwe had already started making contacts in preparation for the rising. He aimed at making his army as widely representative as possible. First he brought the idea to his own friends, those people he felt he could trust the most. Some of these he sent as emissaries to influential people at distant places. He himself concentrated on influential people serving in other missions or who were evangelizing on their own. Among those he approached were Joseph Bismarck, Rev Kambwiri Matecheta and Rev Stephen Kundecha of Blantyre Mission and Pastor K.M. Malinki who had distinguished himself in the Seventh-day Adventist Church, but there he found little fertile ground to sow the seeds of his aspirations. He engaged in long talks and correspondence with Kundecha, who argued from the outset that Africans were not ready to stand on their own and that they still had a lot to learn from the Europeans. To this Chilembwe would retort "And you shall know the truth and the truth shall make you free." Undaunted, Kundecha would reply that the freedom spoken of in John 8:32 meant freedom in spiritual matters and that Chilembwe had wrongly interpreted the gospel. "He had a secret meaning of these verses, but did not explain," Kundecha later told the Commission of Inquiry.

D.D. Phiri argues that towards the end of his life Chilembwe was so charged with nationalistic and black power sentiments that whenever he talked of salvation he had in mind as much freedom from foreign colonial domination as from the dominion of Satan.[20] Once Kundecha's colleague, Harry Matecheta, spent a night at Chilembwe's house. He was not allowed to enjoy sleep. Chilembwe and his church elders spoke and debated all night long of white men and whether they were in Africa truly for the good of the African. Matecheta, like Kundecha, defended the intentions of the white missionaries while Chilembwe and his followers remained skeptical.

Chilembwe's politicization campaign (political evangelism) was more effective with fellow Africans who had already seceded from European churches for reasons of their own. In Zomba there was Simeon Kadewere of Makwangwala

---

[20] D.D. Phiri, *Let Us Die for Africa*, p. 28.

village by the river Namiwawa. Kadewere and Edward Makwangwala had broken away from the Church of Christ when Hollis, the missionary in charge, decided to lengthen the preparation time before admitting converts to the sacraments. At Kadewere's mission Chilembwe's strong man David Kaduya became a frequent visitor interpreting biblical passages in black power terms.[21] He was more successful, however, with Phillip Chinyama of Ntinda village, Ntcheu. In November 1914, Chinyama spent at least one and a half weeks at the PIM as Chilembwe's guest. They discussed the proposed War of Independence, African freedom and unity. They talked of African Independence in political and ecclesiastical matters.

Rev John Chilembwe used his followers, resident on estates, largely as his agents for introducing to others the idea of fighting for freedom. At the Bruce estates, the recruiting was done mainly by Livingstone's head servant Linjesi Khomelera, and ex-employees, Wilson Zimba and Lifeyu. Njilima and Kufa similarly recruited workers on the estates in the Nsoni and Midima areas. Njilima was also responsible for recruiting the *boma* messengers in Blantyre; Morrison made contact with some of the teachers at Nguludi. The greatest campaigner of them all was David Kaduya from Migowi. He was not amongst the best educated of Chilembwe's right hand men, but his ardour for freedom easily rivalled that of Chilembwe. From time to time Chilembwe would hesitate about the prudence of leading unarmed people into a bloody revolt. Up to the moment of his execution Kaduya never doubted it. Kaduya was entrusted with the risky enterprise of contacting and seeking support from policemen, soldiers and chiefs. He visited practically all the chiefs in Chiradzulu and Mulanje, and some in Zomba and Blantyre. It is not known how many actually committed themselves to supporting Chilembwe. However those who refused kept their promise to be silent regarding what they had heard.

In Zomba the leader of the Church of Christ Simon Kadewere and his friend and village headman Edward Makwangwala supported Chilembwe. Kadewere was at this time preaching with conviction about the end of the world. Chilembwe sent Kaduya to him. Within a short time Kadewere's charismatic movement, then spiritual in tone, had become political. People were now being told that those who were on the side of Chilembwe would not perish on the day of judgement; only Europeans who oppressed Africans, as well as their African stooges, would die. George Masangano revealed Kaduya's propaganda methods in a testimony on 26 January 1915, at the Zomba Military Camp. He testified that in February 1914, John Chilembwe had sent to him a man called David Kaduya, who said that he had news from John Chilembwe. Together with a friend Elliot Mitumba, and another, he went into Mitumba's house. Kaduya opened the Bible, Isaiah chapter 52, and asked Masangano if he understood the meaning of the words 'Awake, Awake'. Masangano replied that

---

[21] *Ibid.*, p. 28.

it meant Christians must be aware of the temptations of Satan. Kaduya, in a mood, expressed how ignorant his friend was as regards to the interpretation of the passage. He told Masangano that he was still slumbering and didn't know what he was doing. The words 'Awake, Awake', meant that people must fight for their own nation. Kaduya managed to create a freedom army as large possible.

During the second week of January 1915, Kaduya was addressing meetings at Machemba, a village five kilometers north of Migowi trading centre, in highly inflammatory language about the end of the world and the coming of the millennium. The 'beasts from the sea' mentioned in the book of Revelation, Kaduya asserted, were the white people already in the country. Those Africans who supported Chilembwe were safe as in Noah's ark; those Africans who supported the Europeans would perish with them. On one occasion, having worked himself up to a frenzy, Kaduya picked up the Bible and waved it at the people. 'This is the word of God in which I believe. If something doesn't happen very soon to the *azungu* in this country I shall burn this Bible'. This threat reached the ears of the Rev Archibald Smith of the Church of Scotland, Mulanje, who on 16 January 1915 reported the matter to the Resident at Mulanje. The Resident sent for Kaduya, but found he had slipped out of Mulanje district, back to Chiradzulu. For the next seven days no real attempt was made either by the Mulanje Resident or by the Chiradzulu Resident to arrest Kaduya.[22]

Between 3 January and 22 January 1915, people were busy preparing for the war. More members of Chilembwe's select group were summoned; including chiefs from Mulanje and organizers at the Bruce Estates. They were told that Europeans would be coming to attack Africans on the following Monday, 25 January 1915. Chilembwe put it to them that there was no alternative but to make a pre-emptive attack on Saturday, 23 January 1915. They responded with applause and agreed to bring their people to a pre-attack briefing on Friday 22 January. On the Bruce Estates some people met at the house of Abraham Chimbiya at Namiseche near Ndunde hill. Johnstone Zilongolola was one of the principle speakers. In exhorting the people to come out he warned them they were in greater danger from Europeans than was Chilembwe himself who, having married a *dona*, would not be killed, but would escape to England.[23]

On the afternoon of Friday, 22 January 1915 people gathered at Mbombwe. When Linjesi Khomelera, one of the leading tenants of the Bruce Estates came, he found a large gathering of fellow patriots already assembled. Chilembwe announced that war against their oppressors would start the following evening,

---

[22] *Ibid.*, p. 60.
[23] *Ibid.*, p. 62.

Saturday, 23 January 1915.[24] The details of the mobilization having been revealed, David Kaduya called for silence for Chilembwe to speak:

> Time has come at last to fight against our oppressors. Many times we have asked for redress of grievances. Instead they have forced us to go out and fight their wars. As you have already been told, they are busy now preparing to come here and attack us. Let us go out, and attack them first.
>
> You are going to fight as African patriots, not just for Nyasaland but the whole of Africa, for the whole black race. Africa is one, from the Indian Ocean to the Atlantic Ocean; remember this freedom is the cry of Africa, of the Negro race. I am not saying you are going to win the war and then become kings. We have no weapons with which to fight. They have guns, we have only spears, with our bare hands, our sticks, we must go out and fight the good fight, some of us will die on the battlefield and leave behind widows and orphans, but they will be a free people. Our blood will mean something at last.[25]

On the night of 23 January, 1915 a body of natives armed principally with spears, attacked the houses occupied by Europeans on the Magomero Estates situated about halfway between Zomba and Blantyre. Livingstone, MacCommack and Ferguson were killed. Robertson was wounded and three women and five children were carried off. A lady, guest of the Livingstones, brought news of the attack to the house of a neighbouring planter. Assisted by a native servant, she escaped and was then taken by motorcyclists to Zomba, reaching there in the early hours of Sunday 24 January.[26] The march to Chiradzulu for the captive women and their children was slow. The traumatized women were used to being carried in *machilas*. Their captors did everything to make the journey easier for them. They carried the children and gave them the care that could have been expected of loyal nursemaids. They traveled on foot tracks parallel to the road leading to Chiradzulu *boma*. Between one and two o'clock in the morning they arrived at Jonathan's house[27] and slept there. The following morning a number of armed men came to greet the white women addressing them as 'sisters'. This is what they wanted from Europeans, that they be brothers and sisters, not *bwanas* and *donas* (Sirs and Madams).[28] On Sunday evening they stopped at the house of Stephen Mkulichi close to Sangano hill, on their way to PIM. The following morning news reached Chilembwe that Mrs Livingstone had problems walking, so Chilembwe sent a *machila* for her. After a short distance enroute to the boma the men

---

[24] This was the time at which Europeans were in the habit of socializing in clubs and at functions.
[25] D.D. Phiri, *Let Us Die for Africa*, p. 64. A series of rules of discipline that were to be followed were given them after the speech. See D.D. Phiri, *Let Us Die for Africa* p. 65.
[26] For more details of the attack at Magomero see D.D. Phiri, *Let Us Die for Africa*, pp. 66-69
[27] One of Chilembwe's followers, whose full name was not given.
[28] D.D. Phiri, *Let Us Die for Africa*, p. 71.

carrying the *machila* asked Mrs Livingstone to get down. They fled, for the *askari* (soldiers) were coming.

The group that went to Mandala did not succeed as planned. Captained by Kaduya and seconded by Stephen Mkulichi, they arrived in Limbe about 7:00 pm,[29] in accordance with the plan. John Grey Kufa and his men were nowhere to be seen. Kaduya and Mkulichi waited. Still the group that was to join Kaduya in Blantyre via Nsoni remained conspicuous by its absence. After leading his army half way, Kufa had shrunk from the treasonable act and deserted his group. Without a leader, the fighters scattered. After nearly an hour of fruitless waiting, Kaduya commanded his force to proceed to Blantyre. The watchman at Mandala shouted an alarm. They shot him dead, but it was already too late—his cries had attracted the attention of a European family nearby. The Kaduya group scattered as some Europeans were coming with their guns to protect their place.

They thought the Germans were attacking their colony. Duncan Kunjilima, one of the leaders of the group that was to attack the Mandala shop in Blantyre, also shrunk from the assignment. The PIM headquarters gave him instructions to wait in Blantyre town. He had twelve *askari* who were under the Resident at the *boma* who were to join Kaduya's group as soon as they arrived at Mandala. Duncan Kunjilima and his few men were to attack the *boma* buildings by setting fire to them, for which he was supplied with four tins of paraffin.

John Gray Kufa: The man who deserted his group, a CCAP member.

---

[29] George Simeon Mwase has the information that they arrived in Blantyre at about 9:00 PM. This is probably true as Mwase was writing from the first hand informants imprisoned with him.

Early on Monday, 25 January, Richard Kuchale delivered Chilembwe's letter to Phillip Chinyama, at Dzunje, and Chinyama at once mobilized his own forces. But it was too late. He managed to collect two hundred spear and axe-wielding men. His own brother and the village headman Ntinda warned the Resident Magistrate at Ntcheu. Thus the group scattered.[30]

The Last Sunday at PIM

The worshippers turned up at PIM on Sunday 24 January as usual. It was the first time that most of the wives learned of the revolt and their husbands' participation in it. It had been Chilembwe's idea not to involve women in the agonies of war and to keep them ignorant of the scheming, lest their worries weakened the men's zeal. Livingstone's severed head had been brought up by Abraham Chimbiya and was on display in the PIM church. Chilembwe scribbled some words on it.[31] Chilembwe's act of bringing Livingstone's severed head into the church may symbolize the defeat of evil. As all the people, particularly those working in Bruce Estate, knew how cruel Livingstone was, to them it might have been their day of victory. When the fighters returned on the Sunday, Rev John Chilembwe came from the hill where he was, to receive information on how his army had fought and what casualties it had sustained. Upon learning that some white women had been brought and were kept at Harrison's house,[32] Chilembwe sent bread and other food to them. The failure of the Blantyre group to seize the arsenal, the defection of John Gray Kufa and the reluctance of chiefs and village headmen to bring out their people and reinforce his men, were Chilembwe's main disappointments that day. He took counsel with his leading men: "Suppose we tell the people to disperse [and let] each one try to save his life." David Kaduya and Stephen Mkulichi waived that suggestion aside. "No father, we agreed to fight and die for our country. Let us go on with the fight."[33] Chilembwe advised that all women living at PIM should go and stay in surrounding friendly villages. His own wife and children moved to a village of a friendly Lomwe headman nearby. He also encouraged his army to fight on, and never be discouraged by whatever they saw. He knew they had no weapons to stand against the strong army of the white men. He further advised them that he did not mean for them to succeed

---

[30] For a more detailed information see D.D. Phiri, *Let Us Die for Africa*, pp. 69-74 or George Simeon Mwase's article on The Real Cause for Forming a Rebellion and How the Army was Divided and How they Fought to the End, pamphlet, Chancellor College Library, p. 36-43. It is also said that some of Chinyama's men were seen running towards the direction of Matandani mission as a friendly place from which to escape from the wrath of the government (Yonah Matemba, *Matandani. The Second Adventist Mission in Malawi*, Zomba: Kachere 2004, p. 49).
[31] Interview Sakhula, Lilongwe, 3 May, 1999. It is not known what was scribbled on the head.
[32] George Simeon Mwase "*The Real Cause for forming a Rebellion and how the army was Divided and how they Fought to the End.*" p. 42.
[33] D.D. Phiri, *Let Us Die for Africa*, p. 77.

and defeat the white men. The action was intended only to give a hint to the white men that treatment of the Africans was grieving the whole country; and that on behalf of all their countrymen they had chosen to die for them.

In the afternoon of Monday, 25 January 1915, the Chilembwe men placed some sentries around their station. On Tuesday morning the sentries reported that they had not espied anything, and that there were no signs of approaching enemies. This report made the Chilembwe people relax, but the colonial army had passed between the sentries and Chilimankhwanje hill, where John Chilembwe was camping. Suddenly the Chilembwe people were attacked from the left wing. They scattered disorderly, towards Chilimankhwanje hill. There they found that Chilembwe and the women had left. They thought he might have gone to Thuchila.[34] They went to Machemba but did not find him there. Then they went to Chiradzulu in Mozambique and back to Chisitu in Malawi, where there was still no trace of John Chilembwe.[35] Then they returned to Mauzi twenty kilometers east of Migowi. It derives its name from a hill that forms a boundary between Malawi and Mozambique. In this place lived Christians from the Migowi church.

On 1st February 1915, John Chilembwe was not there. The following day they went to a thick forest called Pyerepyere, where they also failed to trace his whereabouts. They camped at the end of this forest, looking towards Pyerepyere plain. They placed sentries on the other side of the *dambo* (marsh) but not behind them thinking their enemies would not come through the thick forest and would be able to trace their whereabouts. After setting up camp, they sent twelve men as scouts to Magomero and another twelve to Thumbwe. Both groups were instructed to come back and report at the camp on Thursday or Friday of the same week. The group was reduced by 24 to fifty. They waited there for the two groups over Thursday, Friday, Saturday and Sunday. There was no sign of them. On Monday morning one of their Captains, Wallace Kampingo, had a dream, that they should abandon the camp and retreat for safety somewhere. He said, "I am sure those scouts are captured."[36] Wilson Zimba and others rejected the idea because it was from a dream. As Wallace Kampingo was a young man, the elder men did not take notice of his suggestion, though he was captain of the group. When his proposal was refused, Wallace took up a patrol across the *dambo*, accompanied by Andrew Mkulichi, the younger brother of Stephen Mkulichi. Returning to the camp from their patrol after about a quarter of an hour, they were heavily fired on from behind, whence they did not expect their enemy to come. The attack was quite

---

[34] Thuchila is a place found in Mulanje district some fifty kilometres from Limbe if one takes the Midima road.
[35] These areas were probably some of the PIM branches that were known to have been established by that time.
[36] George Simeon Mwase's "*The Real Cause for Forming a Rebellion and how the Army was Divided and how they Fought to the End*, p. 45.

unexpected. They all abandoned the camp in disorderly fashion. None of them picked up his rifle, except Stephen Mkulichi who was shot dead as he ran. At the camp also Nelson Nyamuliwa was killed and Wilson Zimba was wounded. The whole army was in full retreat towards the *dambo*. Wallace was wounded in his left leg and was crippled. His servant helped him by tying a bandage around the leg, but he was unable to walk further and was left lying there. Two of his men tried to carry him to the village but were unable to do so. Andrew Mkulichi was shot at but was unharmed by the bullets, which tore the shirt he wore, but did not wound him in any way. The two men who were killed were left where they died, where hyenas feasted on their flesh through the night. Only the head of Stephen Mkulichi was found the next morning and taken to the *boma*. The colonial soldiers carried Wilson Zimba to the *boma*. This marked the end of the struggle, as it was the largest group of Chilembwe's followers that remained and had fought together as a group.

The Chilembwe Myth

The death of John Chilembwe has been mythologized, spawning an array of different stories. Some believe that Chilembwe was never killed, but entered Mozambique. Others take the story further. They say that from Mozambique he took a ship to Britain, then went to the USA and came back in 1940 under the name of C.C. Adams.[37] On Friday morning of 29 February 1915, Chilembwe's followers found him at Michezime.[38] He was seated on the *khonde* [veranda] of a friend's house. By his side were his nephew Morrison Chilembwe and his black dog called, rather ironically, 'Bruce'. They were singing hymns; the little dog was silent. After the greetings he addressed the crowd, "We are now alone. Chiefs promised us a hand, but they have deserted us; some of them have even turned against us. Some of you have been killed. No doubt more of you will be killed. To America I went and returned to try and liberate our country. Though we have lost the battle someone will come again from there and set our children free. Believe me in this. Our blood is not spilt in vain. Our defeat is only temporary."[39] It is said that after this farewell, Chilembwe tore apart a white cloth and wrote words of surrender on it. The night before, he had handed in a letter to Isaac Chambo addressed to the Resident at Chiradzulu This day he gave him the white cloth shaped into the flag and instructed him to lead the women and children to the Resident and sue for peace.[40] He assured the women that Europeans would not kill them. He had treated white women and

---

[37] Interview Billiat Kaphaidyani, Mitundu, Lilongwe, 2 May, 1999. CC Adams was the Secretary of the Foreign Mission Board of the National Baptist Convention of USA Inc. He made his missionary visit to Malawi in 1940. Probably this was the time that he was mistaken as Chilembwe.
[38] Today at this place there is a Post Office and shops.
[39] Tape Interview Rev Wylie Pilgrim Chigamba, MBC Martyrs Day radio programm, 1988.
[40] D.D. Phiri, *Let Us Die for Africa*, p. 81.

children kindly. He then shook hands with the men who were there including Kaduya; now disabled and squatting in a *machila*, chasing flies from his festering wound. Chilembwe advised each one of them to try to save himself and should anyone be caught alive and taken to court, he should not hesitate to speak of freedom and why they came out to fight. They should tell the truth and speak bravely for they had nothing to gain by beating about the bush.

Isaac Chambo left for the Chiradzulu *boma*, the white flag raised high on a pole. Following were fifty-two women and twenty-four children, including Mrs Chilembwe and her two children as well as four other youth. Before they had gone far security forces approached them, fully armed. They were under the command of A.G. Sherwell, to whom Chambo handed Chilembwe's letter. Sherwell asked where Chilembwe himself was. Chambo said he did not know; that the letter and the flag had been sent to him through a third party. The lieutenant was undeceived. He ordered the soldiers to bind Chambo with ropes against a tree. And Chambo was warned if he did not say where Chilembwe was, he would be shot. Chambo again said he had not seen Chilembwe for several days. Another young man was also tied to a tree. Soldiers were detailed to shoot but at that time another white officer arrived. He ordered the two men to be freed. The soldiers and the captives then went back to Michezime village where Chilembwe had been left sitting.

As they drew nearer the village Sherwell put up his telescope and approached it more cautiously. He was afraid in case an army of his own followers protected Chilembwe. Just at that very moment Chilembwe and his nephew saw the security forces. They entered the house by the front door and left by the back door, closing it behind them. The army surrounded the house, thinking Chilembwe had locked himself inside. But Chilembwe had escaped into the bush opposite.

For nine days Chilembwe moved from village to village between Michezime and Mount Mulanje, particularly north east of Machemba Hill. He was well looked after by the villagers to whom he was already well known. Rev Archibald Smith, a resident of Mulanje then, who was very keen to prove that his church was no breeding ground for disloyal Africans, reported that the person who spotted Chilembwe's whereabouts was the church elder of his church at Machemba. On 3 February 1915, Chilembwe was spotted at Chinolampeni hill towards the Mozambique border. He had a Bible in his hands. When he saw the African soldiers coming he made no attempt to run. He just knelt against a tree and prayed. They fired at him and then seized him. Bleeding, he asked if they would take him to their European masters so that he could explain what he had done. His request was refused. It was not considered safe to travel with a captive (Chilembwe) through the villages all the way to Mulanje or Chiradzulu *boma*. It was feared that villages everywhere were too full of his sympathizers. He prayed and then they shot him dead. The corpse was taken to Likulezi Estate and kept in the house till dusk. It was then taken in a cart to the Mulanje *boma*. The Rev Archibald Smith, the Resident, and few people went to have a look at it; with spectacles still attached to his dusty face. He was buried at a place believed to be within the Esperanza Tea Estate. His grave was unmarked.[41]

John Chilembwe in Migowi

People in Migowi believe that Chilembwe was not killed. They are all convinced that he entered Mozambique. They recollect that William Jervis Livingstone was listed as one of the white men who brought much trouble to the Africans. They are proud that their forefathers participated in the uprising, and explained in detail how they were involved. John Chilembwe and his followers, together with Chinyama, worked out the plan of the rising.[42] Chief Kimu refused to join the Chilembwe group, as he felt that the white men were too strong. He could not take such a risk and be involved in such a dangerous affair. During this time, Benjamin Kaduya, who was nicknamed Changamakuti because of his hunting skills, was called from Nkhande.[43] Chilembwe said to the people *"Tiyeni tisule sompho ndi nthungo"*[44] "Let us make an axe and a spear."[45] People could not understand what he meant. Finally when people knew what this meant they began to sing a song.

> Vala zida, pitikitsa adani.
> Put on the armour and chase the enemy.

When the Europeans and soldiers came to PIM, they found nobody, for Chilembwe and his followers were hiding at Sanjika rock. They prayed there for some days and there was fog [*nkhungu*] at Sanjika rock since Chilembwe went into hiding.[46] When he went into hiding people began to run away.[47] Changamakuti [Benjamin Kaduya] ran to Phalombe at Migowi to tell his relatives that war had broken out at PIM. Together with Roland Namwera, both the church elders ran to Sombani [the name of a place to the east of Migowi some twenty kilometres away from Migowi trading centre] to hide. David Kaduya was shot at Mbombwe. He was shouting from a tree, announcing that the battle would last for six years when he met his fate.[48] He then advised the soldiers not to take him to the hospital but rather to kill him. He demanded that five soldiers should surround him and shoot him at once. He was then buried

---

[41] Ibid., p. 88. D.D. Phiri has it that the grave was unmarked for fear - a very justified fear - that his followers and admirers might make a shrine of it.
[42] Interview Mr Palasa, Mandeule village, 13.10.1994.
[43] Interview Mr Palasa, Mandeule village, 13.10.1994.
[44] Benjamin was Chilembwe's church elder at Migowi, and a brother to David Kaduya.
[45] Interview Mr Palasa, Mandeule village, 13.10.1994.
[46] Interview Mr Palasa, Mandeule village, 13.10.1994.
[47] The actual date that Chilembwe went out of hiding was not known to the informant.
[48] Interview Palasa and Muocha, 13.10.1994 and 14.12.1996 respectively.

at Magomero in Chiradzulu. Chilembwe and his nephew ran to Migowi in Mulanje.[49] "When they arrived at Migowi they had prayers at the back of my house."[50] That night they slept here.[51] They continued their journey and reached Garnet village,[52] where they prayed. From there they reached Mlera, a village along the path that passed through Phaloni and entered Mozambique. At this place they also prayed.[53] It was at Mlera that Chilembwe advised his nephew to go back and show himself to the *boma*. He was strongly advised never to run away. On his way back, Mores Chimpele Chilembwe met the soldiers from the *boma* and was killed. His head was cut off and was taken to the *boma* for identification as to whether it was Chilembwe's. Changamakuti and Roland Namwera heard that Chimpele was killed. They went there by night, took his body and buried it the same night at Garnet village.[54] When the soldiers reached the *boma* with Chimpele's head, they inquired from some of Chilembwe followers, who were imprisoned at the *boma*, to identify if it was Chilembwe's. They all said that it was Chimpele's, his nephew's and that they had missed Chilembwe. All the way from Migowi, Mwananyani, Nandiwo, Mattawa, Namphinga and Phaloni many people were killed.[55]

The death of Chilembwe sometimes becomes a controversial issue. People have mixed ideas about his death. History has it that Chilembwe was killed on 4 February 1915. This is not the case in Migowi. According to what Sandras Mandeule, Mr Palasa, Gogo Salewa believe and the general view of the people of Migowi, Chilembwe entered Mozambique. They strongly refute Chilembwe's death. Sandras Mandeule says, "The grave that is found at Mt Cleveland Ohio Baptist Church is that of Mores Chimpele 1915. According to what I heard, John Chilembwe gave him his jacket and when the government soldiers saw him they thought he was Chilembwe and they killed him. When the head was brought to the *boma*, it was discovered that it was not Chilembwe's head. John Chilembwe entered Mozambique. But if the *boma* claims that Chilembwe was killed, then where is his grave?"[56] Even the people at Phaloni, just close to Chinolampeni, which D.D. Phiri identifies as the place where Chilembwe was killed, still believe that Chilembwe entered

---

[49] Interview Mr Palasa, Mandeule village, 13.10.1994.
[50] Interview Gogo Salewa, Nandolo village, 14.10.1994.
[51] Interview Mr Palasa, Mandeule village, 13.10.1994. 'Here' referred to Mandeule village.
[52] This is the place where Morris Chimpele Chilembwe's grave is found and where PIM's Mt Cleveland Ohio Baptist Church is situated.
[53] It is not known what sort of prayers they were, however there is evidence that a few sympathizers and some PIM members attended such prayers whenever they were around.
[54] Interview Mr Palasa, Mandeule village, 13.10.1994.
[55] The graves of those people who were killed are still found today along this path from Migowi to Phaloni. I failed to identify the names of the people that were buried in those graves. Some of my informants explained to me that some of those people were not even known to the people that buried them as they were on the run from other places.
[56] Interview Sandras Mandeule, 10.10.1994.

Mozambique. Chinolampeni is currently known as Pachibwerera nkhondo.[57] This was the place where the colonial forces returned.

However, Rev Muocha offers an alternative version suggesting Chilembwe was killed at Nandiwo River just some distance from Migowi. The soldiers followed the shoe prints, as it was the rainy season. When they reached the Nandiwo River, there was no continuation of the shoe prints on the other side of the river. The soldiers were stranded and could not trace which direction the person followed. It would be either from or to the direction the river was flowing. They decided to return. As they returned a short distance, Chilembwe decided to proceed from where he was hiding. As he came out of the river, he was seen by the soldiers, and then was killed. When his body was taken to the *boma*, the Resident denied responsibility for his death, as he had only advised the men on the hunt to arrest him. Fearing some questioning, the men who carried the body disposed of him in the nearest forest and disappeared. This is why till this day, Chilembwe's grave cannot be spotted.

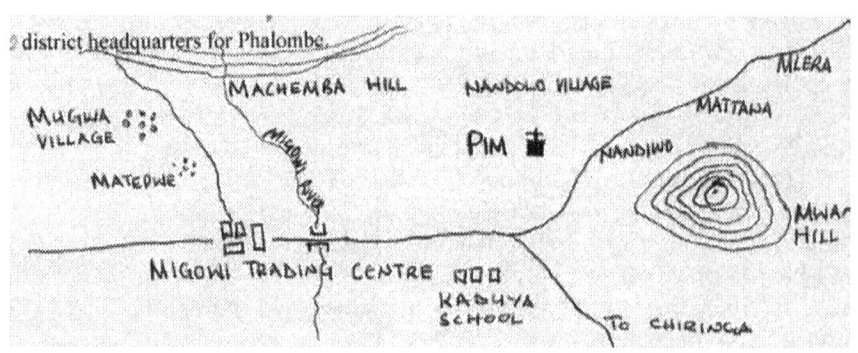

Map Showing Chilembwe's Potential Movements

George Nasolo's field research shows that Chilembwe was killed at Fort Lister in Phalombe. Today the area is known as Mata. The late Lieutenant Njilima claims to have known the whereabouts of Chilembwe's grave in Mozambique. This further complicates the issue about the death of Chilembwe. However, Rev Wylie Pilgrim Chigamba acknowledges that not even one of Chilembwe's Christians knew or claimed to know the whereabouts of Chilembwe's grave.[58] So his death remains a mystery. Possibly further research would establish the real truth of the matter or his death will remain a legend. The truth that remains is that his ministry of justice cost him his life or forced him into exile.

---

[57] These words literally mean "where war turned around".
[58] Tape, MBC radio programme, Martyrs Day, 3 March, 1988.

Chapter Seven

THE DARK PERIOD OF PIM MINISTRY 1915-1926

IMMEDIATELY AFTER THE UPRISING, THE PIM CHURCH WAS BANNED AND THE Christians were scattered. The Secretary of the Foreign Mission Board of the National Baptist Convention of USA Inc, Dr Jordan, asked $40000 compensation for the destruction of the PIM church, but it was not granted.[1] Many people began to write about their views on the uprising, such as Kundecha, Matecheta, Manatee, Chisuse and Kamwana.[2] This was particularly prompted by the Commission of Inquiry, which was constituted to establish the truth about the cause of the uprising. Within a few months and years, the news of the uprising spread all over including outside the country. Clement Kalaile, then coming to the peak of his power as leader of the Industrial and Commercial Workers Union of South Africa, wrote the following to a correspondent in Nyasaland in 1921:

> Yes I have heard about that African Patriot John Chilembwe and I am indeed proud of his name. It was a few days ago that I was relating his adventures to my staff at this office and they were indeed inspired. Further particulars about him will be much appreciated, as I would like to obtain this information for the future history of Africa, as I believe that whitemen will not preserve the genuine history of the blackman.[3]

One of the PIM members, who played a very important role as a Christian and as one of the leaders in the uprising, was Mr Andrew G. Mkulichi. In the early 1950s he wrote this for Thomas Price in a forty-page account entitled *Maziko a Prov. Ind. Mission, Chiradzulu. Nyasaland. 1900 AD*. Mkulichi put only brief speeches into Chilembwe's mouth. With one exception these were in the vernacular. The exception was the following representation of three memorable sentiments of Chilembwe's, which are all given in English, 1. "I hear the cry of my Africans." 2. "My people are destroyed through lack of knowledge." 3. "It is better for me to die than to live". Mkulichi wrote the following in vernacular:

---

[1] Rev M.B.K. Chipuliko, *A Brief History of Rev John Chilembwe*, Chilembwe Day Celebration, 1995, Chiradzulu, p. 2.
[2] For more information on this see George Shepperson, *The Place of John Chilembwe in Malawi Historiography*, in Pachai.
[3] George Shepperson, *The Place of John Chilembwe in Malawi Historiography* in Pachai, p. 416.

> Anayamba kuphunzitsa mwa mphamvu, nati limbikani musafoke mu mzimu ngakhale mudzaone zovuta. Pakuti ambiri adzafika mdzina la Kristu, nadzati ife ndife a Khristu. Ndipo anaphunzitsa Machitidwe 20:29-32. Iye analimbikitsa ndi mawu akuti Tiyenera kumva zowawa chifukwa omwe anali patsogolo pathu anamva zowawa chifukwa chache ndifulumizani inu nonse kuti mukondane wina ndi wina ndikuwapempheleranso iwo amene anakuzunzani inu mwa ambuye.
>
> He began strong teaching. He said 'Be strong. Don't be wearied in the spirit even in the face of trouble. For many will arrive in Christ's name and will say we are of Christ.' And then he taught Acts chapter 20 verses 29-32. He strengthened them with these words, "We ought to experience hardships because those who went before us had bitter experiences. That is why I urge you all that you love one another and pray to the Lord again for those who have been cruel to you".[4]

Acts 20:25-32 reads as follows: "For I know this, that after my departing shall grievous wolves enter in among you, not sparing the flock. Also of your own selves shall men arise, speaking perverse things, to draw away disciples after them. Therefore watch and remember, that by the space of three years I ceased not to warn every one night and day with tears. And now brethren, I commend you to God, and to the word of his grace, which is able to build you up, and to give you an inheritance among all them which are sanctified."[5] This chapter represents some kind of a prophetic warning to PIM followers as to what would become of them after their leader's departure.[6] This may also show that Chilembwe foresaw some kind of trouble after the rising. As he had a glimpse of what might become of his followers, he strengthened them and prepared them to be strong and of good courage for the impending trouble. What the PIM pastor envisaged happening came into reality between the period 1915-1926. Many of the PIM converts were betrayed by their own relatives, killed, hanged and some imprisoned. However they faced all those troubles with courage and determination.

---

[4] Ibid., p. 417. As quoted by Pachai from a fourty page document said to have been written by A.G. Mkulichi.
[5] King James Version, Acts 20:29-32.
[6] Departure in this sense would either mean his death or absence from his flock.

The Dark Period of PIM Ministry 1915-1926

PIM followers being led to prison in 1915

It is this mixture of religion and politics which brings the PIM close to what has been called in European history the 'Radical Reformation'. This kind of teaching that came from the PIM pastor seems to have strengthened the followers wherever they went. Most of them were courageous enough not to hide their identity as PIM Christians. Though there were some who tried to deny their involvement in the rising, in the end they were found guilty. As many people scattered and disappeared, either into Mozambique or Tanzania (in the case of Yotamu Bango), still some were arrested and faced trial. Of those who faced trial, many were killed, hanged or imprisoned.

Early PIM Outstations and the Rising

The PIM outstations were greatly affected by the uprising. Some of its members were arrested and some were killed. It became dangerous to be identified as a PIM member. Even chiefs did not want to be identified with PIM in their villages. Village headman Garinet Kaduya was one of these. He worked very hard to assure the government that he did not favour the uprising, by hunting the PIM members who were hiding on his own initiative. When the war reached its climax and the people dispersed, Benjamin Kaduya and Roland Namwera, prominent members of the church at Migowi, left Migowi to go into hiding at Sombani, a distance of about twenty kilometres from Migowi towards Lake Chirwa. David Kaduya was killed and his body was buried at Magomero after he had shown publicly that he was a strong Chilembwe supporter. When it was declared that the war should come to an end, village headman Garinet Kaduya said *"Nkhondo isathe nsanga ena sanapezeke"* (The war should not come to an end, others still have not been found).[7] Garinet wanted to ensure that the two prominent PIM members at Migowi, Changamakuti and Namwera, were arrested. While at Sombani, Changamakuti and Namwera sent Mandeule, a PIM Christian, to Migowi to check if the war had come to an end. While there, he was found by the colonial forces and denied knowledge of the whereabouts of Namwera and Changamakuti. At his own effort village headman Garinet Kaduya found Namwera and Changamakuti at Sombani and betrayed them, bringing them to the *boma*; from there they were taken to Blantyre for trial. Changamakuti (Benjamin Kaduya) was hanged and Namwera was imprisoned. He was immediately sent to Zomba prison. Then the end of war was declared.[8]

When Benjamin was killed, and Namwera and Wylie Chigamba were imprisoned, the church at Migowi lacked leadership. Christians were dispersed and nobody wished to identify themselves with the PIM. When Roland Namwera and Wylie Chigamba were released from prison in 1920 they revived the church. Village headman Garinet Kaduya discouraged the people of his village from joining the church. This did not discourage the PIM local leaders. As the church at Migowi was revived, it extended its influence as far as Mauzi, a distance of about twenty kilometres from Migowi. Other Christians who had been gathering secretly at Chiringa began to emerge from hiding. Wiskes Matengo and his brother Yokoniya Matengo led this group. The church they started is known today as St Paul Baptist Church at Nkome village in T/A Nazombe in Phalombe district.

The other PIM outstations that were affected during the uprising were the churches at Wallani and Boloweza in T/A Mwambo in Zomba district. Wallani and his friend Phambalawo hid themselves in a beer basket at Bakali village. Fearing the threats of the colonial forces that occupied Wallani and Boloweza village, the people of the village helped the forces in hunting Wallani and his friend. In the process they found Symon Kadewere: Wallani's brother and a brother to Wallani and a member of the Church of Christ at Namiwawa in Zomba. He was mistaken for Wallani and was hanged at Zomba prison. When Wallani heard this he fled to Mozambique, where he stayed for eight years. He came back and stayed at Chinkhwangwa village in Phalombe district. At Chinkhwangwa, he started a PIM church in 1923 and named it Mt Olivett Baptist Church.[9] It is possible that many churches were started during this time, as it was, in my opinion, the period of PIM diaspora during which members were scattered to various places.

---

[7] Interview Mr Palasa, Migowi, 14.10.1994.
[8] Interview Mr Palasa, Migowi, 14.8.1994.
[9] Wallani died there at Chinkhwangwa village and his body was taken to his original village at Likangala in Zomba where he was buried. It was not known when he died to the informant.

Stefano of Ntcheu was one of the PIM member hanged in Zomba in 1915. At the time of his execution, he was singing hymn number 114 of *Nyimbo za Mulungu*. The residing strength of his faith is reflected in the hymn: "What can cleanse me, nothing but the blood of Jesus."[10]

At the end of 1915, Peter Kalemba was brought to court in Zomba to answer charges on his involvement in the uprising. He was asked three questions. The first one was "Are you a PIM member and follower of Chilembwe?" His answer was "Yes, I am". The second question was "Where were you when Chilembwe sent his people to kill the white settlers at Magomero?" Kalemba answered, "I was in the central region". The third question was "If you were there in the southern region would you join and participate in the killing?" His answer was, "Yes, and I would probably be the first one to kill". Then the white judge said, "Very good, this now clearly shows that you are Chilembwe's follower, you will not be hanged, instead you will be tortured and then released". In the process of torturing Kalemba, part of his ear was chopped off. He was then sent back to the central region.[11] When Kalemba reached the central region he continued with PIM work.

Secret Gatherings

Between the year 1915 and 1924, the colonial government seemed to have been working towards the total destruction of PIM work. PIM members were followed and had no chance of conducting services in public. They conducted their worship secretly. In Migowi, secret services were conducted in the house of Roland Namwera. In Chiringa, services were conducted in the house of Wiskes Matengo. At PIM, Mbombwe, services were conducted in the house of Andrew Mkulichi and Wallace Kampingo. Later they started gathering at the PIM mission campus during the daytime, and a shelter was constructed for that purpose. In November 1922, the colonial Government sent a representative to spy on the activities of the PIM in Lilongwe and Dedza districts. The report, submitted to the Chief Commissioner of Police on November 15, 1922, reads as follows:

> I will explain the habits of the youths of the P.I. Mission. I arrived at Nkhoma at the village of Chipira where there is a youth pastor Bizayi Kachiwanda. He said to me let us go into the bush. Then we went far to the water at Linthipe, and then he commenced to ask me where I came from, I said I came from Zomba and I was the head Capitao to go along and see the roads, then he asked me who told me about them. I said that I had inquired from the natives on the road where the people stay who

---

[10] Interview Billiat Kaphaidyani, Mitundu, Lilongwe, 2.5.1999. The Chichewa version of the song that Joshua Chateka sang on the way to execution was "Chitha nchiyani kundiyeretsa, mwazi wa ambuye Yesu, nchiyani chindipulumutsa, mwazi wa Ambuye Yesu."
[11] Interview Billiat Kaphaidyani, Mitundu, Lilongwe, 2.5.1999.

are praying by themselves in the evenings and they replied at Nkhoma at the village of Chipira, and so I came to talk with you. He asked me how I found him, to what mission did I belong? I told him that long ago I used to stay with John Chilembwe at Chiradzulu but now I belong to the Watch Tower, thereupon he said alright you have said well truly. He then went on to say that although the white men oppress us they will see a time when our head John Chilembwe will arrive and they will be ashamed because now he is near 1923 perhaps he will arrive here. At the time they wanted to kill him, he ran away to America and then there came his brother Anderson? Who wanted to put things right at Chiradzulu but the whiteman at the *boma* told him that he should do another year and to return to America, he returned there, he will come back here 1923 next year.

He further said that the whitemen do not know what God will do, there will be war with them and they will leave this country and all the Chiefs who helped them to oppress us will be ashamed of themselves.

Thereupon I went to the village of Kalumbu where I found another head of theirs, he is looking after all the youths of Lilongwe and Dedza, he is Peter Kalemba and he said of the same things as Bizayi, he also said that if you send a person to listen to what they are saying they will kill him truly because the whitemen are them for no reason, You will see trouble another time and your Chieftainship will come to an end. This country of Nyasaland the lord will give them great strength to fight with a whitemen and although you oppress you will fail, you wont accomplish anything.

But I saw terrible bad people. I have been with you a long time Bwana in this work but I have never seen such people as them, they are really terrible youths. If I had made a mistake when speaking they would have killed me as they are people who have hardened their hearts indeed.

I am going on because of your orders Bwana on that account even if they kill me it does not matter for you Bwana have trusted me in your work and I go on wherever you say Bwana. I am not afraid of them but I want to say exactly what they told me to my face.

The things of which I have spoken are the same which they told me and all that they are saying are such words indeed my Bwana.

Peter Kalemba. Mnyanja. Kalumbu's village, chief Mazengera

Steven Kalumbu. Mnyanja Kalumbu's village, chief Mazengera

Anderson Nyangu. Mnyanja Kalumbu's village, chief Mazengera

Jonathan Kalumbu. Mnyanja. Kalumbu's village, chief Mazengera

Zenas Mnyanja. Dowokos village, chief Mazengera.

Gabriel Mnyanja. Santhes village, chief Mazengera

Joshua Chatheka. Mngoni. Kapala's village, chief Chimdidi

Robert Mngoni. Chimpele's village, chief Chimdidi.

Gabriel Tongo. Mngoni. Chadza village, chief Masula

All leaders of the PIM. in the Lilongwe district who are bad people.

Bizayi Kachiwanda. Mchewa. Chipira's village, chief Kapuka. Fanwell Senzani. Mchewa. Kanalo's village, chief Kapuka, Lutere Ntachi. Mchewa. Tumbwe's village, chief Kapuka Abisaye Chonde. Mchewa. Chonde's village, chief Pemba, Naboti Manondo. Mwamvu's village. Chief Tambala Aziyele, Pemba's village, Chief Pemba

Leaders of the PIM. in the Dedza District who are bad people.[12]

This report, which was submitted to the Commissioner of Police in Lilongwe, conveys the thoroughness of the investigation. This is evidence that the PIM was still operating underground even though it was banned, and it displayed an element of growth. The church had only started in Lilongwe in November 1914, now it had reached as far as Dedza. What seemed to be the period of silence proved to be a period of spiritual awakening to some people who risked their lives to proclaim their faith as PIM members, despite the fact that PIM was banned. The report reveals that PIM members in the central region believed that their leader, Rev John Chilembwe, had not been killed. They still hoped he would return from America where he went after the uprising. In this context, the belief that Chilembwe came to Lilongwe in 1940 under the name C.C. Adams is not an entirely illogical conclusion to draw.[13] At the same time, rumours of the coming of Dr Malekebu were circulating. This is evident from Bizayi Kachiwanda's report. Possibily he had some knowledge of the coming of Dr Malekebu in 1921 when he was advised to go back for a while for some clearance. The church in the central region fulfilled Chilembwe's intention of having a fully operational church in the central region when the PIM in the Southern region was completely destroyed.

Trials

During the period of 1915 to 1926, most of the PIM Christians were arrested and large numbers of Christians were captured and some four hundred were put on trial. Capital punishment was meted out to forty-six of the ringleaders, of whom thirty-six were hanged. Some three hundred more received varying sentences. A collective fine in the shape of an extra hut tax was imposed on all the disaffected villages as a general punishment and as part of the contribution towards the indemnification of those whose property had been destroyed by the PIM supporters who were involved in the war.[14] Some of them stood to

---

[12] Letter from a correspondent to the Chief Commissioner of Police, Lilongwe, 15.11.1922.

[13] C.C. Adams was the secretary of the FMB. During this time he was on his missionary tour to the FMB stations in East and Central Africa, to which Malekebu was Supervisor of Missions.

[14] Unsigned and untitled pamphlet, PIM Pavilion, p. 8. Some of the villages include Golden village in Chiradzulu, Masanjala and numerous villages in Kadewere's area.

their faith and confessed they were PIM Christians. Others tried to defend themselves by denying their involvement in the uprising; however, investigations found them and they were executed. Both Mrs Kathleen Livingstone and Mrs Ida Chilembwe were used as key witnesses for the prosecution, although Mrs Livingstone's memory proved to be of limited range due to her recent trauma. The first trials that took place in Zomba were swift and impatient. The courts and the prosecutors were interested mostly in whether a prisoner had taken part in the murder, attended an illegal assembly such as that on Friday 22 January, or had known about the plot. It was in the screening of such information that Mrs Chilembwe figured most and she spoke recklessly about who had been plotting with her husband.[15] The other women in court, by means of a special gaze, tried to intimidate her. She ignored them. Thereupon Wilson Zimba jumped up and shouted at the court that it was

---

[15] Case of Aida (John Chilembwe's Widow), 8.2.1915. (half caste, Magololo). "On Saturday night I was ill and I saw none of the men. All of them left on Saturday night. John Chilembwe told us to run away. We went eventually to Johnston's village on the Thursday after hiding in Chirimangwanje hill. I saw at Chilembwe's village on the Friday 22 January Duncan Njilima, John Gray, Wilson Zimba (Mtonga), Lifeyu an elder at Magomero, Lee a Ngoni, Wallace Kampingo deacon, a Ngoni, Witness a tailor at Chilembwe's a Ngoni, David Kaduya, Daniel Mangulama Nyanja deacon of John Chilembwe, Douglas a Nyanja a teacher at Matiti, Barnett Kadangwe a Nyanja teacher, Andrack Jamali a Yao of Zomba, Stephen Mkulichi a Yao, Andrew Mkulichi a Brother Yao and a teacher at Sangano, Isaac Chambo, Yotamu S. Bango, Alias Saiti Chikunda Stephen Mkulichi's cook, Dickson Magololo, Morris Chilembwe son of Chimpele, Wilfred Mtambo a teacher at Chingoli, Nelson Nyamuliwa a teacher at John Chilembwe's Andrack's assistant, Headman Mtipasanjo, Johnstone elder at Namadzi, Master Nyimbili deacon at Nangundi, Jonathan Maniwa elder at Chilembwe's and a church bell ringer, Babylon Kamfumu. I did not see Robin Edward Mkombesi on the Friday or Saturday but I saw him at the village talking to John Chilembwe from time to time. Wilson Daniel Kusita is John Chilembwe's teacher in Angoniland. I have seen him. John Chilembwe and Stephen Mkulichi were alone in the church. I never saw any European in John Chilembwe. My mother ran off. I did not see the men".
9.2.1915. "On Saturday during the day time I saw David Kaduya, Morris Chilembwe, Wallace Kampingo, Andrack Jamali, Stephen Mkulichi, Isaac Chambo, Yotamu Bango, Dickson, Wilfred Mtambo, Nelson, Petros Kampingo Ngoni. I never saw Ex serg. Chimwaza there, he is not a Christian. I did not see Damson teacher of Ndunde on Friday or Saturday, Fred Maganga, James Samuti, Dovite, David of Ndundi Jam. I did not see Anderson Magombo scholar at John Chilembwe's on Friday or Saturday. I did not see Maynard Ebella formerly one of John Chilembwe's teachers. I do not know George Masangano, Simon Kadewere, Robert Masache, Fredrick Singani, Elliot Yohane Achirwa, Peter Kambona, Edward Peters, Mungo Park, Oliver Kwidio, Augustine Mlanga. I did not see Malinki or Chisuse. Gordon Matakathe, younger brother of Duncan Njilima by a different father, used to come to John Chilembwe's some time ago but was absent on ulendo. Headman Kumlata and Ntipasanjo used to come to Chilembwe's kuchedaza. On Sunday I slept in the hut of Nguru sympathizers at the Thumbwe. On Monday I was at the Thumbwe. On Thursday I was at Johnston's village and my husband John Chilembwe came at night and told me that he had given Isaac Chambo a letter to Chiradzulu *boma* to take care of us. I met Isaac Chambo on the Friday. I do not know why he wanted to kill the white people. I live quite contentedly. I heard him once complain about the school being destroyed by Europeans at Namadzi."

getting false information from Mrs Chilembwe. "This plotting was only done by a few of us: Chilembwe, Kaduya, Kufa, Stephen Mkulichi and myself. Women knew nothing about it, not even Mrs Chilembwe", he said. Then he went on to demand that the women be sent back. "We treated your women with respect, how can you keep ours here in prison, compelling them to break stones and cut grass? You are cruel, you people. We have been fighting with mere spears and sticks and you have the guns. And yet you panic like this?"[16]

Those who witnessed this audacity talked decades later of the bravery of that Tonga man. The women and children were released after one week. By that time a number of them had witnessed their husbands being led to the scaffold and dying bravely, singing hymns as they climbed up.

As the days went by, trials became more British in method and fairness. In Blantyre, the judge asked Benjamin Changamakuti Kaduya why he had taken up arms against the Crown. He replied, "Sir, suppose we black people went to your country, grabbed land from your people, made laws that forbade them to hunt or make use of their trees, what would your people do to us?"[17] The judge did not reply directly. He said instead that he was convinced that Changamakuti was indeed in the top category of the conspirators. He sentenced him to death and ordered that he be executed at Mulanje, his hometown, for the local people to witness.[18]

Duncan Njilima, one of the strongest PIM supporters, was also executed. He was convicted of high treason and of being an accessory to the murder of the watchman at Mandala, Blantyre, on 24 January 1915. Although he did not make a full confession, there was not the slightest doubt of his active participation in the plans for the insurrection.

---

[16] D.D. Phiri, *Let Us Die for Africa. An African Perspective on the Life and Death of John Chilembwe of Nyasaland/Malawi*, Blantyre: Central Africana, p. 90. This was a statement given to D.D. Phiri by Ntambo, Wylie Chigamba and Gogo Juwa. All were eye Witnesses of the 1915 rising.
[17] Interview Rev Wylie P. Chigamba, Tape, MBC Radio, Matyrs' Day programme, 1988.
[18] Ibid.

The public execution at Zomba of convicted Chilembwe insurgents
(Central Africana Archives)

When he made his statement he was under the impression that his father, Ndambe Njilima, his wife Harriet and one of his daughters (Mary) were dead. But they were all alive: Harriet his wife and six children, namely Matthew C. Njilima (19) Fredrick, (18) Mary (14), Edith (8), Elizabeth (7) and Dyson (2). At this time Matthew and Fredrick were at school in the USA, at Natchez College, Missouri and at Lincoln Ridge College, Kentucky respectively. Both of these colleges were founded by Negro Baptists and were under the tutelage of a Negro Baptist named Jordan, the secretary of the Foreign Mission Board of the National Baptist Convention, USA Inc. In petitioning the Government, Duncan wished his estate to be divided between his widow and surviving children. His widow and his daughter Mary were not mentioned owing to his belief that they had been killed in the war. However he was informed before his execution that they were alive and that the Government in its military operations did not harm women and children. Considering that Duncan took so prominent a part in engineering the rebellion and that he was one of the most influential members of PIM and that his brother Msalule cut the telegraph line near Mikolongwe and led the party that brutally murdered a Mulanje policeman, and that his brother Clair Njilima was also involved though not tried, the magistrate saw no reason why Duncan's real and personal estate should not be forfeited to the Crown.[19] At the time of his execution Duncan Njilima trusted his property into the hands of Robin. He wrote the following:

---

[19] Magistrate, Zomba camp Chief Secretary, Zomba, 2.3.1915.

Dear Robin

Goodbye, I am going to die and now all things belongs to you and Kunsalule if the *boma* will agree: the house Kunsalule will built it again and stay in the same place; the *boma* will make the people to stay in their villages again. Do not depart with your sister from the land. Nelson must stay there also when he will return from Livingstone: You will see me to God; good bye, do not leave the place where your father was staying. My land is 125 acres, Cattle twelve, I gave £54:12:0 to Jessie to hide long ago.

I am Yours

(Signed) D. Njilima.[20]

Among those who were tried was Moses alias Manyanja, his father's name being Masongola of Mbamera, a Nyanja by tribe. When asked to give an account of his involvement in the war, he gave the following explanation.

"I was working as carpenter for Mr James in Blantyre and on Sunday [24th], I heard that people had come with war to Mandala, had broken and opened a house and had taken some guns. I heard it from people who were passing on the road and whom I did not recognize. On Monday I heard that there was war at Chilembwe's. I do not know who told me. I remained in Blantyre till Thursday and on that day I returned to my village to see if the people were still there. All the people were there except my wife Rebeka who I was told had gone to her father Mpolameli who lives at Ndunde. I do not remember the name of the village. I was going to follow her on Friday but on the way I met some Lomwe who took me to Chiradzulu *boma*. I have never seen John Chilembwe and have not heard the war talked about before the 24th January. I lived in Blantyre most of the time. I worked for Mr James for three months and two weeks and left there on Thursday [28th January]. Sometimes I was employed painting, other times making doors and window frames. I worked in the shop. Mr James has my labour ticket. I left my work on Saturday and did not go to work on Monday because other people were not working. I did not go on Tuesday or Wednesday. I am a Christian of Chilembwe. I have no witnesses to prove my statement."[21]

The Magistrate evaluated the statement given by Moses alias Manyanja and came up with the following conclusions:

"The accused stated that he worked for James for three months and two weeks and left on Thursday. He worked for six days and left on Saturday 23rd January as his labour ticket (Ex 1) shows. He denied any knowledge of Chilembwe but the evidence proves that he is a Christian and now he admits it. He does not

---

[20] A letter from D. Njilima, Zomba prison to Robin, 19.2.1915.

[21] A report of case number 9, held in the Magistrate's court at the camp, Zomba on the 7 April, 1915, before Ranald Macdonald, Magistrate.

give a satisfactory account of his movements from the 23rd January. FINDING: Guilty; SENTENCE: Two years hard labour and 16 lashes."[22]

It was a common thing that most of those who were tried denied their involvement in the uprising and connection with the PIM, but later were found guilty. Those who were tried include Tamangisa of Chema, Magomero (case No. 1), Manawira of Chiwewa, Chiradzulu (case No. 2), Allan Morris of Chilembwe village (case No. 3), Stephen of Likangala (case No. 4), Akombo of Chiwewa (case No. 5), Gide of Gomanos (case No. 6), Lait of Chimpesa (case No. 7), Mitete of Mpere (case No. 7a), Garneti Alias Lali of Mwambo in Zomba (case No. 8), Moses Alias Manyanja (case No. 9), Tablu of Somani (case No. 10), Nelson Addison Sosola of Chisau (case No. 11), Steamer of Mtiko (case No. 13), Mikua of Mtiko (case No. 14), Ndakuonani of Kalimanjira (case No. 16), Skotimwayembele Sumbeya of Mtiko (case No. 19), and White of Namaka (case No. 20).[23]

At the time when the uprising was launched, it appears the school was about to open. But with the plan of the uprising, the holiday was extended. This is evidenced in the case of Stephen of Likangala, who left Likangala in Zomba for the school at the PIM. This area of Likangala refers to numerous villages close to Govala in Zomba district, in T/A Mwambo area. Upon his arrival at his friend's village, which was close to the school at PIM, he was told that the school would not open on that particular week. This is what he reports in his defence to the magistrate.

> I left my village at Likangala and went to Chilembwe's to school about the 11th January. I went there because I had friends staying near the school. When I reached there I heard the school would not be opened till the following week, I was not told the reason. I decided to stay on at Chilembwe's until the school started, but the following week I heard that there was war and I ran away. I did not see any signs of war. I run away to *dambo* and stayed there with four other boys and we stayed three days. There were also some women there. At the end of this time, we decided to go to *boma* and we made white flags so that *askari* should not fire at us. I do not know who suggested that we should have white flags. On the way we met two *askari* who took us to the *boma*. I slept in Wallace's house. I did not see meetings of the people nor any men with spears about the village. I ran away on Saturday."

Among those whose cases were heard in court some were released on the basis that they were not involved in the war and had no knowledge of it, and above all, that they were not PIM members. Such individuals include Gide of Gomano's at Namaka, who professed to be a Muslim. Among those who were questioned was a woman, Namitete, of Mpere village. Chilembwe gave a letter

---

[22] Ibid., p. 2.
[23] Those were the people whose accounts of the case were available to me during the time of the research. The information was found in the PIM Pavilion.

to this woman stating that she must lead other women and children to the *boma* while carrying a white flag for their safety. She made the following statement:

> I am the wife of Mpera whom I have not seen for three weeks. My village is on one side of the Nasalani stream and Chilembwe's is on the other side. On Saturday [23rd] and Sunday I remained in my village and everything appeared to be in the usual state. I saw no sign of war but my house is some distance from Chilembwe's. On Monday Chilembwe came to me and said 'because you are a woman and do not know everything you must not go far in the bush'. He gave a letter, which he told me to give to any European that I might meet. He also told me to make a white flag. I gave the letter to one of the Europeans who was with the *askari*."

She, together with other women, was released the following week in response to Wilson Zimba's strong protest against keeping women in custody.

Some who faced trial were those who had less direct links with PIM. These were the likes of David Shirt, a member of the Church of Christ, who claimed to teach Chilembwe's doctrine. Shirt's stance was somewhat confusing, as he identified himself as a follower of John Chilembwe. Possibly he was referring to Chilembwe's ideology. But Shirt seemed to be a member of the Church of Christ. This shows that Chilembwe's teaching influenced the central region in one way or another. In his defense David Shirt, a Ngoni from Kwataine in Ntcheu district, admitted that he was teaching the same creed as did the late John Chilembwe: Christianity from the Bible. It is from this statement that he was imprisoned as he had clearly admitted that he was a follower of Chilembwe's teaching although he was not a baptized member of the PIM. In his second trial in December 1923, Shirt is accused of teaching a doctrine that was dangerous to peace, order and good government. Shirt admitted that he preached the doctrine of the Church of Christ as expounded by Jordan Njirayafa, a disciple of Mr Hollis who was deported after the rebellion of 1915. Being connected to Njirayafa who was imprisoned following the 1915 rising, Shirt was sentenced by Magistrate Cecil Walker to imprisonment on charges that his teaching was dangerous and disapproved of by the government.

PIM in Relation to other Churches 1915-1926

By 1915, a difference between Catholic and Protestant converts had already emerged. The Catholics were not only encouraged in habits of submission, but were also less familiar with the Bible and thus missed exposure to the rich political and religious ideology that fed both the Independent Churches and the Native Associations. This difference was especially evident at the time of the uprising in 1915, when priests received warnings of impending trouble from their catechists and were able to pass on the warnings to the government.

During the rising, the Catholic missions were a special target. The attack on Nguludi led by David Kaduya came around 3:30 in the morning, when the moon had gone down. During the government attempt to capture the PIM, he had defended the mission professionally enough to repulse *boma* troops. Swelsen was caught half asleep on his bed but managed to bludgeon his way through the Chilembwe army only to fall, clubbed to the ground and bleeding profusely from six stab wounds, in the mission cemetery. Fortunately for him, the crowd's attention was diverted by the wounding of Kaduya who was shot in the leg by Sumani, the headman, from a hiding place in the bushes. Kaduya was taken into the half built shell of Nguludi Cathedral where a service with hymns and prayers was held. From this action it be easily deduced that the PIM followers were genuinely convinced that they were fighting a holy war. After the rising the Catholic school spread triumphantly into the old area of the Providence Industrial Mission at Masanjala's, Tembeta's and Maleta's.[24] These areas are within the boundaries of the Bruce Estate.

> Nguludi was burnt down, and an assault on Nzama, the oldest Roman Catholic mission in Ntcheu District, was planned. Nguludi mission, four miles west from PIM headquarters at Mbombwe had been having struggles with the PIM. In 1913 there had been friction over prayer houses. Two hundred members of PIM pleaded to build a prayer house at Nawani village on Bruce's plantation land. The request was refused, but the prayer house was built. Livingstone sacked their leader, Lifeyu, and burnt down the prayer house. It was widely believed that Livingstone had given permission to the Catholics, however this claim is denied.[25] The PIM school was pulled down by order of the District Commissioner after complaints from Catholic catechists about its proximity to a Catholic school. It is said that Chilembwe spoke to the Catholic catechist at Masanjala's who reported back to the school director, Fr Swelsen, that if these incidents continued there would be an exchange of blows.[26]

The uprising affected anyone who had connections with PIM; it even provoked a crisis in Blantyre Synod. Some of the rebels, such as John Gray Kufa Mapantha, were baptized members of the Synod. This aroused a strong suspicion in the British administration and amongst the white settlers that the Blantyre Mission educational policy was subversive. When the Commission of Inquiry was set up to investigate the causes of the rising, Blantyre Mission was among the prime suspects.

Missionaries of other churches such as Cockerill who came as an independent Seventh Day Baptist Missionary 1914, who were made scapegoats for

---

[24] Nguludi Diary, 7 December 1916, MNA.
[25] A. Nielsen, M. Schoffeleers, H. Reijnaerts, *Montfortians in Malawi: Their Spirituality and Pastoral Approach*, Blantyre: CLAIM-Kachere, 1997, p. 139.
[26] Ibid., p. 139.

The Dark Period of PIM Ministry 1915-1926

the Chilembwe rising, were expelled from Malawi in 1915.[27] Joshua Chateka, who had close relations to the PIM Christians in Lilongwe but was a member of the Seventh Day Baptists, was also arrested. He was questioned in Zomba, his eyes were plucked out. He was then released. He died at Chinoko village in T/A Chimutu in Lilongwe district. Sometime before his death he sent his followers to ask Kamuzu, if he was the right person to rule the country. Kamuzu's response to them was "Go and tell him what you see I am doing". Then he advised his followers to accept and follow Kamuzu as their right leader.[28] This statement may back the belief that Chilembwe predicted Kamuzu's leadership.

A few devout followers of PIM met in private houses and conducted religious meetings between 1915 and 1924. These meetings grew in size as many of those imprisoned in the aftermath of the uprising were released. While some were in prison, the PIM members at Mbombwe were still meeting under the leadership of Andrew Mkulichi.[29] Those who registered for baptism he taught basic teachings of the Bible and sent them to Zomba prison where Jordan Njirayafa of the Church of Christ was responsible for baptism, as there was no other minister ordained to baptize. The leaders in prison were Wilson Zimba and Wallace Kampingo.

The meetings at Mbombwe were boldly held during the day: "No one could threaten us, this is the holy city of Africa".[30] In 1921 Andrew Mkulichi, a brother of Stephen Mkulichi, built a grass shelter at PIM, for their gatherings.[31] This move might have been possible since after 1920 the government tacitly accepted PIM congregations, so gathering during the day for PIM members was no longer a threat.

As the colonial government did all it could to suppress PIM, other churches excelled very much in their ministry during this period. The iron sheets from Mbombwe were given by the Nyasaland government to Nguludi Mission in compensation for the damage that had been inflicted by the so called rebels. Father Regent led the procession of the Catholics who went to carry them from the PIM mission site to their own.[32] While this was happening, many PIM members were suffering through imprisonment and executions. The remaining members were made safe through the request of the Foreign Mission Board of the National Baptist Convention of USA Inc to the colonial government.[33] At the subsequent Commission of Inquiry, the two Catholic bishops were more than compensated for being able to state with confidence that no Catholics had

---

[27] K.R. Ross (ed.) *Christianity in Malawi: A Source Book*, Gweru: Mambo-Kachere. 1996, p. 131.
[28] Interview Billiat Kaphaidyani, Mitundu, Lilongwe, 2.5.1999.
[29] Interview Daniel Wasiya, Mbombwe, Chiradzulu, 26.2.99.
[30] Interview Daniel Wasiya, Mbombwe, 26.2.1999.
[31] Interview Herbert Mkulichi, 11.8.1999.
[32] Nielsen A; Schoffeleers M; Reijnaerts H., *Montfortians in Malawi*, p. 43.
[33] Muocha's speech, 26.2.1999.

been involved in this biblically inspired rebellion. Any lingering doubt concerning previous Catholic association with the Portuguese was dissolved and they enjoyed a rather favourable position in the eyes of government and planters, who regarded them as especially knowledgeable about "native opinion". This contributed to the rapid expansion by the Montfort Fathers who descended into the steamy heat of the Shire Valley and opened Chikwawa in 1918, and Nsanje in 1921, bringing Catholicism into the area of the South Africa General Mission.

There was rise of African leadership in churches. This was particularly true between 1915 and 1926 when PIM was in a state of dormancy. In one of his sermons, Dr Harvey, Secretary of the FMB, preached that the colonial government thought they had destroyed the church by dismantling the mission station. It was utter naivety to believe the church was not stronger than the building within which it stood.[34] Dr Harvey's sermon could imply that the church that the colonial government managed to destroy during the period 1915-1926 was the church as an institution and not the church as invisible. This then means that the church as invisible, which is the body of Christ, was still operational hence the secret gatherings. These secret gatherings had their leaders. It would not be wrong to say that during this time leadership skills developed even in PIM itself. People were able to run their own church programmes secretly even in the absence of their leader, John Chilembwe. Possibly this time would be the most difficult time for one to be attributed a leadership position particularly when the church was not legally accepted by the government. However these local leaders were able to run their activities till such a time when the church was officially re-opened. It was this local leadership that took an initiative to approach the government to allow them to worship publicly without interference from the government. This may show how this local leadership was growing within the PIM itself and the African community in general. The African leadership in other churches also developed as a significant number of missionaries of the smaller churches had been deported from the country. It was after this deportation that the African leaders took charge of the mission work. At the time when a handful of these missionaries returned or others were sent out to take charge of the work, the African leaders who had already established a wide personal following resisted this overlordship. One example was Alexander Makwinya, a former Watchtower leader, who had joined the Seventh Day Baptist Church after his release in 1925.

The PIM's ministry of justice brought a positive contribution to the society. The colonial government established a Commission of Inquiry to discover the cause of the rising, so that they become aware of the African grievances. Although there had been efforts from the Africans to highlight their grievances

---

[34] Tape, Dr Harvey's sermon, PIM, March 1999.

to the government, they were never taken seriously until the rising. Therefore it can be concluded that the PIM ministry of justice liberated Africans from some forms of oppression, as the Commission of Inquiry brought in several recommendations that improved treatment of Africans and abolished many abuses. This was probably what Chilembwe meant when he encouraged his followers to bravely engage themselves in the rising not with the intention of winning and becoming kings. But rather their death should carry a message to their oppressors. The PIM pastor was sure that this would no doubt bring change in the future. It was a prophetic statement for the future glory of Malawi. It is no wonder then that during the one party era in Malawi, the Ngwazi, Kamuzu Banda, in some circles was looked at as the man Chilembwe prophesied. One of the songs of the *Mbumba za Kamuzu* portrays this. The song goes like this *John Chilembwe ananena anthu anga musalire adzabwera wina Mtsogoleri*. ("John Chilembwe said 'my people do not cry, there will come another leader.") This very statement was also said by one of Chilembwe's followers who survived the rising, Rev Wylie Pilgrim Chigamba, in an interview with the MBC in 1988. If it was really true that Chilembwe spoke these words, it might have been related to church leadership if one considers the type of audience that he was addressing. Yet on the other hand the very fact that this statement was put in a song in praise of a political figure implied that Chilembwe prophesied about the political leadership that was divinely approved by God.

The rise of African leadership in churches after the rising can also be looked at as a positive contribution of PIM's ministry of justice towards the ecclesiastical independency and development of a remarkably early indigenous liberation theology.

Chapter Eight

PIM's Dawn of Hope

Chilembwe's Foresight for the PIM Land

AT THE TIME WHEN THE RISING WAS TO BE LAUNCHED, CHILEMBWE HAD ALready entrusted the property of the mission to the Foreign Mission Board of the National Baptist Convention of USA Inc. According to the Nyasaland government's record, the Chiradzulu estate of 93 acres was attributed by Crown procedures to John Chilembwe by Deed No. 687 dated the 6th March 1901.[1] By Deed No. 800 dated 18th April 1902, Chilembwe conveyed the estate to the Providence Industrial Mission.[2] The government later used these documents to convince Chilembwe's relations who were claiming legal right to occupy the PIM land. The government's stance was that neither Chilembwe nor his children had any interest in any land in the protectorate.[3] The land at Mbombwe belonged to the church as it was transferred to the Trustees of the Foreign Mission Board of the National Baptist Convention of USA Inc in 1902 and not to individuals. Among the relations who were claiming PIM land was Donald Chilembwe, Chilembwe's son, in 1933. He submitted to the government a letter of inquiry about his late father's estate.[4] Chilembwe's vision for the future PIM helped in safeguarding the PIM land. He totally dedicated the land to the work of God and none of his relations could claim it.

> As early as the 1920s some PIM members expressed an interest in reopening a PIM church. The government did not allow them to put up structures at PIM Mbombwe premises. To the government, the land belonged to the Foreign Missions Board of the National Baptist Convention of USA Inc.

In June 1924, three members of PIM who had been imprisoned and then released expressed an interest in the land to reopen the mission station. They wrote to the government asking permission to worship and gather publicly.

---

[1] An attached document from a magistrate, Chiradzulu Chief Secretary, 18.4.33.
[2] Ibid.
[3] The government arrived at this decision after looking at the title deeds. They showed that the land legally belonged to PIM owned by the Foreign Mission Board of USA Inc.
[4] Document from the Magistrate, Chiradzulu to the Chief Secretary, 18.4.33, PIM Pavilion, Mbombwe, Chiradzulu.

These three people were Andrew Mkulichi, Jackson Chiwayula and Isaac Chambo:

> We humbly beg to forward our petition for his Excellency's consideration and approval, as we are aware that we cannot do anything without his Excellency's consent. We are John Chilembwe's Christians, we have been imprisoned (now released) some killed, others still in prison for life, for what we have done to the government. For reason we have now learned a good lesson, we have to bring all our needs to your notice. The writing of this petition is 1. We want the government to allow us to read our Bibles and preach in the name of Jesus to anyone who comes to us.
>
> We will appreciate and thank the government most highly if this petition will meet with your favourable consideration.
>
> We have the honour to be,
>
> Sir
>
> Your most obedient servants
>
> (Signed) Andrew Mkulichi, Jackson Chiwayula, Isaac Chambo[5]

When this letter was handed to the government, there was a thorough investigation of its authors. The following recommendations were given about them.

> "Jackson seemed to have some common sense, Andrew, I think, should be watched, promptly dealt with if he is found holding meetings or services of any sort. A confessed belief that there is no redemption except by blood, and that John Chilembwe was a prophet martyr, are not sound foundations for a church."[6]

When the three PIM members wrote to the Government, I.M. Lawrence, husband to Ruth Malekebu, Daniel's sister, helped them to communicate with the FMB of NBC Inc in the United States of America. He played a great role in acting as a mediator between the church in Malawi and the FMB. I.M. Lawrence seemed to be a good writer and communicator, very enthusiastic to see the FMB resuming its work in Malawi. In his letter of 20 July 1924 to the FMB, he pleaded that the board had to do something with the PIM church in Malawi. He states:

> Moreover as the three of our leading members were very much moved with the spirit, they risked their lives, and went straight to the Nyasaland Governor to apply for the rebuilding of the ruins, his reply was I am willing to give you back the place, but only it requires your principals to apply and mentioning your names, as to that they have entrusted you with the plot now the very thing that we require is: please write us a guarantee and contract us to open and rebuild the 'Providence Industrial

---

[5] Letter from Andrew Mkulichi, Jackson Chiwayula, Isaac Chambo through the Resident Chiradzulu to the Chief Secretary Zomba, 16.6.1924.
[6] Memorandum to the Chief Secretary, 30.7.1924.

Mission' for your board, and whenever convenient, it will be at your liberty to send us a minister to lead us. Only we can start the work if we receive the guarantee.[7]

PIM members were anxious to reopen their church, but seeking the approval of the FMB was a lengthy process. I.M. Lawrence alluded to this in the same letter "as this place we understood belongs to you, so the Government did not wish to take this place with the very understanding that the principals are in America, and so we wrote you about this same in 1923, but had no confirmation about it."[8] I.M. Lawrence emphasized that the people were willing to start the work at once if only the board would issue them the authority. He tried all the means at his disposal to communicate with the FMB asking for permission, as the natives were eager and ready to do the work by themselves. When the three members approached the Government, they were allowed to build their houses at the site but not the church building, till they consulted the board. In another letter to Dr East through Dr Malekebu while at Risk Institute, in Monrovia, Liberia, I.M. Lawrence wrote:

> I am very pleased to write you this letter, so as to inform you that I have also today written you another letter which I have posted to America to the parent body If you are indeed willing to save us from misery and help us, in sending literature, books etc we are even ready to commence the foundation ourselves at once, as we are now allowed to build our own houses at the mission ground with the exception of the 'HOUSE OF GOD', which we are earnestly asking your permission, so that we can at once erect the said house.[9]

He also wrote to Dr Malekebu while at Risk Institute in Liberia. He persuaded him to communicate with the FMB in the best way he could so that their request could pass. After sending letters to Dr East and Dr Malekebu, he wrote another to Andrew Mkulichi, informing him of the progress he had made so far in dispatching the letters. He also encouraged him to go ahead with the work he had started. He wrote:

> I was very much pleased when I heard you have tried your very best by presenting your petition to the chief secretary to allow you to preach openly, and to which he allowed you with the understanding that, should you require to repair the ruins, then you are to ask for a permission to the

---

[7]   I.M. Lawrence to Dr James E. East, Secretary of the FMB, 20.7.1924.
[8]   Ibid. It seemed that individuals resumed interest in the reopening of the PIM correspondence with the FMB of the NBC of USA Inc immediately through I.M. Lawrence, however it took much time for the FMB to respond to their requests. This might also have contributed to the return of Dr Malekebu when he visited Nyasaland in 1921. The government saw him as a danger to the peace of the country and required approval from the FMB of NBC of USA. After the FMB confirmed to the Nyasaland government, and indeed Malekebu's own effort through the Aborigines' Society, he was cleared and came to Nyasaland. This led to the reopening of PIM in 1926.
[9]   I.M. Lawrence to Dr East through Dr Malekebu, Monrovia, 20.7.1924.

right owners of the plot, and that you have now moved from Chingoli, and are now staying just opposite to where Miss Delany's house was i.e. to the Big rock near the Mbombwe River, to this I am very much pleased to hear, for I have a good faith that, should we succeed, we are all going to rebuild our church for there is nothing hard and impossible with God, who is the author of everything visible and invisible, therefore dear brother don't lose your courage, at any time, should you surely be successful, I am sure that we are all to come and make up our houses at the mission with the understanding that, we are to serve God and not the living individual, which exists today and none tomorrow, so therefore be of courage and faithfully stand to the right, and the lord will reward you openly.[10]

The chief commissioner of Police intercepted all the letters that I.M. Lawrence sent to Mkulichi. He then forwarded them to the Chief Secretary Zomba, as the mail was of interest in view of the application that Andrew Mkulichi and friends had submitted. The Chief Commissioner of Police described in detail I.M. Lawrence and analyzed his life and character. He ended the letter by discouraging the reopening of Providence Industrial Mission. He described I.M. Lawrence as a native of Nyasaland Protectorate who formerly resided in Chiradzulu District, and first came under the notice of the police department in February 1921, when he was found in possession of stolen whiskey and was sentenced to three months imprisonment with Hard Labour at Blantyre. At that time he lived at Mkwaila village, about one and half miles from the site of John Chilembwe's church. After his release, he left the protectorate and proceeded to Chinde where he worked until the time when he moved to Beira and was employed by the Companhia Industrial da Beira. His wife Ruth was a sister of Dr D.S Malekebu, who left Nyasaland when about 16 years of age and proceeded to America where he was educated.

Malekebu returned to Nyasaland in February 1921 on the pretence of visiting his mother who lived at Mkwaila village: But a pamphlet, written by him entitled "A Plea for Africa" found in the Hotel at Chinde clearly indicated that the object of his visit was to resuscitate Chilembwe's old mission. He stayed with his mother and sister at Mkwaila village and left the protectorate again in June 1921 for Liberia and took up missionary work at Monrovia. Since Isa M. Lawrence had been away from the protectorate he carried on voluminous correspondence with his wife who lived at Malabvi hill in Blantyre District, and members of the late Chilembwe's mission, and sent pamphlets and tracts to Andrew Mkulichi. He also corresponded with Dr Malekebu to whom he had been sending begging letters from time to time. He appeared to have spent most of his time in corresponding with various people and was most methodical in the way he numbered and kept copies of all his letters.

---

[10] I.M. Lawrence - Mkulichi, Beira, 20.7.1924.

The Commissioner of Police further described I.M. Lawrence as a hypocrite. Although he pretended to be a good Christian and condemned the teaching of the Watchtower Society, he appeared to lead a double life, as the letters to his wife generally written in English, sometimes contained disgusting expressions. The CP concluded from Lawrence's correspondence with his wife that at one point he was suffering from venereal diseases with which he infected his wife at the time she visited him at Chinde. For a short time he corresponded in a secret cipher, which was found to be a modification of concluded morse code. Lawrence paid a short visit to his wife in May 1924. On his arrival at Port Herald, the Principal Immigration Officer took various letters and literature, including a prohibited publication "The Negro World" from him. From copies of letters from Malekebu to Lawrence it appears that Malekebu was trying to leave Liberia on the grounds of ill heath, but the letters did not indicate that there was any likelihood of his coming to Nyasaland then. As nothing was known against him and as he was a native of Nyasaland, the Police Commissioner presumed that he could not be refused re-admission should he desire to return to Nyasaland. But seeing that he started his education under Chilembwe and was related to his followers, the Commissioner had no doubt that he would do his best to re-establish the Providence Industrial Mission. He therefore advised the government not to allow that move.[11]

The Fruitful Results of the Laymen's Efforts

The efforts of the three PIM members' and I.M. Lawrence to communicate with the FMB eventually reaped results. The FMB responded to their request and wrote to the Government of Nyasaland to allow the PIM Christian natives of Nyasaland to reopen the mission. The letter was signed by FMB Chairman JCA and FMB Secretary JEE itself.

> We, The Foreign Mission Board of The National Baptist Convention, beg first to express our very deep regret for the unfortunate uprising of the natives years ago that led to the destruction of life and property and the closing of the Providence Mission. We have been slow in asking for the reopening of this Station for we had wanted evidence that the workers in connection therewith, would no circumstance breed, abet, or be in any way associated with sedition and rebellion against your Excellency's Government. Many times we had been pleaded with to approach your Excellency for the opening of this Mission Station, but have kept silent. Now that we hear some of the native workers have made advances to your Excellency, and believing they will build and operate and develop a loyal Mission for the betterment of themselves and their neighbours; we beg to advise your Excellency that we have given permission to the believers, who were formerly connected with the Mission, to take posses-

---

[11] Chief Commissioner of Police - Chief Secretary, Zomba, 28.7.1924.

sion of the plot of ground and to reopen the Station. These workers are represented by the following: Jackson Chiwayula, Isaac Chambo, and Andrew G. Nkulichi. We graciously pray that your Excellency will approve of the same. It shall ever be our pleasure to insist that the Mission be conducted peaceably and harmoniously with your Excellency's Government.[12]

Then the FMB issued another letter entitled TO WHOM IT MAY CONCERN, which said

"This is to certify that The Foreign Mission Board of the National Baptist Convention, has given permission to Jackson Chiwayula, Isaac Chambo, and Andrew G. Mkulichi, to act in behalf of the Providence Mission, taking charge of the plot of ground deeded to the above named Board, and reopening The Providence Mission. Done by order of the Board."[13]

On November 28, 1924 the FMB wrote to Andrew Mkulichi, Jackson Chiwayula, and Isaac Chambo notifying them that permission had been granted for them to reopen the Providence Industrial Mission.

Your letter dated September 10th came to hand. We thank God with you that you are permitted to open the Providence Mission. May you go very carefully now for by your previous act the work has been much set back. Many lives have been lost and there has been much suffering by many who are still alive. We have already written letters to the Government requesting them to allow you to reoccupy the mission ground. We will gladly pay the taxes due as soon as we can find out the amount. We arranged to have Rev Malekebu return to you from Liberia as soon as funds are available, he and his wife. We hope that will be in the early part of 1925. May God bless you and the work there.[14]

Revival Meetings

When the PIM leaders were given permission to hold meetings they became very mobile. They conducted public religious meetings in the centres where PIM existed before 1915, at Mulaeje village and Lambulira village in Magomero area. The Chief Commissioner of Police was very quick to note that religious activities of PIM had resumed in some villages. In his report to the Chief Secretary he states

On Sunday last about 100 natives including men, women, youths and children, attended a service conducted by John Lulanga at Mulaeje village, Andrew Mkulichi and Jackson Chiwayula being amongst those present. John Lulanga was connected with the John Chilembwe rising and was convicted for unlawful assembly and sentenced to 10 years I.H.L.

---

[12] FMB - Governor of Nyasaland, 24.1.1924.
[13] The Foreign Mission Board letter 24.10.1924.
[14] FMB to PIM addressed Andrew Mkulichi, Jackson Chiwayula and Isaac Chambo, 28.11.1924.

and 16 lashes. On Sunday, Isaac Chambo held a service at Lambulira village, when about 20 people comprised the congregation. The services appear to be purely of religious nature and consist of singing and prayers.[15]

The Chief Commissioner of Police's concerted efforts to investigate the PIM members could not indicate that he had no knowledge that they had been pemitted to conduct their prayers publicly. However this could have been a way of monitoring their gathering in case they presented any danger to the peace of the country. Several times he reported to the Chief Secretary of Court about the increased religious activities of PIM, on 15 September 1925 reporting that:

> I have the honour to inform you that the leaders of the above sect are continuing their activities. On 27th July 1925, a service was held by John Lulanga at his hut in village Maeje, district Chiradzulu from 6-7 pm. There were 30 men and 20 women present, among those were noticed Andrew Mkulichi, Jackson Chiwayula and Isaac Chambo. On 4 August 1925 a service was held at Chingoli village by Andrew Mkulichi and continued from 8 pm to 7 am on 5th August 1925. The congregation consisted of 74 men and women, some coming from 11 miles away to attend. I have suggested to the Resident Chiradzulu that in view of the increased activities of the leaders contrary to orders, proceedings should be instituted against them.[16]

The Coming of Dr and Mrs Malekebu (Missionaries to their own People)

While services were conducted in various places and villages, communication with the FMB was ongoing. The man behind this was I.M. Lawrence, who received instruction from Dr Malekebu and passed it on to the church and the leaders. He informed them that Dr Malekebu would come shortly and preparations for his coming had to start. He further instructed the leaders and the church that Dr Malekebu expected to find the following things when he came: A house built at PIM, six table chairs, three easy chairs, one table, and a garden planted with all kinds of edible relish. He further instructed that the hammock (*machila*) was to be in good order.[17]

---

[15] Chief Commissioner of Police - Chief Secretary, 16.1.1925.
[16] Chief Commissioner of Police and Chief Inspector of Prisons - Chief Secretary, 15.9.1925.
[17] I.M. Lawrence to Andrew Mkulichi and the PIM church, Beira, 7.10.25. Since the following people were issued with copies of the letter, which was addressed to the church, they were probably prominent leaders of the church: Andrew Mkulichi, Isaac Chambo, Jackson Chiwayula, Elmo Mtipasonjo, Amos Melo, John Lulanga, Miss Kapingo (Deaconess), Josquam Kaojole and Wilfred Mtambo.

At long last the people's prayers and wishes were finally fulfilled with the coming of Dr and Mrs Malekebu. In the autumn of 1925 they sailed from Liberia to the United States for a brief leave. Then they left the States for Africa. They arrived in Malawi 3 February 1926. The following day, immigration and customs having this time been swiftly and successfully cleared, the Malekebu's train was met at Mikolongwe, south of Blantyre, by hundreds upon hundreds of people with a hammock (*machila*) to carry them to the Providence Industrial Mission in Chiradzulu. Mrs Malekebu noted, "Conditions have changed greatly since we were here in 1920; we have been cordially received and happily welcomed by the Nyasaland Government, as well as the people themselves."[18]

Malekebu was born probably in 1890; on his grandfather's side there were three brothers and one sister. Chief Chambo was the oldest, a Yao of the Ambewe clan, a great hunter, a warrior and a slave trader in east and central Africa. He died of a snakebite received while hunting. Malekebu recalls "My mother told me that he was a very handsome man, women went crazy over him. For this reason some jealous women bewitched him in this way and he died."[19] On his grandmother's side there were three sisters and one brother. Chief Chambo married Akwatongolaga, Malekebu's grandmother, who was sometimes called 'Lisoka' the spirit. She was a Yao of the Amilasi clan, which boasts of having been the greatest warriors, because they were the ones that made and held war mascots.

In chief Chambo's family there were four girls and two boys. Malekebu's mother was the second child. Concerning his family, Malekebu said:

> In my family, the first child was a boy, died while young, I never saw him. I was the second. We were then four boys and four girls. Now coming to myself. I was born on the southeastern side of Mulanje mountain, the year and date is not known because our people did not know how to write, what they did was to count time and years by how many moons they stayed at a place or by seasons."[20]

Malekebu, himself a member of PIM, who went to the USA in 1905 for an education, recalls his conversion story.

> In 1903, I was converted and accepted Christ as my saviour. When the news that I was to be baptized reached my people, they came in from the village in large numbers to get me away from the mission. It happened that my sister was now on the mission with Miss DeLany and both of us were to be baptized on the same day. Our people came to get us away saying we must not follow the customs of the Europeans. But we refused.

---

[18] Daniel Malekebu, "My Life and My Work", 1940.
[19] Ibid., pp. 4-5.
[20] Ibid., p. 1. "Southeastern of Mulanje side" referred to by Malekebu is probably Mozambique: Malekebu himself did not explain exactly where. However his parents moved from that place and settled at Mkwaila village in Chiradzulu. Malekebu attended school at PIM Mbombwe.from this village.

They said if you do not obey us, we shall not give you anything to eat. On Sunday morning March 1, 1903, we were baptized by Rev L.N. Cheek, then the missionary of Central Africa. True to their word, our people did not give us food. The missionary was not able to feed us, but she did the best she could for us. We stayed on nevertheless eating field mice and locusts and trusting on the Lord..[21]

It is from this background of Christianity that Malekebu eventually took over responsibility of the church after his predecessor Rev John Chilembwe. The efforts he put in studying was planting the seed of the future church's leadership. After his training, fully equipped as a Baptist pastor, Malekebu returned to his homeland with his wife Flora Zeto, also an African (from Zaire) brought up in America. Malekebu himself wrote that in the year 1926 Mrs Malekebu and her husband sailed from the USA for the purpose of reopening the Station. Arriving in Nyasaland 3 February 1926, they found the mission had grown into bush, and wild animals had taken possession of the place. Witchdoctors had made it a place for hiding their medicine, horns and charms. It was a weird and fearful place. Their services were held under a *thundu* tree. On June 3, 1926, they started clearing up the place and getting ready for building, killing many large snakes, deer, leopards, hyenas and other wild beasts. They started putting up one building after another. A few Former members of the church who were scattered began to come in one by one.[22]

The New Jerusalem Baptist Temple

By 1929 the mission was well established. In early June, Mr Richard Paterson, an educationist from the Church of Scotland Mission at Blantyre, laid the cornerstone for an ambitiously conceived brick church. The involvement of the members of other churches in laying the foundation might show how the church freely mixed with people of other denominations. The first foundations of the church were demolished at the suggestion of women who saw that the first foundations were too small to accommodate their future children. The women had a vision of the growing church. Their suggestion was accepted and a new foundation was laid.[23] This may also show that the church was able to listen to the voice of women in the church. In this case the women had a say in the church and were capable of making constructive decisions. It was their church: they were not spectators but rather contributors to the propagation of the gospel of Christ. Their vision for a growing church was even better than that of the men. At the same time, the men were able to listen to the women and treated them as fellow servants of Christ: their equals in the spread of the

---

[21] Ibid., pp. 4-5.
[22] Daniel Malekebu, "My Vision", p. 3.
[23] Interview Mrs Chilumpha, PIM, Mbombwe, August 2000.

gospel. Today New Jerusalem alone has over two thousand members, which are accommodated in this church.

It appears that for some time, overtures had been made to the PIM with a view to it joining the Federation of Protestant Missions. Dr Malekebu had received permission from the Foreign Mission Board to apply for membership, and in that same month June 1929, he did so. The Dutch Reformed Church Mission objected strenuously, however, on grounds that are unclear but possessed suspiciously racial overtones. In the event the PIM application was not acted upon, ostensibly because the FMB of the National Baptist Convention objected both to the generally accepted practice of delimiting mission fields, and to the length of the probationary periods established by the Protestants for candidates waiting for baptism.

Highlighting this early period of PIM's dawn of hope was the completion and dedication of the church in September 1933. Over four years had passed since the cornerstone had been laid. Very little financial support for the building's construction had been forthcoming from the Board. The Board was probably in financial hardship due the USA being in deep economic depression after 1929. This affected the black community greatly, and surely did not spare the FMB. When the time came for the roof to be put in place, Dr Malekebu prevailed upon a local trading company, Mandala, to provide corrugated iron sheets on credit. About four hundred church members made the thirty kilometres round trip to Blantyre on foot, triumphantly carrying the iron roofing on their heads.

The New Jerusalem Baptist Temple at Mbombwe PIM built 1928-1933

Completion of the church, replacing the equally impressive structure destroyed by Government order almost twenty years previously, served to confirm symbolically the reconstitution of the mission. Dr Malekebu emphasized this fact in a joyful mood:

> To us in Africa the building is a dream and a wonderful piece of work ... what makes it great, is when we think it was conceived, planned, by Africans; built by Africans, built almost entirely by the poor people's money. But the love of Christ constrains them. This is great.[24]

Rev Ernest Gray of the neighbouring Church of Christ Mission conducted the dedication service, held on 10 September to coincide with the National Baptist Convention's annual conference in the United States. A large congregation of the thousands assembled for the occasion, some having come over a hundred kilometres on foot from outlying PIM branches. A solo of 'The Holy City' sung by Mrs Malekebu followed Gray's 'powerful' sermon. The singing moved the great congregation and made a fitting climax. Writing at the time Dr Malekebu took note of both African and European reactions to the church. Many of the PIM's older members were quoted as saying that "If I could only live long enough to go into this church I would say I have lived my days and now I am ready to go". Recalling a conversation with "a good European friend of ours" some years previously, Malekebu quoted him as remarking "when this church is finished, I will never say again that the Africans cannot do anything by themselves."[25] Malekebu also emphasized the fact that virtually all of Nyasaland's many tribes were represented at the various ceremonies held in conjunction with the dedication. Prayers were made and songs were sung in many tongues including Negro melodies taught by Mrs Malekebu to the school children, which they sung beautifully.

Seven years after its reopening, the mission was very much a going concern of education and evangelization. The work for which Dr Malekebu had been most highly trained—medicine and the provision of health services—tended to lag behind. There were several reasons for this but especially the innate conservatism of the people, which made them loath to seek out the Doctor for his professional services. As he describes the situation,

> In those days, particularly women were very sensitive. They were shy. They would not want me to come to help them. They would not want my services because of our custom about the mid wife, you see. But what opened up the way was this. Sometimes they had difficulty, the midwife in delivering. And they said then, oh yes, we have heard there is a doctor who might help you. But they would not come in daylight to me. They would come at night to tell me such and such a woman is sick. That I must get up from my bed and walk that distance and deliver her and

---

[24] Daniel Malekebu, "My Life and my Work", 1940.
[25] Ibid.

when she is delivered, then the next one who is in trouble also just like this one; they say to her, such and such a woman was in difficulty and the doctor helped her. Now we are going to call him. And that opened up the way, so much so that the hospital was crowded.[26]

The hospital was crowded and, although well built, clean and well ventilated, it suffered from a shortage of drugs. The Mission's members could by their labour construct schools, dormitories, a hospital building and provide them with simple furnishings but medical supplies required cash. Again the problem arose in retaining the services of those young men and women he trained as nurses and medical orderlies. As for the nurses, they could help, they were very useful, but the trouble, was these girls after training, they looked so nice, and such a way, that they wouldn't let me keep them long. Boys, you know. They came all the way from Blantyre; to see our girls. Constantly came and constantly going. Proposing marriage first this one, then that one. Now as for the boys, yes, I trained quite a number of boys. Some of them served well for a time, but then perhaps they would get an inducement, a rise in pay, to leave. And then very naturally perhaps, somebody would get them. Well I am losing him. I've got to start again. But that's a difficult thing.[27]

Throughout this period both Dr and particularly Mrs Malekebu were subject to bouts of ill heath. Dr Malekebu, although a most vigorous and active man, was approaching 50 years of age. The lack of any form of transport at the mission made for exhausting work. Commencing in the late 1920s, the letters sent regularly to the headquarters of the FMB in Philadelphia by both the Malekebus included requests for assistance or home leave. Though apparently sympathetic up to a point, as these often explicit letters were published in the Board's monthly periodical, the Mission Herald, neither request was granted. Presumably the funds required were simply not available. Though their salaries were sent promptly, as was the personal medication and the eyeglasses that they requested, the Malekebus served unassisted and unrelieved for over twelve years until at long last they were recalled to the States in the spring of 1938.

Still, until their departure for the United States on leave in May 1938, the Malekebus continued to consolidate and expand their Christian community. While the focus, lacking qualified assistants, inevitably remained upon the headquarters at Mbombwe, small outposts of the mission mushroomed throughout the country as well as across its borders in Mozambique and Zimbabwe. Annually Dr Malekebu would personally tour these outstations. Conversely, representatives of villages and larger communities would visit Mbombwe seeking the mission's presence. Dr Malekebu relates several examples of this:

---

[26] Ibid.
[27] Ibid.

> I was deeply touched one day when a chief came in from behind Mulanje Mountain. He said 'I have come to ask you bambo [Sir] to build a church in my country. I did not want to send these men [a four man delegation] alone because I was afraid you will not hear [believe] them. I did not want to write because you might take too long to do this.' These calls come from many others saying the same thing. ... A delegation came and is here now from a northern province. [Northern region]—one month journey, saying 'come the people are calling and are waiting to be baptised.' In Transvaal which we just left, the cry comes, come back, the people are waiting on you.[28]

During the early period of the PIM dawn of hope, the church was very active and experienced rapid growth in terms of its influence and expansion. Travel was often arduous as it was mostly done on foot. Sometimes there was the opportunity to use lorries, but even with these many kilometres would have to be covered on foot.

> Many people were converted and baptised through our preaching. The growth and expansion of the work was wonderful. Churches and prayer houses were built throughout Nyasaland, B.E. Africa. In 1934, I made my first visit into Southern Rhodesia. The atmosphere here was not very cordial at first, but when the officials got information from Nyasaland government about me, things took on a big change for the better. Today the government in Southern Rhodesia thinks well of our work and we are going in a very big way there. As a minister of the gospel, I was alone from 1926 to 1938, preaching and baptising many people, as many as 150 to 300 people per day. At the end of 1938, I had baptised 17 000 souls. Our work extends all over Nyasaland going up to Tanganyika Territory into Northern Rhodesia, Southern Rhodesia, Union of South Africa and Portuguese East Africa. Embracing many, many tribes of East, Central and South Africa into one big Christian family.[29]

---

[28] Ibid.
[29] Daniel Malekebu, "My Vision", p. 5.

Conclusion

It is in the exploration of its historical reality that one begins to appreciate PIM's contribution to the church history of Malawi. Just like any of the other churches that existed during the period discussed in this book, PIM provided for both the spiritual and social needs of the people. There is a clear connection between the existence of PIM and the radical Baptist preacher Joseph Booth. He influenced Nyasaland native John Chilembwe and promoted him to attain higher education by introducing him to the Foreign Mission Board of the National Baptist Convention of the USA Inc. It is this kind of interaction between Booth and Chilembwe that finally acted as a catalyst for the events that helped the latter realize his dream and establish a church that was run in almost the same way as the white man's.

Chilembwe attributed his presence in the United States of America to God and not to Booth. Several times he acknowledged that it was God's divine plan for the people of Africa to receive the light. He became a missionary to his own people and country. His successor Dr Daniel Malekebu continued his legacy and vision for the people of Africa. Several times he wrote 'My desire and my impression was greatly deepened to go to America to study to be a preacher and a doctor to help my people'. A common attribute of these PIM pastors was their concern for the welfare of the people of Africa both spiritually and socially. Throughout the period covered in this book, the PIM endeavoured to work very hard to improve society's standards in these spheres. The church built schools and a hospital, and opened farms as part of its call to ministry. It provided much needed help both to the surrounding communities and to the communities at large. Wherever the church existed, people felt its presence and most of them participated in its activities at the local branches and at headquarters. The inclusion of local leaders from the outstations into the executive committee at the mission made the church break the unstated tradition that such responsibilities were only for the whites or the educated. However this can better be understood if one compares it with how other churches were operating at the time.

Despite the fact that at times the church was struggling financially, it still carried its call to ministry. It also addressed the social evils of the society at that particular time. This led to the death of many PIM followers including its first pastor Rev John Chilembwe in 1915. Chilembwe's political views seemed to be radical as he was convinced that Africans and Europeans were equal not only in the eyes of God, but also in real life. He alluded to this concept in response to Caldwell, concerning the Ham and Japheth passage. In the same way, his successor Malekebu described Africans as "diamonds in the rough." He believed that if an African were given an equal opportunity to that of the white man, he would easily develop and hold better positions in society.

The church's vision of the liberation in various sectors of life was in some ways realized after the rising of 1915. Although the rising could be seen as a failure, it still contributed to liberation in various ways. It contributed to the rise of African leadership as the deportation of some missionaries following the rising gave the opportunity of leadership roles to Africans. The rising initiated by PIM liberated those people who had the potential to serve in their respective churches but had no opportunity of doing so. Despite their low level of education, the Africans were able to participate in church positions, which were normally regarded as roles for whites or the educated. The memory of the rising can be seen as a potent factor in the evolution of the nationalist consciousness, which finally resulted in independence for Malawi in 1964. Therefore the PIM pastor who emerged as the harbinger of political independence for Malawi was recognized in the first years of the Second Republic of Malawi when Chilembwe Day (15 January) was gazetted as a public holiday. Furthermore, his portrait is used on Malawian bank notes. The PIM can therefore be considered an outstanding example of the connection between ecclesiastical independency and political nationalism. From PIM's ministry of justice, one can see how the PIM leadership drew political conclusions from their Christian faith and developed a remarkably indigenous liberation theology.

Throughout the period of 1900 to 1940, the church developed tremendously in its spiritual and social activities. It experienced growth both in membership and geographical spheres. Despite problems, the church succeeded in building up a Christian community wherever it existed.

BIBLIOGRAPHY

A. Primary Sources

Oral Informants

Binali, C.L., Chiradzulu, February 1999.
Chamba, Brown, Mambala Farm, Thyolo, February 1999.
Chibwana, B.G. (Rev), Milepa, Chiradzulu, February 1999.
Chikuni, D.B. (Rev), PIM, Chiradzulu, August 2000.
Chikwengwe, C.J. (Rev), Mt Cleveland Ohio Baptist Church, Migowi, 14 August 1994.
Chilunda, Molle, Malindi village, Chiradzulu, August 2000.
Chilumpha, (Mrs), Mitete village, Mpama, Chiradzulu, 14 August 2000, 23 March 2001.
Chitseko, Ellen, Nyungwi, Chiradzulu west, April 1996.
Chipungu, C., Mphanda, Lilongwe, 15 December 1998.
Dini, (Mr), Mulanje, August 2000.
Elefe, (Miss), Nandolo village, Migowi, March 2001.
Garinet, (Mrs), Village Headwoman, Garinet village, Migowi, 14 August 1994.
Gawani, Esime, St Paul Baptist Church, Mphatama village, Zomba, August 2000.
Goodson, Justin, Mambala farm, Thyolo, 10 December 1998.
Kadangwe, S., Sikita village, T/A Nkhumba, 28 March 2001.
Kaduya,, Sub T/A, Kaduya village, Migowi, Phalombe, 30 March 2001.
Kachulu, Alena J, Chingoli village, Chiradzulu, 26 February 1999.
Kafadala, M. (Rev), Lilongwe, 4 May 1999.
Kafulatira, H., Mitundu, Lilongwe, 3 May 1999.
Kamchotseni, W.D. (Rev), PIM, Mbombwe, Chiradzulu, February 1999.
Kampingo, W., Mbombwe, Chiradzulu, February 1999.
Kaphaidyani, Billiat, Mitundu, Lilongwe, 3 May 1999.
Kaunde, Mellissa, Matapila, Lilongwe, January 2001.
Kaunde, Velina (Mrs), Matapila, Lilongwe, January 2001.
Kaunde, Feliat, Matapila, Lilongwe, January 2001.
Komiha, D.B., PIM, Mbombwe, Chiradzulu, August 2000.
Likungwa, Esnala, Mambala farm, Thyolo, 12 December 2001.
Magombo, Effe, Namulu village, Chiradzulu, 23 March 2001.
Makondesa, F. (Rev), Chiringa, Phalombe, December 2000.
Maneya, G. (Rev), PIM, Chiradzulu, February 1999.
Mandala, B.G. (Rev), Zomba, February 1999.
Mandeule, James, Garinet village, Migowi, 10 October 1994.
Mandeule, Sandras, Garinet village, Migowi, 10 October 1994.
Masuku, Gese, Mambala farm, Thyolo, 11 December 1998.
Maulidi, Lydia, Gona village, Migowi, August 1994.

Mkulichi, Herbert, Mitete village, Chiradzulu, February 1999.
Mawaya, R.G., Thyolo, February 1999.
Mityala, Emma, Mtipasanjo village, Mpama, Chiradzulu, March 2001.
Mononga,, Namuthokoni village, Mpama, Chiradzulu, 24 March 2001, 19 March 2001.
Mpeleya, Saidi, Mambala farm, Thyolo, 9 December 1998.
Mulinga, T. (Mrs), Namuhe village, Thumbwe, Chiradzulu, March 2001.
Mugwa, L. (Mrs), Gona village, Migowi, August 1994.
Mugwa, Lucy Naluso, Gona village, Migowi, August 1994.
Muocha, L.C. (Rev), Chairman emeritus, Nyungwe, CZ, 14 Dec 1996, 12 Apr 1996, Aug 1998.
Nakoma, Mebo (Mrs), Mambala farm, Thyolo, 9 December 1998.
Namakhwa, Mabuka village, Mulanje, 23 March 2001.
Nandolo, (Rev), Mozambique, February 1999.
Palasa, Kaduya village, Migowi, 14 Aug 1994, 13 Oct 1994, 14 Oct 1996.
Phiri, Faransia, Chiawelo, Soweto, Republic of South Africa, December 1997, 7 Feb 1998.
Saidi, Stephen, Mambala farm, Thyolo, 12 December 1998.
Sakhula, Lilongwe, 3 May 1999.
Salewa, (gogo), Nandolo village, Migowi, 14 August 1994, 14 October 1996.
Siyamanda, Elefe, Nandolo village, Migowi, 22 March 2001.
Wallani, Fredrick, Wallani village, Mwambo, Zomba, August 2000.
Wallani, Nkhondo, Wallani village, Mwambo, Zomba, 14 August 2000, March 2001.
Wasiya, G, Chiradzulu, 26 February 1999, August 2000.

Papers

Dambo, E., "Sectarianism in the Providence Industrial Mission: An Assessment of Background Causes", Seminar paper, Chancellor College, Zomba, 1980/81.
Macdonald, Rodreck J., "The Rev Dr Daniel Sharpe Malekebu and the Reopening of Providence Industrial Mission 1926-1939: An Appreciation', 1975.
Makondesa, Patrick, "The Life and Ministry of Rev and Mrs Muocha of the Providence Industrial Mission", BEd Dissertation, University of Malawi, 1996.
Parrat, John K., "Mbombwe: Dr Daniel Malekebu and the Second Era of the Providence Industrial Mission", History seminar paper, Chancellor College, Zomba, 1984-1985

Articles

Malekebu, Daniel, "My Life and My Work", 1940
Malekebu, Daniel, "A Plea for Africans", 1918
Malekebu, Daniel, "My Vision: East, Central and Southern Africa Today", 1951
Mwase, G., *Strike a Blow and Die*, ed. Robert I. Rotberg, Cambridge: Harvard University Press, 1967.
Pachai, Bridglal, "Assessment of events leading to the Nyasaland Rising of 1915", in Gordon W. Smith, Bridglal Pachai and Roger K. Tangri (eds), *Malawi Past and Present*, Blantyre: CLAIM, 1971.
Shepperson, George, "The Place of John Chilembwe in Malawi Historiography", in Bridglal Pachai (eds), *The Early History of Malawi*, London: Longman 1972.

BIBLIOGRAPHY

Documents

Compiled list of cases of the captured Chilembwe supporters of the 1915 Native rising.
File containing educational correspondence between the department of education and the PIM School 1926-1928.
List of the baptized member believers of the First African Baptist Church as of November 1914.
Hardcover containing names of baptized members of PIM from 1926 in Malekebu's own handwriting.
Native Rebellion – Revised list of Natives wanted.
Poster of the early missionaries of PIM.
Poster showing Malekebu's activities prepared by the FMB of the NBC of USA Inc.

Tapes

Tape recording, Dr Harvey's sermon, March 1999.
Tape interview, Rev Wylie Pilgrim Chigamba, MBC Martyrs Day Programme, 1988.
Tape recording, Rev Muocha's speech, March 1999.
Tape recording, Mrs Carolyn McDonald speech, Chilembwe Day Celebration, January 1995.
Tape recording, Dr Bakili Muluzi (President), Address, Chilembwe Day, PIM Pavilion. 1995.
Tape, Dr Walker's Sermon, Chairman Emeritus of the FMB of the NBC, USA, Inc. 2000.

Letters

Acting Chief Secretary to Acting Intelligence Officer, Kings African Rifles, dated 29 July 1919.
Acting Chief Secretary to the Government to Secretary for Native Affairs, Salisbury, 24 November 1936.
Acting Provincial Commissioner Lilongwe, to the Honourable Chief Secretary, Zomba, titled 'Native churches and religious propaganda', dated 18 October, 1923.
Acting Provincial Commissioner to the Chief Secretary, dated December 14, 1923
Attorney General to Right Rev the Bishop of Nyasaland, Universities Mission to Central Africa, Likoma, dated 18 December 1918
Casson, J.C., to the Chief Secretary, dated, 22 April, 1915
Chief Commissioner of Police and Chief Inspector of Prisons Headquarters to the Chief Secretary, Zomba addressing the resumed religious activities of the PIM, dated 16 January 1925
Chief Commissioner of Police and Chief Inspector of Prisons headquarters to the Chief Secretary, Zomba reporting on further activities of PIM members, dated, 15 September, 1925
Chief Commissioner of Police to Chief Secretary, 24.11.36
Chief Commissioner of Police to Chief Secretary, 31 7.1924
Chief Commissioner of Police to the Chief Secretary, 28.7.1924
Chief Secretary Nyasaland to Secretary for Native Affairs, Salisbury, 11 2 1937
Chilembwe to H.E. Peters Mlelemba, 05.7.1909
Chilembwe to H.E. Peters Mlelemba, 13.11.1910

Chilembwe to H.E. Peters Mlelemba, 24.4.1912
Chilembwe to H.E. Peters Mlelemba, 26.3.1914
Chilembwe to the Resident, Chiradzulu, 12.01.1914
FMB to Andrew Mkulichi, Jackson Chiwayula, Isaac Chambo, November 28, 1924
FMB to the Nyasaland government requesting the opening of the PIM, 24 October 1924
FMB, notification letter regarding the authorization of Isaac Chambo, Andrew Mkulichi, Jackson Chiwayula in reopening of PIM, dated 30.7.1924
Head Capitao Lilongwe to the Chief Commissioner, dated November 15, 1922
Intelligence Officer, Kings African Rifles, Zomba to Nairobi, inquiring about Chilembwe man Yortam Bango who walked to Tunduru to deliver Chilembwe's letter to German authorities and was caught on his way back, dated 20 February 1919. (secret copy)
Lands Officer to Chief Secretary, 10 January, 1925
Lawrence, I.M., Beira, to A.G. Mkulichi, Chiradzulu, dated 20 July 1924
Lawrence, I.M., Beira, to Dr Jas. E. East, Monrovia, 20 July 1924
Lawrence, I.M., Beira, to Dr Jas. E. East, Philadelphia, 20 July 1924
Lawrence, I.M., Beira, to Dr Malekebu, Liberia, dated 20 July 1924
Lawrence, I.M., to Providence Industrial Mission members, 8th October 1925
Magistrate A.M. Tomball, Zomba Camp to the Secretary, Zomba, dated 2 March 1915
Magistrate Ntcheu to the Chief Secretary Zomba, dated 11 December 1923
Memorandum on Natives interested in the reopening of PIM, dated, 30.07.1924
Mkulichi, Andrew, Jackson Chiwayula, Isaac Chambo to the Chief Secretary, 16 June 1924
Moggridge, C.E., Major, to the Intelligence Officer, Kings African Rifles, dated Nairobi, 20 February 1919
Njilima, Duncan, Zomba Prison to his nephew Robin, dated 19 February 1915
Panum, M. (Lawrence) to Mkulichi, Beira, 7 October 1925
Provincial Commissioner, Southern Province to Chief Secretary, 31 July 1924
Resident Ntcheu to the Acting Chief Secretary, Zomba, dated, 14 October, 1923
Resident Ntcheu to the Chief Secretary, Zomba through the Provincial Commissioner, Lilongwe, date not visible
Secretary for Native Affairs, Salisbury to Chief Secretary, Nyasaland, 15 January 1937
Secretary for Native Affairs, Salisbury, Southern Rhodesia to the Chief Secretary to the Government, the Secretariat, Zomba, inquiring a Native preacher who went their as PIM member, 6 November 1936

B. Secondary Sources

Banda, Kelvin N., *A Brief History of Education in Malawi*, Blantyre: Dzuka, 1982.
Berkhof, Louis, *Systematic Theology*, London: Cox and Wyman, 1976.
Boff, C. and Pixley G.V., *The Bible, the Church, and the Poor*, New York: Burns and Oates/Search, 1989.
Boff, C. and Boff L., *Salvation and Liberation: In Search of a Balance between Faith and Politics*, New York: Burns and Oates/Search, 1989.
Chakanza, J.C. and Ross, K.R., (ed), *Religion in Malawi: An Annotated Bibliography*, A Kachere Text, Blantyre: CLAIM, 1998.
Gibson, Alan F., *The Church and its Unity*, England: Intervarsity, 1992.

Kritzinger, J.J., Meiring, P.G.J. and Saayman WA., *On Being Witness*, Johannesburg: Orion, 1994.
Kritzinger, J.J., *The South African Context for Mission*, Cape Town: Lux Verbi, 1988.
Makondesa, Patrick, *Moyo ndi Utumiki wa Mbusa ndi Mayi Muocha a Providence Industrial Mission*, Mvunguti Book, Blantyre: CLAIM-Kachere, 2000.
Moltmann, J., *The Crucified God*, London: SCM, 1974.
Paas, Steven, *Digging out the Ancestral Church: Researching and Communicating Church History*, Blantyre: CLAIM, 2000.
Phiri, D.D., *Let us Die for Africa: An African Perspective on the Life and Death of John Chilembwe of Nyasaland/Malawi*, Blantyre: Central Africana, 1999.
Phiri, D.D., *Malawians to Remember. John Chilembwe*, London: Longman, 1976.
Phiri, D.D., *The Rev John Chilembwe*, London: Longman, 1976.
Reijnaerts, H., A. Nielsen and M. Schoffeleers, *Montfortians in Malawi: Their Spirituality and Pastoral Approach*, A Kachere Text, Blantyre: CLAIM-Kachere 1997.
Ross, K.R. (ed), *Christianity in Malawi: A Source Book*, Gweru: Mambo-Kachere 1996.
Ross, K.R. (ed), *Church, University and Theological Education in Malawi*, Zomba-Kachere, 1995.
Scot, Charis A.F., *The Story of Malindi Mission near Mangochi in Malawi (Nyasaland) 1898-1998*, Blantyre: Montfort, 1998.
Shepperson, G. and T. Price, *Independent African: John Chilembwe and the Nyasaland Rising of 1915*, Blantyre: CLAIM, 2000.
Weller, J. and J. Linden, *Mainstream Christianity to 1980 in Malawi, Zambia and Zimbabwe*, Gweru: Mambo, 1984.

Appendices

Appendix 1: Letters

A letter from Rev John Chilembwe to Mr H.E. Peters encouraging him to keep on informing others about the Native Industrial Mission, dated 5.7.1909

PROVIDENCE INDUSTRIAL MISSION,
CHIRADZULU,
BLANTYRE.
5/7/09.

Mr H.E. Peters,
Blantyre,

Dear Bro:—

Thanks for your letter, but there are another reason which could be mentioned, if one had time. And I want to remind you, that you must stand as a man, and be not discouraged or be coward enough, but stand in God's His own will. Please don't you be tired to preach the gospel of Native, Industrial, Union to every Christian man and to every Christian woman. You can reach them by writing to them, and telling necessity of being a member, of the said Union. I think the future of the Christian is very largely depends on true understanding that when Christian joine with Christian, and are brought in continuous contact with men of intellectual and spiritual strength; it will benifite both part. Should also enterpert the meaning of the great intercessory prayer, in the same literal

P. t. o.

A letter from Rev John Chilembwe to Mr H.E. Peters notifying him that his letter have been forwarded to the FMB about the balance of the £84.10 debt that he owed him, dated, 13.11.1910.

P. I. Mission
Chiradzulo
13/11/1910

My Dear Bro-

I thank you very much for kind and thoughtful letter. Indeed you are quite right in all, I am sending this very your letter to Dr. Jordan for the balance of £84.10. I hope you will be quite sure to wait, I know next December was our agreement and it will not go beyond that, but the time of your grace is needed you had been so good in the beginning toward this first African Church, and I hope you will be the same to the end. You understand me that it is motto in my heart to live honestly before God and my fellow countrymen, I shall be very happy when you shall get all your money in your hands. Yes I had returned from my Hunting trip nothing successful to please men, but I have done a great work in preaching the words of God to our poor people until the Portuguese thought to lay hand on me, but they failed.
I know this is the work I was born for.
God bless you.

Yours sincerely,
John Chilembwe

A letter from Rev John Chilembwe to Peters, emphasizing his call to gospel ministry, dated 24.04.1912

(2)

And the remainder I am sending and I shall pay you only give me time. May Lord, I Value and if you not Value you I am not responsible. I have the balance of £23 of you. Please find enclosed £1. leaving £22. Pray for me that I may not fail. for the Money in my heart I value nothing for I have weighed the world and its riches and find nothing. Comparing the love I got for my people and our God. And as for you my dear friend I owed a great thanks I shall never forgot the kindness you showed me in this world and in the world yet to come. I shall be very please when I shall pay the amount. Remember there was good words the prospect of help from that you you said I remain in prayer that God may raise some friends to loose me the chain prepared for my neck. God bless you! Bleave me

I am yours for ever,
John Chilembwe.

A letter from Andrew Mkulichi I, Jackson Chiwayula, Isaac Chambo addressed to the Honourable, Chief Secretary, Zomba asking for permission to hold their services publicly, dated 16th June, 1924

Conf Series
22
1924

Chiradzulo
16th June, 1924

Sir,

We humbly beg to forward our petition for His Excellency's consideration and approval as we are aware that we cannot do anything without His Excellency's consent.

We are John Chilembwe's Christians, we have been imprisoned (now released) some killed and others still imprison for life, for what we have done to Government. For this reason we have now learned a good lesson, we have to bring all our needs to your notice.

The writing of this petition is:—

1. We want the Government to allow us to read our Bibles and preach in the name of Jesus to anyone who comes to us.

We will appreciate and thank the Government most highly if this petition will meet with your favourable consideration.

We have the honour to be,
Sir,
Your most obedient Servants,
Andrew Mkulichi
Jackson Chiwayula
Isaac Chambo

Honourable,
Chief Secretary,
Zomba.

go The Resident, Chiradzulu.

A memorandum giving comments on the Natives who had interest in the reopening of the PIM, dated 30.07.1924

Memorandum. Conf Series 22/1924

saw these natives with Mr Jennings at Chiradzulu on July 12th. Andrew Mkhulichi is a nephew of John Chilembwe's whom he appears to regard as a great teacher. I could not find that their professed doctrines differed from those of the Baptist Missions in the country and they agreed that there was no doctrinal bar to their becoming members of several other existing Missions. Their desire to be resuscitate the Chilembwe community seemed to be based on a sentimental respect for his memory.

They asked for the address of the Providence Industrial Mission and I gathered that they were not in touch with any outside body.

Though they professed to regard the rising as a great error, they could not explain how it could have occurred if Chilembwe's teaching were good or why similar teaching should not produce similar outbreaks.

Jackson seemed to have some common sense and to be best observed by tacts and catchwords; Andrew I think should be watched & promptly dealt with if he is found holding meetings or services of any sort. A confessed belief that 'there is no redemption except by blood' and that John Chilembwe was a prophet-martyr are not sound found of this for a Church.

The letter from the Foreign Mission Board of the National Baptist Convention of USA Inc. to the Government of Nyasaland applying for the reopening of the Providence Industrial Mission, dated, 24th October, 1924

2   10/24/24

develop a loyal Mission for the betterment of themselves and their neighbors; we beg to advise Your Excellency that we have given permission to the believers, who were formerly connected with the Mission, to take possession of the plot of ground and to reopen the Station. These workers are represented by the following : Jackson Chiwayula, Isaac Chambo, and Andrew G. Mkulichi.

     We graciously pray that Your Excellency will approve of the same. It shall ever be our pleasure to insist that the Mission be conducted peaceably and harmoniously with Your Excellency's Government.

     We have the honor to be

                 Respectfully yours,

                 FOREIGN MISSION BOARD,

                               Chairman

                               Secretary

JEE/JEB

The letter of notification to whom it may concern regarding the authorization of Isaac Chambo, Andrew Mkulichi, Jackson Chiwayula in the reopening of the Providence Industrial Mission, dated 24th October, 1924.

October 24, 1924.

TO WHOM IT MAY CONCERN:

                              This is certify that The Foreign Mission Board of the National Baptist Convention, has given permission to Jackson Chiwayula, Isaac Chambo, and Andrew G. Mkulichi, to act in behalf of the Providence Mission, taking charge of the plot of ground deeded to the above named Board, and reopening The Providence Mission.

                                                  Done by order of the Board.

                      FOREIGN MISSION BOARD,

                                        Chairman

                                        Secretary

JEE/JEB

Appendix 2: Table

The following is a complete list of early PIM Christians whose names were registered at the PIM headquarters as of November 1914.[1] G.L. Kapitao signed the list in November 1914

THE FIRST AFRICAN BAPTIST CHURCH STANDING MEMBERSHIP

The Baptized Member Believers

Name	Name	Name	Name	Name	Name
D.L. Kaduya*	J. Chigwinya	A. Nampeya****	J. Chuchu	Mrs B. Maunda	
W. Kampingo***	K. Kanyang'ama	F. Mamakwa	Mrs A. Ntaka	Mrs J. Mlakala	
. Wasiya***	L. Mikwaja	A. Maganga	Mrs C. Nsanyira	Mrs J. Malekebu***	
W. Kusita******	S. Maganisya	F. Guwo	Mrs B. Chimpele***	Mrs E. Mtambalika**	
A. Jamali**	M. Linya**	Y. Kumukumu	Mrs F. Chimpele***	Mrs E. Juma****	
D. Boloweza**	S. kaliati	C. Napago	Mr T. Ngwazi	C. Chimbiya**	
D. Mankhokwe**	K. Makaika	M. Namalawa	P. Chidote**	I. Mangokwe**	
M. Punguya	A. Lipulo	L. Chilewani	N. Lekenya	S. Yalabi	
. Chapasuka	B. Sasera	B. Mulelemba	M. Chifisi	K. Kalongonda*	
. Kabanda	Y. Manjawira	H. Makwati	A. Mkamula	J. Mkango	
. Kadangwanya	J. Kumukumu	J. Keselema	G. Mwikomana*	J. Maneya*	
. Chambo***	S. Kapire	W. Ntaka	B. Nakalaka*	M. Makatanje	
F. Nsanyira	L. Namalawa*	M. Salamba	S. Dawati	T. Chinangwa*	
. Kuwombola	Y. Kulula	T. Mwanamulo	J. Kubvala	D. Smith	
A. Chimpele***	R. Lipipa	Y. Bango***	N. Nyamuliwa***	D. Mpumila	
. Gordon***	S.M. Majawa*	Mrs J. Kanfumu***	M. Chikwewu	J. Kaitana	
B. Kamfumu***	A. Mmelo	Mrs R. Chidothe**	B. Matonga	F. Mlowa	
. Mlaeje***	Mrs I. Chilembwe	S. Chimombo*	S. Mpanda*	L. Nantumbi	
. Kampingo***	Mrs Kampingo***	A. Nguluwe	J. Nachiula	C. Kapeleche***	
F. Ntaka	Mrs R. Kaduya*	B. Kadangwe	B.D. Mangulama**	L. Mjojo	
W. Ntambo***	Mrs N. Wasiya***	R. Mmero	Mrs Nyamuliwa***	S. Mkango	
. Manjombe	Mrs A. Kusita* 6	J. Matambo	Mrs D. Nakalare	P. Mkumbi****	
. Kuneriwa	Mrs J. Nsomba	D. Rapechu	Mrs E. Chimpele***	M. Kubvala	
N. Chibwana	Mrs A. Mpanda*	S. Mangulama**	Mrs J. Maloza	Mrs L. Kubvala	
. Malondo	Mrs M. Mkulichi***	S. Ntandeni*	Mrs J. Ng'onga	F. Katamba	

[1] The original list is kept at the PIM Pavilion at Mbombwe.

S. Kalima	Mrs J Punguya***	J. Kalinde	Mrs J. Nsumwa	M. Namilopa*
H. Kolimbo	Mrs B. Chapasuka	P. Mang'andira	G. R. Makina*	B. Chingolo
A. Chiunda	Mrs Kadangwanya	S. Nsomba	W. Matare	H.M.C. Malenga***
J. Mwachatayo	Mrs Kampingo***	D. Mwawa	L. Siteven	Mrs L. Malenga***
M Chiwalo***	Mrs D. Mulera*	W. Chilambula	J. Namanya*	Mrs A. Mpumira
W. kumbuyo	Mrs Chiwalo***	R. Kuchale	H. Paliani	Y. Ziguluche
A. Likungwa	Mrs R. Kumbuyo	M. Gordon***	H. Kapyola**	G. Liguluche
P. Boloweza**	Mrs Mankokwe**	S. Mtala**	E Nyimbiri	C. Zolomani
S. Kumwaza**	Mrs DBoloweza**	W. Maneya*	L. Kachele	L. Puka
L. Kataika	Mrs L. Nsamila*	C. Maneya*	K. Kachele	J. Maniwa***
K. Ngolomondo	Mrs A Makwata*8	J. Kabvalo	D. Mwili*	D. Chewonga
Y. Mlulera*	Mrs Mandelumbe	G. Chabwera***	T. Jumbe*	M. Pilingo
A. Lolo*	Mrs R. Kapenuka	J. Katunga	Mrs J. Jumbe*	W. Matipa
S. Verua*	Mrs M. Matuwira	C. Manjawira	B. Magoro	R. Chipata
L. Mkolola	Mrs R. Mulembe	M. Kanyera	J. Sabora	M. Chisanga
H. Matonga	Mrs A. Lipulo	A. Mangulama***	Mrs A. Pambala	W. Mangasanja
C. Mlama	Mrs M. Kuchale	B. Maneya*	Mrs F. Tambalika**	A. Mpezeni*
T. Sulumba**	Mrs Kampingo***	D. Chabwera***	Mrs D. Chikweza	D. Malowa
I. Jaiti	Mrs Malangano**	A. Kalimba	Mrs R. Namalawa*	I. Tamangitsa
Y. Dembe	L. Kalongonda*	Y. Kabvalo	S. Chikwezu	A. Kobiri
J. Matoga	M. Malonda	J. Nakawa	H. Mcheze	S. Tinire
J. Chendelamo	A. Mauwa	I. Meneya*	L. Kachamba	Mrs E. Maniwa***
P. Kuna**	H. Kapenuka	Y. Ndamuwa	J. Chiundiza*	Mrs E. Chewonga
J. Sumbululu	M. Zabula	B. Nachapa	D. Ching'anda	Mrs L. Pilingo
J. Lipulo	S. Nkwangwanya	B. Maneya	L. Maunda	I. Siliya
M. Bwanahaji	Y. Muyebva	W. Gumulira*	D. Chimbalanga	B. Kasiana
R. Maloza	S. Mathuwa	A. Nyimbili	J.Kanena	J. Kafusi
J. Tonde	C. Lombola	F. Kankute	R. Chisau	M. Boloweza**
D. Malekebu***	J. Ekwawila	A. Nkomera	R. Chikuni****	B. Mfuta
E. Kundawanje	D. Magolola	P. Malumo	K. Chinyama*8	K.Makana
E. Mkwaila***	R. Bonongwe	H. Piye++	J. Chinyama*8	E Charlie
L. Mpachika	G. Nsamila	A. Chiwale	J. Nsembiya	S. Chumula
C. Chisulo	J. Baluwa	B. Mina	A. Muripa*	J. Siamanda****
C. Ndamwa	S. Baluwa	N. Matumbo	B. Mwiri*	S. Mataka***
F. Chikwaza	M. Fasana	M. Chiuta	J. Namalombe***	D. Maluwa
F. Nsamila	A. Masunga	M. Matope	A. Tikina	B. Chakhuta*
B. Malenga***	H. Bukini	B.Kamfumu***	J. Chekacheka	E Matewe
Y. Kasilinya	L. Makasali	S. Longo	John Mveka	M. Msamila

Appendicies

F. Mlakala	A. Nkanyila	N. Sambilamavu	C. Walika	B. Sitolo	
T. Zulupi	S. Chiwoko	J. Namalemba	J. Seyani*	S. Njenjema	
A. Bvoleka	D. Nachokolo	K. Mangaule	S. Mkawa	H. Namwera*	
H. Masanga	C. Kapendama	A. Mangaule	A. Kasyoni	J. Matiyera	
Mrs J. Giya	P. Paso	A. Chintongo	R. Twenu	S. Chitera	
Mrs F. Masunga	D.Mwendawamba	C. Nkaula	P.Tamani	A. Napiyo++	
Mrs M. Chikweu	B. Mkwawila*	M. Kaugala	J. chilumba	D. Mwiliapo	
Mrs E. Chilunda	N. Kwalanyiwa	G. Seani*	Y. Malonda	S. Mbwatu	
Mrs J. Chinziri	G. Mwawa	T. Nazombe*	W. Titiwa	N. Salawa	
Mrs Zilongolola**	W. Kambalame	P. Kawe	T. Sawasawa****	S. Mpwelemwe*	
Mrs M. Mzunga	J. Nampatiwa*	J. Kalilangwe	J. Kondamwanasi	R. Mukawa	
Mrs N. Kalemba* 5	F. Namasiku*	S. Namangatwe	A. Mina	J. Matope	
P. Kalemba* 5	J. Likomwe*	D. Namondi	A. Paliwina	K. Chiputo	
J. Zilongolola**	B. Likakazi	A. Chibaya	Nawan***	M. Tepeka	
A. Bwana	M.Taula	I. Maneya*	M. Chembe	J. Kafisi	
H. Mazunga**	A. Makawa***	W. Chimbaila	A. Chembe	B.namelo	
I Chinziri	L. Roka	M. Chimbaila	S. Nawani***	J. James	
J. Chikweu	J. Lula	D. Chabwela***	D. Matemba	L. Boyd	
D. Sulumba**	A. Kuvira	A. Nedson	B. Pindani	R. Kavina	
M. Kalongonda*	D. Dimuwa	M. Matope	D. Mulenga***	E. Marten	
J. Matohana	F. Kaponya	N. Magwiri	E. Chomola	A Chanje	
H. Chumba	Y. Mageleta*	A. Liwawa	T. Voliwa	B. Mpwalogo	
J. Chikweu	A. Ntopola	C. Namasiku*	G. Topesa	A Person	
Mrs M. Chikwewu	A. Marten	L. Kapina	L. Salawa	D. Jailosi	
N. Mkulichi***	A. Moses	A. Mauwa	N. Matope	B. Njenjema	
John Nkulama	L. Potokosi	C. Magombo*	A. Namale	M. Boazi	
E. Makonja	M. Camulon	S. Kwajama	R. Sumaili**	A. Likule	
J. Nyozani	D. Mark	J. Tuluwa	D. Chiteze**	M. Mokowa	
Y. Nengolo	M. Mataka***	b. Mononga****	A. Peter	A. Mokowa	
G. Phuka	E. Magombo*	A. Chopembere	J. John	G. Mombesi	
P. Chinangwa	A. Kopeka	J. Namalaka	G. Wamalombe	M.Mpwele	
D. Mwawa	A. Goodson	I. Kapanga	J. Nkawa	J. Chigwiri	
I. Mwali	J. Paladi	B. Chitedze**	S. Mwandiuza	I. Kasiye	
W. Niwaro	A. Lifeyu	K. Chidyamoto	M. Zilongolola***	A. Kapango	
B. Komiha***	C. Matumba	W. Kudzi	D.Maloya	B. Likalanga	
D. Matumba	A. Mizimbe	A. Chiteze**	A.Nyiwa	Alice	
S. Makombi	S. Mwalinje	L. Mwatinzi	J.Turuna	R. Morris	
S. Manyuwa	D. Nkopeka	S. Zilongolola***	N. Namanya*	L. Baired	

J. Chongola	D. Likangala	A. Chitambuli	A. Clement	B. Mvuu
P. Maile	F. Gulandu	J. Maloya	I. Mverenga	A. Teyela
J. Kanyongo	P. Gwegwede	S.Likakazi	F. Benett	H. Amweya
B. Mabutawo	S. Thom	N. Mulero	J. Chomola	M. Felosi
J. Ndiamava	L. Manji	P. chilumba	A. Nankwinjimbi	J. Nyiwa
B. Mbayire	J. Mangoni	F. Mkulichi***	S. Michenga	A. Chilumba
C. Kachala	J. Job	J. Nkupu	S. Fatachi	N.Person
U. Kanyongo	A. Chintengo	J. Likule	A. Boloweza**	G. Namachila
A. Kasiye	Y. Ndamuwa	B. Mkawa	M.Krisawo	S. Namachila
C. Ndiyamavu	G. Chiwayula***	J. Namanya*	R. Makawa	W. Manea*
J. Chitala	F. Chimwadule	S. Namonde	J. Sumaili**	J. Kasila
O. Mtalika****	R. Namwera*	J. Makasu	A. Kamala	W. Pambala
S. Muliva	A. Kumukumu*	C. Ngunguni	N. Chimwaza**	R. Kumkalapa
A. Kapine	S. Lula	P. Makawa	C. Mtitima	E. Kumkalapa
G. Mwaliwa	N. Masanga	K. Kutayali	L.Lula	L. Chongolela
E. Somba	A. Mwawa***	J. Makandanje	P. Muyapa	A. Chongolela
A. Mlongola	L. Mbaile	F. Mwalula	Thos Nambamba	H. Kalumba
E. Mulinga***	M. Maulidi	J. afonso	L. Nambamba	T. Amilele
R. Luku	S. Lipinga	B. Mkong'a	S. Kuvala	J. Magombo*
D. Sitolo	S. Chituwa	L. Mkong'a	M.Mukiwa	R. Machika
N. Chilembwe***	W. Matengo*	A. Nyangu* 5	D. Mukiwa	S. Mkwawila
D. Najiwa	Y. Matengo*	A. Nyangu* 5	S. Chisau	A. Chambo***
H. Momba	M. Matengo*	J. Nachamba	J. Kamdalika	J. Chambo***
S. Kamazana	A. Matengo*	D. Chikwana***	S. Kambwata	A. Ntala**
M. Kabanda	J. Chiwayula***	A Msaka	J. Nachala	C. Mtambalika**
B. Lamya*	S. Chinyula	M. Kalongonda*	A. Mpumila	L. Kampingo***
R. Chewasili	B. Kadangwe	W. Lomoliwa	B. Kunkalapa	P. Mtambalika**
F. Bakuwa	I. Waruni	S. Mlongola	J. Manunje	G. Chamba***
A. Chitambuli	M. Namilonzi	I. Mawenga	M. Manunje	R. Kalidadya
J. Mangokwe**	K. Chisulo	A. Mlongola	I. Manyenje*	B. Njima
K. Chazemba	J. Nachalala	B. Kotamo	A. Manunje	Scott Chambo***
D. Mangwere	J. Katamba	C. Muliya*	N. Manunje	S. Mkwawila
N. Chidothe**	Y. Kalongonda*	C. Tikiwa	G. Maneya*	N. Kampingo***
B. Tausi	L. Nakopa	S. Susani	A. Mikwajaja	K. Kampingo***
I. Gomeza	D. Lipeta	J. Maganga	M. Maeta	B. Tambala*
N.Matira	K. Nyanya	S. Mvuluma	G. Kumula	M. Moses
J.mpoola	J. Kawojole**	A. Chitimbe	M. Kumula	K. Ndozi
N. Mwili*	A. Musa***	S. Matine	J. Mpemvu	K. Nkono

Appendicies

K. Mamia	D. Lamuli	K. Tamani	A. Kavala	S. Chiwambo	
R. Samaniko	S.L. Mkulichi***	S. Luleya	A. Mukuluwa	E. Lulanga	
M.Manea*	I. Mpokwa	M. Tikiwa	A. Chisao	K. Tambala*	
K. Mtambalika**	M. Amwanamwa	L. Nankwinyimbi	L. Nazembe	D. Kampingo***	
L.Nakumwa	P. Njenjema	J. Luleya	A Chikwewo	C. Jamali	
K. Tiremuno	L. Ngomanje	I. Chidiamoto	P. Nkumbi****	A. Namwela*	
M. Venya	R. Mkwaila	B. Mausa	J. Tonde	J. Namaunda	
A. Masabiti	P. Kabweremawa	E Chitanda	L. Nkumbi	E. Lijulo	
F. Maloza	K. Mkemba	M. Makwati	A. Mwiri*	M. Mangulama**	
J. Chikweu	M. Nasolo***	W. Makwati	L. Mchekeni	J. Mangulama**	
M. Chikweu	K. Ntawira*	Chenyangu Chilembwe	L. Kapilikwete	R. Sema	
J. Nachala	Y. Sawe	L. Maloza	Y. Ndembo	M. Sema	
W. Matipo	G. Nampatiwa	M. Gorden***	M. Kapirikwete	M. Mulongo	
D. Matipo	S. Nakoma	J. Namizinga	K. Kapirikwete	C. Sanjika	
A. Namasiku*	M. Mreko	M. Bwanaisa	G. Mtembanji	S. Chipere***	
S. Totolo	C. Kaelama	H. Gwegwede	P. Kafisi	A. Chipere***	
B. Mandawala	N. Fumulani	M. Paulosi	J. Ntambo***	M. Nakahi	
P.Chiwembe	K. Fumulani	D. Nache	M. Maloya	J. Lulanga	
M.Chapola*	W. Naura*	L. Minyala	K. Matengo*	A. Lulanga	
E. Chituwa	M. Naura*	M. Konye	A. Ngomana	E. Kalonga* 5	
H. Makowa	A. Tiyera	L. Tongwe	L. Chingale	A. Kalonga* 5	
B. Mataya	R. Sameta++	K. Mkango	M. Matengo*	E. Ntawila*	
M. Masambiti	B. Jumbe*	L. Peula	E. Matengo*	J. Matuwila	
B. Masambiti	L. Chidiamoto	J. Somoniko	J. Ndala***	R. Magwira	
R. Chiteze**	M. Makawa	R. Noniwa	L. Chajiya	S. Chiwayula	
M. Maoni	S. Nayuma	J. Kaponde	S. Kahiye	A. Bwana	
R. Chitungu	J. Chimwaza**	S. Sonjoma	D. Nasolo***	R. Chiwayula	
H. Chiwayula	L. Nsamila	N. Kachamba	L. Topanawo	M. Nachiula	
M. Chiwayula	J. Kopakopa	W. Chenjema	E. Sokonombwe	A. Sonjoma	
R. Warika	A. M. Bwana	L. Khuzi	A. Mkwate	L. Chanta	
A. Kaduya*	J. Pumani	D. Chikumba***	M. Kafisi	J. Kachamba***	
R. Noniwa	B. Pumani	M. Katambo	S. Manyenje*	J.mkwawila	
A. Namasiku*	A. Temuwa	L. Chikumba***	A.Ntawila*	U.S Chigwa	
J. Turuwa*	J. Katamba	R. Tambala*	S. Ndala*	A. Chigwa	
E. Masambiti	D. Katamba	G. Peula	S.Mkawa	A. Mwili*	
L. Taimu	L. Niwaru	M. Tambala*	M.Kahiye	Golu Nyingeni	
M. Lamuli	J. Makuwa	M. Chikanga	N. Mlenga***	L. Juma	

F. Lamuli	J. Makuwa	S. Mbalame	K. Nasolo***	H. Mtelela
B. Chifisi	S. Kalumba	L. Noniwa	M.. Nasolo***	M. Chiwalika
M. Chifisi	D. Malemia	J. Chalala	L.Mtipasonjo***	P. Mtipa
B. Chisemula	B. Kumbila	M. Kamenya* 6	A. Mlenga***	E. Majiwa
G. Bisa	A. Kumbila	A. Mchekeni	Y. Sokonombwe***	E. Kamwa
A. Bisa	A. Makuwa	M. Nanthabwe	D. Mlenga***	W. Chisulo
D. Bisa	P. Makala	J. Chasemba	S. Kolamana	M. Tande
A. Bisa	J. Tepeka	P. Sapanga	A. Kwelete	M. Magwela*
A. Kumbanya	J. Kutayali	L. Katema	M. Chabwela***	A. Magwela*
W. Mpumila	D. Kalilangwe	J. Mankokwe**	A. Kanyong'o	M. Nyengeni
M. Salangwa	D. Kalilangwe	K. Masanjala***	K. Makawa	J. Nasambo
K. Mokowa	C. Tomeya	J. Nkomela	F. Gumulira*	E. Namikangozo
R. Muronya	A. Tomeya	J. Kuvala	J. Chikwana	M. Kachilambo
V. Mdereko	B. Mbamira	Y. Mkwawila	B. Matengo*	W. Chazemba
B. Chikwana	T. Chisima	j. Namasika	G. Chiwayula***	S. Matiya
K. Chikwana	L. Lumuli	N. Melo	J. Gunya*	M. Tambo
B. Namikangozo	E. Rapeohu	W. Chilambo	D. Mitembo	H. Ngwale
P. Masambo	J. Nyamaliwa***	G. Lumbwa	L. Likangala	B. Kaduya*
L. Katamba	R. Kolokole	A. Ntambo***	S. Mitembo	e. Samuka
G. Chamba	G. Chikoja	L. Lumba	E.M.Mataya	R. Ntamila
S. Njojo	E. Kalongonda*	T. Mwanyanje	J.Wilson	F. Namulu*
I. Wareta	L. Mokowa	E. Nsamila	E. Wilson	a. Kaduya*
A. Pulaisi	L. Nanambe	J. Njilima*	P.Kalumbi	E. Namwera*
E. Namakanya	A. Mataya	M. Kambalame	E. Kalumbi	J. Matipwili*
J. Kamicheni	J. Kalilangwe	A. Kambalame	D. Topesa***	G. Chinguwo
J. Matuwila	T. Noniwa	B. Mangasanja	B. Mlenga***	E. Samuka
B. Katopola	M. Bwana	M. Chisulo	W. Mbeta	S. Chanungira
S. Zagwa	L. Chigwiri	A. Kachilombo	J.Tamila	M. Naluso*
C. Chawaka	L. Muruta	L. Ntiwa	S. Kalongonda*	W. Chazemba
K. Sanjika	B. Malemeka	M. Gomeza	T. Mmeta	S. Matiya
A. Tomola	K. Makwapala	M. Timbwinya	S. Kaliyati****	A. Ntambo***
A. Tomola	L. Ntamila	E. Kunyawa	I. Sulumba**	E. Baluti
B. Chilamo	W. Chigamba*	A. Lati	G. Menyani	D. Kachembele
J. Chilamo	T. Mahele*	T. Matonga	A. Katema	J. Nchocholo
A. Chilambula	B. Kaduya*	T. Chizimba	M. Livevela	H. Chindevu***
A. Fundi	A. Chilimba*	K. Makata	M. Chauya	J. Kuloka
W. Nyongonya	M. Chikwana*	O.Makawa	Y. Manyenje*	H. Kupasati
Y. Namahasa	A. Chkwana*	B. Mulolo	M. Mpumila	L. Mbeza

APPENDICIES

M. Misasa	D. Kwalala*	J. Liva	D. Kwirima	Y. Komelela***
P. Namanya*	I. Kalinde*	S. Movera	S. Mwakamo	B. Tonde
A. Chilanga	M. Kaduya*	J. Bandawe*	A. Dozola	J. Nlasa
M. Mbombwe	E. Namasengwera	EM. Amosa	A. Lulanga	E. Nlasa
D. Kaundo	W. Mukama	A. Kawinga	L. Lulanga	E. Chiwayula
M. Maonga*	L. Chisowile	M. Wahela	L. Musanya	D. Sulumba**
A. Kasindo	Y. Liso	J. Naketo	L. Mangulama**	M. Topanawo
M. Kalamba	J. Kolokole	M. Mwenela	M. Nazombe*	A. Chikweo
A. Chimbalanga	M. Kolowa	N. Nihilo	S ndala**	M. Chikwewo
E. Namakanya	M. Chuchu	B. Chitimbe	S. Sumbululu	S. Kachepa
I. Kwemba	U. Chilimba	A. Ntowa	B. Chikwana	A. Chisulo
K. Isa	P. Muhole	A. Kulomve	S. Chilunga	W. Muzananji
T. Kolomana	N. Kalanga	M. Liwara	L. Maunda	S. Chintendele
H. Mombanya	G. Nasolo***	B. Namizinga	A. Chepondani	N. Namakala
I Chilima	E. Nkagula	A. Namizinga	B. Likwanya	N. Chabwera***
N. Chilombo	E. Kaduya*	J. Kainga*	E. Nlapula	Annie Sulumba**
K. Kachilombo	E. Namwera*	D. Namalemba	U. Nchimala	B. Chakana
Kachilombo	M. Malekebu***	W. Mkuzi	A. Vuluma	S. Mzimu
L. Mambo	E. Msamila	Y. Lingwalanya	L. Vuluma	I. Mzimu
H. Namingwe	M. Chilimba	M. Liva	R. Makata	E. Chipembele
B. Zerela	Lucy Chambo***	S. Tayali	N. Vuluma	A. Kapote
A. Seyani*	Y. Makawa	H. Mpaso	S. Mpona	M. Mbagaliwa***
H. Chimbalanga	K. Nemwala	N.Mveka	A. Mipasanje	D. Chipembele
B. Chitanda	S. Leyi	A. Kwalanyiwa	D. Salima	G. Kunjilima*
M. Chitanda	M. Makumba	M. Namakwa	J. Kondwani	S. Makole*
I. Kapukusa	Simon Kadiwala	A. Omosa	I.M.Bwana	
S. Mkwembe	B. Kamala	D. Mpalika	I. Chituwa	
M. Kwilima	N. Njojo	A. Mwili*	L. Nambili	
B. Mwachande	D. Pumila	M.Mpaso	E. Nlapula	
L. Kaulesi	B. Kwacha	E. Wanyowa	S. Malemia	
R. Chigwiya	M. Kapewa	E. Nalimbwi	G. Nazimela	
N. Nameta	J. Lolo	L. Nalimbwi	J. Chongo	
G. Ntimula	J. Lumwila*****	A. Nangawa	A. Ndeleko	
A. Sameta++	H. Kanyenga	W. Chilombo	D. Masala	
A. Kaulesi	N. Kwapitla	I.Ngulu	S. Chitembe	
A. Chatamoto	Storey Mpaso	R. Nangawa	G. Kulanda	
A. Waruni	L. Kobili	A. Maneya*	A. Makete	
A. Namunda	B. Malombe	A.Mwela	M. Nantambwe	

D. Namakanya	K. Masanga	A. Malenga*	E. Liwawa	
W. Mrika	B. Ntambo***	P.Mazera	A. Suedi	
K. Malonda	F. Namusilika	L. Tuluma	J. Likangala	
I. Mkuna	P. Monihe	J. Sasa	J.Likangala	
K. Kusimika	A. Katembwe	M. Kaduya*	G. Mwili*	
A. Gorden***	R. Mwanyanje	S. Sumbululu	R. Sinyanga	
D. Mbamira	Ch. Nserembwe	J. Matengo*	M. Naluso*	

Key to the* in the membership list

Mulanje   *
Zomba   **
`Chiradzulu   ***
Thyolo   ****
Lilongwe   * 5
Ntcheu   * 6
Salima   * 8
Magomero   **
Mozambique ++

www.ingramcontent.com/pod-product-compliance
Lightning Source LLC
Chambersburg PA
CBHW031552300426
44111CB00006BA/281